ELIZABETHAN SONNETS

VOL. II

ELIZABETHAN SONNETS

NEWLY ARRANGED AND INDEXED

WITH AN INTRODUCTION BY

SIDNEY LEE

Editor of 'The Dictionary of National Biography'
Author of 'A Life of William Shakespeare' and
'Queen Victoria: A Biography'

VOL. II

NEW YORK

COOPER SQUARE PUBLISHERS, INC.

1964

PUBLISHERS' NOTE

THE texts contained in the present volume are reprinted with very slight alterations from the *English
Garner* issued in eight volumes (1877-1890, London,
8vo) by Professor Arber, whose name is sufficient
guarantee for the accurate collation of the texts
with the rare originals, the old spelling being in
most cases carefully modernised.   The contents of
the original *Garner* have been rearranged and now
for the first time classified, under the general
editorial supervision of Mr. Thomas Seccombe.
Certain lacunae have been filled by the interpolation
of fresh matter.   The Introductions are wholly
new and have been written specially for this issue.

4332

Published by
Cooper Square Publishers, Inc.
59 Fourth Avenue, New York, N. Y. 10003
Library of Congress Catalog Card No. 64-16741
Printed in the United States of America

821.008
L51e

CONTENTS

v

---

* The items indicated by an asterisk are new additions to *An English Garner.*

PHILLIS

Honoured with Pa-

ftorall Sonnets, Elegies, and amo-

rous delights.

VVhere-vnto is annexed, the tragicall
complaynt of *Elftred.*

*Iam Phoebus difiungit equos, iam Cin-
thia iungit.*

At London,
Printed for Iohn Busbie, and are to
be fold at his fhoppe, at the Weft-doore
of Paules. 1593.

[In the complete *Phillis* collection of poems were included, together with the poems of sonnet character, numbered consecutively I.-XL., an 'Induction' in eight (6-line) stanzas, two eclogues—one in twenty-six (6-line) stanzas and the other in twenty (4-line) stanzas—an elegy in fifty alternately-rhyming (5-iambic) lines, and an ode in five (8-line) stanzas. There are only printed here thirty-eight of the poems of the sonnet character, numbered I.-XL. ; those numbered XV. and XVI. are omitted, because they have another metrical character, being each twenty-lines long and variously rhymed.]

Lodge.]
1593.]
    PHILLIS.
    3

SONNET I.

O H PLEASING thoughts, apprentices of love,
    Fore-runners of desire, sweet mithridates
    The poison of my sorrows to remove,
    With whom my hopes and fear full oft debates!
Enrich yourselves and me by your self riches,
Which are the thoughts you spend on heaven-bred beauty,
Rouse you my muse beyond our poets' pitches,
And, working wonders, yet say all is duty!
Use you no eaglets' eyes, nor phœnix' feathers,
To tower the heaven from whence heaven's wonder sallies.
For why? Your sun sings sweetly to her weathers,
Making a spring of winter in the valleys.
    Show to the world, though poor and scant my skill is,
    How sweet thoughts be, that are but thoughts on
        Phillis.

SONNET II.

Y OU sacred sea-nymphs pleasantly disporting
    Amidst this wat'ry world, where now I sail;
    If ever love, or lovers sad reporting,
    Had power sweet tears from your fair eyes to
        hail;
And you, more gentle-hearted than the rest,
Under the northern noon-stead sweetly streaming
Lend those moist riches of your crystal crest,
To quench the flames from my heart's Ætna streaming;
    And thou, kind Triton, in thy trumpet relish
The ruthful accents of my discontent,
    That midst this travel desolate and hellish,
Some gentle wind that listens my lament
    May prattle in the north in Phillis' ears:
    " Where Phillis wants, Damon consumes in tears."

SONNET III.

N FANCY'S world an Atlas have I been,
Where yet the chaos of my ceaseless care
Is by her eyes unpitied and unseen,
In whom all gifts but pity planted are,
For mercy though still cries my moan-clad muse,
And every paper that she sends to beauty,
In tract of sable tears brings woeful news,
Of my true heart, kind thoughts, and loyal duty.
But ah the strings of her hard heart are strained
Beyond the harmony of my desires ;
And though the happy heavens themselves have pained,
To tame her heart whose will so far aspires,
Yet she who claims the title of world's wonder,
Thinks all deserts too base to bring her under.

SONNET IV.

ONG hath my sufferance laboured to enforce
One pearl of pity from her pretty eyes,
Whilst I with restless rivers of remorse,
Have bathed the banks where my fair Phillis
lies.
The moaning lines which weeping I have written,
And writing read unto my ruthful sheep,
And reading sent with tears that never fitten,
To my love's queen, that hath my heart in keep,
Have made my lambkins lay them down and sigh ;
But Phillis sits, and reads, and calls them trifles.
Oh heavens, why climb not happy lines so high,
To rent that ruthless heart that all hearts rifles !
None writes with truer faith, or greater love ;
Yet out, alas ! I have no power to move.

SONNET V.

H PALE and dying infant of the spring,
How rightly now do I resemble thee!
That self same hand that thee from stalk did
wring,
Hath rent my breast and robbed my heart from me.
Yet shalt thou live. For why? Thy native vigour
Shall thrive by woeful dew-drops of my dolour;
And from the wounds I bear through fancy's rigour,
My streaming blood shall yield the crimson colour.
The ravished sighs that ceaseless take their issue
From out the furnace of my heart inflamed,
To yield you lasting springs shall never miss you;
So by my plaints and pains, you shall be famed.
Let my heart's heat and cold, thy crimson nourish,
And by my sorrows let thy beauty flourish.

SONNET VI.

T IS not death which wretched men call dying,
But that is very death which I endure,
When my coy-looking nymph, her grace
envying,
By fatal frowns my domage doth procure.
It is not life which we for life approve,
But that is life when on her wool-soft paps
I seal sweet kisses which do batten love,
And doubling them do treble my good haps.
'Tis neither love the son, nor love the mother,
Which lovers praise and pray to; but that love is
Which she in eye and I in heart do smother.
Then muse not though I glory in my miss,
Since she who holds my heart and me in durance,
Hath life, death, love and all in her procurance.

SONNET VII.

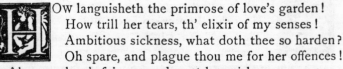

Ow languisheth the primrose of love's garden!
How trill her tears, th' elixir of my senses!
Ambitious sickness, what doth thee so harden?
Oh spare, and plague thou me for her offences!
Ah roses, love's fair roses, do not languish;
Blush through the milk-white veil that holds you
covered.
If heat or cold may mitigate your anguish,
I 'll burn, I 'll freeze, but you shall be recovered.
Good God, would beauty mark how she is crased,
How but one shower of sickness makes her tender,
Her judgments then to mark my woes amazed,
To mercy should opinion's fort surrender!
And I,—oh would I might, or would she meant it!
Should hery[1] love, who now in heart lament it.

[1] *i.e.* praise.

SONNET VIII.

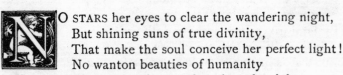

O STARS her eyes to clear the wandering night,
But shining suns of true divinity,
That make the soul conceive her perfect light!
No wanton beauties of humanity
Her pretty brows, but beams that clear the sight
Of him that seeks the true philosophy!
No coral is her lip, no rose her fair,
But even that crimson that adorns the sun.
No nymph is she, but mistress of the air,
By whom my glories are but new begun.
But when I touch and taste as others do,
I then shall write, and you shall wonder too.

SONNET IX.

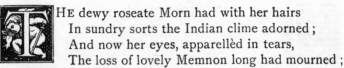

HE dewy roseate Morn had with her hairs
    In sundry sorts the Indian clime adorned ;
    And now her eyes, apparellèd in tears,
    The loss of lovely Memnon long had mourned ;
When as she spied the nymph whom I admire,
Combing her locks, of which the yellow gold
Made blush the beauties of her curlèd wire,
Which heaven itself with wonder might behold,
    Then, red with shame, her reverend locks she rent,
And weeping hid the beauty of her face ;
The flower of fancy wrought such discontent.
The sighs, which midst the air she breathed a space,
    A three-days' stormy tempest did maintain,
    Her shame a fire, her eyes a swelling rain.

SONNET X.

HE rumour runs that here in Isis swim
    Such stately swans so confident in dying,
    That when they feel themselves near Lethe's
        brim,
They sing their fatal dirge when death is nighing.
    And I, like these, that feel my wounds are mortal,
Contented die for her whom I adore ;
And in my joyful hymns do still exhort all
To die for such a saint or love no more.
    Not that my torments or her tyranny
Enforce me to enjoin so hard a task,
But for I know, and yield no reason why,
But will them try that have desire to ask.
    As love hath wreaths his pretty eyes to seel,
    So lovers must keep secret what they feel.

SONNET XI.

Y FRAIL and earthly bark, by reason's guide,
    Which holds the helm, whilst will doth wield
       the sail,
    By my desires, the winds of bad betide,
Hath sailed these worldly seas with small avail,
  Vain objects serve for dreadful rocks to quail
My brittle boat from haven of life that flies
To haunt the sea of mundane miseries.
My soul that draws impressions from above,
  And views my course, and sees the winds aspire,
Bids reason watch to 'scape the shoals of love;
But lawless will enflamed with endless ire
Doth steer empoop, whilst reason doth retire.
  The streams increase; love's waves my bark do fill;
  Thus are they wracked that guide their course by will.

SONNET XII.

H, TREES, why fall your leaves so fast?
    Ah rocks, where are your robes of moss?
    Ah flocks, why stand you all aghast?
    Trees, rocks, and flocks, what, are you pensive
      for my loss?
  The birds, methinks, tune naught but moan,
The winds breathe naught but bitter plaint,
The beasts forsake their dens to groan ;
Birds, winds, and beasts, what doth my loss your powers
    attaint?
  Floods weep their springs above their bounds,
And echo wails to see my woe,
The robe of ruth doth clothe the grounds;
Floods, echo, grounds, why do you all these tears bestow?
    The trees, the rocks, and flocks reply,
    The birds, the winds, the beasts report,
    Floods, echo, grounds, for sorrow cry,
We grieve since Phillis nill kind Damon's love consort.

SONNET XIII.

OVE guides the roses of thy lips,
    And flies about them like a bee;
    If I approach he forward skips,
    And if I kiss he stingeth me.
Love in thine eyes doth build his bower,
And sleeps within their pretty shine;
And if I look the boy will lower,
And from their orbs shoot shafts divine.
    Love works thy heart within his fire,
And in my tears doth firm the same;
And if I tempt it will retire,
And of my plaints doth make a game.
    Love, let me cull her choicest flowers,
And pity me, and calm her eye,
Make soft her heart, dissolve her lowers,
Then will I praise thy deity.
    But if thou do not love, I'll truly serve her.
    In spite of thee, and by firm faith deserve her.

SONNET XIV.

WROTE in Mirrha's bark, and as I wrote,
    Poor Mirrha wept because I wrote forsaken;
    'Twas of thy pride I sung in weeping note,
    When as her leaves great moan for pity maken.
The falling fountains from the mountains falling,
Cried out, alas, so fair and be so cruel!
And babbling echo never ceasèd calling,
Phillis, disdain is fit for none but truthless.
    The rising pines wherein I had engraved
Thy memory consulting with the wind,
Are trucemen to thy heart and thoughts depraved,
And say, thy kind should not be so unkind.
    But, out alas! so fell is Phillis fearless,
    That she hath made her Damon well-nigh tearless.

XV. and XVI.—These poems are not in sonnet form and are omitted.

SONNET XVII.

H, FLEETING weal! ah, sly deluding sleep,
That in one moment giv'st me joy and pain!
How do my hopes dissolve to tears in vain,
As wont the snows, 'fore angry sun to weep!
Ah, noisome life that hath no weal in keep!
My forward grief hath form and working might;
My pleasures, like the shadows, take their flight;
My path to bliss is tedious, long, and steep.
Twice happy thou Endymion that embracest
The live-long night thy love within thy arms,
Where thou fond dream my longèd weal defacest
Whilst fleeting and uncertain shades thou placest
Before my eyes with false deluding charms!
Ah, instant sweets which do my heart revive,
How should I joy if you were true alive!

SONNET XVIII.

S WHERE two raging venoms are united,
Which of themselves dissevered life would
sever,
The sickly wretch of sickness is acquited,
Which else should die, or pine in torments ever;
So fire and frost, that hold my heart in seizure,
Restore those ruins which themselves have wrought,
Where if apart they both had had their pleasure,
The earth long since her fatal claim had caught.
Thus two united deaths keep me from dying;
I burn in ice, and quake amidst the fire,
No hope midst these extremes or favour spying;
Thus love makes me a martyr in his ire.
So that both cold and heat do rather feed
My ceaseless pains, than any comfort breed.

SONNET XIX.

Hou tyrannising monarch that dost tire
   My love-sick heart through those assaulting
     eyes,
   That are the lamps which lighten my desire!
If nought but death thy fury may suffice,
  Not for my peace, but for thy pleasure be it,
That Phillis, wrathful Phillis, that repines me
All grace but death, may deign to come and see it,
And seeing grieve at that which she assigns me.
  This only boon for all my mortal bane
I crave and cry for at thy mercy seat:
That when her wrath a faithful heart hath slain,
And soul is fled, and body reft of heat,
   She might perceive how much she might command
   That had my life and death within her hand.

SONNET XX.

Ome praise the looks, and others praise the locks
   Of their fair queens, in love with curious words;
   Some laud the breast where love his treasure
     locks
All like the eye that life and love affords.
  But none of these frail beauties and unstable
Shall make my pen riot in pompous style;
More greater gifts shall my grave muse enable,
Whereat severer brows shall never smile.
  I praise her honey-sweeter eloquence,
Which from the fountain of true wisdom floweth,
Her modest mien that matcheth excellence,
Her matchless faith which from her virtue groweth;
   And could my style her happy virtues equal,
   Time had no power her glories to enthral.

SONNET XXI.

E HERALDS of my heart, mine ardent groans,
 Oh, tears which gladly would burst out to
  brooks,
 Oh, spent on fruitless sand my surging moans,
Oh, thoughts enthralled unto care-boding looks!
 Ah, just laments of my unjust distress,
Ah, fond desires whom reason could not guide!
Oh, hopes of love that intimate redress,
Yet prove the load-stars unto bad betide!
 When will you cease? Or shall pain never-ceasing,
Seize on my heart? Oh, mollify your rage,
Lest your assaults with over-swift increasing,
Procure my death, or call on timeless age.
 What if they do? They shall but feed the fire,
 Which I have kindled by my fond desire.

SONNET XXII.

AIR art thou, Phillis, ay, so fair, sweet maid
 As nor the sun, nor I have seen more fair,
 For in thy cheeks sweet roses are embayed,
 And gold more pure than gold doth gild thy
  hair.
Sweet bees have hived their honey on thy tongue,
And Hebe spiced her nectar with thy breath;
About thy neck do all the graces throng,
And lay such baits as might entangle death.
 In such a breast what heart would not be thrall
From such sweet arms who would not wish embraces?
At thy fair hands who wonders not at all,
Wonder itself through ignorance embases?
 Yet natheless though wondrous gifts you call these,
 My faith is far more wonderful than all these.

SONNET XXIII.

URST, burst, poor heart! Thou hast no longer
    hope;
    Captive mine eyes unto eternal sleep;
    Let all my senses have no further scope;
Let death be lord of me and all my sheep!
    For Phillis hath betrothèd fierce disdain,
That makes his mortal mansion in her heart;
And though my tongue have long time taken pain
To sue divorce and wed her to desert.
    She will not yield, my words can have no power;
She scorns my faith, she laughs at my sad lays,
She fills my soul with never-ceasing sour,
Who filled the world with volumes of her praise.
    In such extremes what wretch can cease to crave
    His peace from death, who can no mercy have!

SONNET XXIV.

O GLORY makes me glorious or glad,
    Nor pleasure may to pleasure me dispose,
    No comfort can revive my senses sad,
    Nor hope enfranchise me with one repose.
    Nor in her absence taste I one delight.
Nor in her presence am I well content;
Was never time gave term to my despite,
Nor joy that dried the tears of my lament.
    Nor hold I hope of weal in memory,
Nor have I thought to change my restless grief,
Nor doth my conquest yield me sovereignty,
Nor hope repose, nor confidence relief.
    For why? She sorts her frowns and favours so,
    As when I gain or lose I cannot know.

SONNET XXV.

 WAGE the combat with two mighty foes,
　　Which are more strong than I ten thousand fold;
　　The one is when thy pleasure I do lose,
　　The other, when thy person I behold.
In seeing thee a swarm of loves confound me
And cause my death in spite of my resist,
And if I see thee not, thy want doth wound me,
For in thy sight my comfort doth consist.
　The one in me continual care createth,
　The other doth occasion my desire;
　The one the edge of all my joy rebateth,
　The other makes me a phœnix in love's fire.
　　So that I grieve when I enjoy your presence,
　　And die for grief by reason of your absence.

SONNET XXVI.

 'LL teach thee, lovely Phillis, what love is.
　　It is a vision seeming such as thou,
　　That flies as fast as it assaults mine eyes;
　　It is affection that doth reason miss;
　It is a shape of pleasure like to you,
Which meets the eye, and seen on sudden dies;
It is a double grief, a spark of pleasure
Begot by vain desire.　And this is love
　Whom in our youth we count our chiefest treasure,
In age for want of power we do reprove.
　　Yea, such a power is love, whose loss is pain,
　　And having got him we repent our gain.

SONNET XXVII.

AIR eyes, whilst fearful I your fair admire,
     By unexpressèd sweetness that I gain,
     My memory of sorrow doth expire,
     And falcon-like I tower joy's heavens amain,
But when your suns in oceans of their glory
Shut up their day-bright shine, I die for thought;
So pass my joys as doth a new-played story,
And one poor sigh breaths all delight to naught.
    So to myself I live not, but for you;
For you I live, and you I love, but none else.
Oh then, fair eyes, whose light I live to view,
Or poor forlorn despised to live alone else,
     Look sweet, since from the pith of contemplation
     Love gathereth life, and living, breedeth passion.

SONNET XXVIII.

OT causeless were you christened, gentle flowers,
     The one of faith, the other fancy's pride;
     For she who guides both faith and fancy's
        power,
In your fair colours wraps her ivory side.
    As one of you hath whiteness without stain,
So spotless is my love and never tainted;
And as the other shadoweth faith again,
Such is my lass, with no fond change acquainted.
    And as nor tyrant sun nor winter weather
May ever change sweet amaranthus' hue,
So she though love and fortune join together,
Will never leave to be both fair and true.
     And should I leave thee there, thou pretty elf?
     Nay, first let Damon quite forget himself.

SONNET XXIX.

FEEL myself endangered beyond reason,
My death already 'twixt the cup and lip,
Because my proud desire through cursèd treason
Would make my hopes mount heaven, which
cannot skip;
My fancy still requireth at my hands
Such things as are not, cannot, may not be,
And my desire although my power withstands
Will give me wings, who never yet could flee.
What then remains except my maimed soul
Extort compassion from love-flying age,
Or if naught else their fury may control,
To call on death that quells affection's rage;
Which death shall dwell with me and never fly,
Since vain desire seeks that hope doth deny.

SONNET XXX.

DO compare unto thy youthly clear,
Which always bides within thy flow'ring prime,
The month of April, that bedews our clime
With pleasant flowers, when as his showers
appear.
Before thy face shall fly false cruelty,
Before his face the doly season fleets;
Mild been his looks, thine eyes are full of sweets;
Firm is his course, firm is thy loyalty.
He paints the fields through liquid crystal showers,
Thou paint'st my verse with Pallas' learned flowers;
With Zephirus' sweet breath he fills the plains,
And thou my heart with weeping sighs dost wring;
His brows are dewed with morning's crystal spring,
Thou mak'st my eyes with tears bemoan my pains.

SONNET XXXI.

EVOID of reason, thrall to foolish ire,
　I walk and chase a savage fairy still,
　Now near the flood, straight on the mounting
　　hill,
Now midst the woods of youth, and vain desire.
　For leash I bear a cord of careful grief;
For brach I lead an over-forward mind;
My hounds are thoughts, and rage despairing blind,
Pain, cruelty, and care without relief.
　But they perceiving that my swift pursuit
My flying fairy cannot overtake,
With open mouths their prey on me do make,
Like hungry hounds that lately lost their suit.
　　And full of fury on their master feed,
　　To hasten on my hapless death with speed.

SONNET XXXII.

THOUSAND times to think and think the same
　To two fair eyes to show a naked heart,
　Great thirst with bitter liquor to restrain,
　To take repast of care and crooked smart;
　To sigh full oft without relent of ire,
To die for grief and yet conceal the tale,
To others' will to fashion my desire,
To pine in looks disguised through pensive-pale;
　A short despite, a faith unfeigned true,
To love my foe, and set my life at naught,
With heedless eyes mine endless harms to view
A will to speak, a fear to tell the thought;
　　To hope for all, yet for despair to die,
　　Is of my life the certain destiny.

II.　　　　　　　　B　　　　　　　　9

SONNET XXXIII.

HEN first sweet Phillis, whom I must adore,
    'Gan with her beauties bless our wond'ring sky,
    The son of Rhea, from their fatal store
    Make all the gods to grace her majesty.
Apollo first his golden rays among,
Did form the beauty of her bounteous eyes;
He graced her with his sweet melodious song,
And made her subject of his poesies.
    The warrior Mars bequeathed her fierce disdain,
Venus her smile, and Phœbe all her fair,
Python his voice, and Ceres all her grain,
The moon her locks and fingers did repair.
    Young Love, his bow, and Thetis gave her feet;
    Clio her praise, Pallas her science sweet.

SONNET XXXIV.

WOULD in rich and golden-coloured rain,
    With tempting showers in pleasant sort descend
    Into fair Phillis' lap, my lovely friend,
    When sleep her sense with slumber doth restrain.
I would be changèd to a milk-white bull,
When midst the gladsome field she should appear,
By pleasant fineness to surprise my dear,
Whilst from their stalks, she pleasant flowers did pull.
    I were content to weary out my pain,
To be Narcissus so she were a spring,
To drown in her those woes my heart do ring,
And more; I wish transformèd to remain,
    That whilst I thus in pleasure's lap did lie,
    I might refresh desire, which else would die.

SONNET XXXV.

HOPE and fear, I pray and hold my peace,
   Now freeze my thoughts and straight they fry
     again,
   I now admire and straight my wonders cease,
I loose my bonds and yet myself restrain ;
  This likes me most that leaves me discontent,
My courage serves and yet my heart doth fail,
My will doth climb whereas my hopes are spent,
I laugh at love, yet when he comes I quail ;
  The more I strive, the duller bide I still,
I would be thanked, and yet I freedom love,
I would redress, yet hourly feed my ill,
I would repine, and dare not once reprove ;
   And for my love I am bereft of power,
   And strengthless strive my weakness to devour.

SONNET XXXVI.

IF so I seek the shades, I presently do see
   The god of love forsakes his bow and sit me by ;
   If that I think to write, his Muses pliant be,
   If so I plain my grief, the wanton boy will cry,
  If I lament his pride, he doth increase my pain ;
If tears my cheeks attaint, his cheeks are moist with moan ;
If I disclose the wounds the which my heart hath slain,
He takes his fascia off, and wipes them dry anon.
  If so I walk the woods, the woods are his delight,
If I myself torment, he bathes him in my blood ;
He will my soldier be if once I wend to fight,
If seas delight, he steers my bark amidst the flood.
   In brief, the cruel god doth never from me go,
   But makes my lasting love eternal with my woe.

SONNET XXXVII.

THESE fierce incessant waves that stream along my
          face,
     Which show the certain proof of my ne'er-
          ceasing pains,
Fair Phillis, are no tears that trickle from my brains;
For why?   Such streams of ruth within me find no place.
These floods that wet my cheeks are gathered from thy
     grace
And thy perfections, and from hundred thousand flowers
Which from thy beauties spring; whereto I medley
     showers
Of rose and lilies too, the colours of thy face.
My love doth serve for fire, my heart the furnace is,
The aperries of my sighs augment the burning flame,
The limbec is mine eye that doth distil the same;
And by how much my fire is violent and sly,
By so much doth it cause the waters mount on high,
That shower from out mine eyes, for to assuage my
     miss.

SONNET XXXVIII.

HO lives enthralled to Cupid and his flame,
     From day to day is changed in sundry sort;
     The proof whereof myself may well report,
     Who oft transformed by him may teach the
          same.
   I first was turned into a wounded hart,
That bare the bloody arrow in my side ;
Then to a swan that midst the waters glide,
With piteous voice presaged my deadly smart;

Eftsoons I waxed a faint and fading flower;
Then was I made a fountain sudden dry,
Distilling all my tears from troubled eye;
Now am I salamander by his power,
  Living in flames, but hope ere long to be
  A voice, to talk my mistress' majesty.

SONNET XXXIX.

Y MATCHLESS mistress, whose delicious eyes
Have power to perfect nature's privy wants,
Even when the sun in greatest pomp did rise,
With pretty tread did press the tender plants.
Each stalk, whilst forth she stalks, to kiss her feet
Is proud with pomp, and prodigal of sweet.
Her fingers fair in favouring every flower
That wooed their ivory for a wishèd touch,
By chance—sweet chance—upon a blessed hour
Did pluck the flower where Love himself did couch,
  Where Love did couch by summer toil suppressed,
  And sought his sleep within so sweet a nest.
The virgin's hand that held the wanton thrall,
Imprisoned him within the roseate leaves;
And twixt her teats, with favour did install
The lovely rose, where Love his rest receives.
  The lad that felt the soft and sweet so nigh,
  Drowned in delights, disdains his liberty,
And said, let Venus seek another son,
For here my only matchless mother is;
From whose fair orient orbs the drink doth run,
That deifies my state with greater bliss.
  This said, he sucked, my mistress blushing smiled,
  Since Love was both her prisoner and her child.

SONNET XL.

ESEMBLING none, and none so poor as I,
Poor to the world, and poor in each esteem,
Whose first-born loves at first obscured did die,
And bred no fame but flame of base misdeem,
Under the ensign of whose tirèd pen,
Love's legions forth have masked, by others masked;
Think how I live wrongèd by ill-tongued men,
Not master of myself, to all wrongs tasked!
Oh thou that canst, and she that may do all things,
Support these languishing conceits that perish!
Look on their growth; perhaps these silly small things
May win this worthy palm, so you do cherish.
Homer hath vowed, and I with him do vow this,
He will and shall revive, if you allow this.

LICIA,

or

POEMS OF LOVE

in honour of
the admirable and singular virtues of
his Lady.
To the imitation of
the best Latin Poets, and others.

WHEREUNTO IS ADDED
The Rising to the Crown of
RICHARD THE THIRD.

Auxit Musarum numerum SAPPHO *addita Musis.*
Fælix si sævus, sic voluisset Amor.

Ad Amorem.

Si cœlum patria est puer beatum,
Si vero peperit VENUS benigna,
Si Nectar tibi Massicum ministrat;
Si sancta Ambrosia est cibus petitus,
Quid noctes habitas, diesque mecum?
Quid victum face supplicemque aduris?
Quid longam lachrimis sitim repellis?
Quid nostræ dape pasceris medullæ?
O vere rabidum genus fœrarum:
O domo stige patriaque digne:
Jam levis sumus umbra, quid lacessis?

Ad Lectorem.

Non convitia, nec latrationes,
Nec Ronchos timeo, calumniasve,
Nec ullos obelos severiores.
Non quod judicio meo Poeta
Sim tantus, nihil ut queat reprehendi:
Sed quod judicio meo Poeta
Sim tam ridiculus, parumque doctus,
Ut nullum fore judicem eruditum,
Meos carpere qui velit labores:
Nam quis Æthiopem velit lavare?

*To the Worshipful, kind, wise, and
virtuous Lady, the Lady MOLLINEUX,
Wife to the right Worshipful
Sir RICHARD MOLLINEUX Knight.*

OWSOEVER, in the settled opinions of some
wise heads, this trifling labour may easily incur
the suspicion of two evils; either to be of an
idle subject, and so frivolous; or vainly handled,
and so odious: yet my resolute purpose was to proceed so far as the indifferent [*impartial*] Reader might
think this small pains to be rather an effect, than a cause, of
idleness. And howsoever LOVE, in this Age, hath behaved
himself in that loose manner as it is counted a disgrace to
give him but a kind look: yet I take the passion in itself to
be of that honour and credit as it is the perfect resemblance
of the greatest happiness; and rightly valued at his just
price, in a mind that is sincerely and truly amorous, an affection of the greatest virtue, and able of himself to eternize the
meanest vassal.

Concerning the handling of it, especially in this Age, men
may wonder, if a Scholar, How I come by so much leisure?
If otherwise, Why a Writer? Indeed to say truth, though I
cannot justly challenge the first name; yet I wish none to
be Writers, save only such as know Learning. And whereas
my thoughts and some reasons drew me rather to have dealt
in causes of greater weight; yet the present jar of this dis-
agreeing Age drives me into a fit so melancholy as I only
had leisure to grow passionate. And I see not why, upon
our dissensions, I may not sit down idle, forsake my study,

and go sing of Love; as well as our Brownists forsake the
Church, and write of malice.

And that this is a matter not so unfit for a man, either
that respecteth himself, or is a Scholar; peruse but the
writings of former times: and you shall see, not only others
in other countries, as Italy and France, Men of Learning and
great parts to have written Poems and Sonnets of Love;
but even amongst us, men of best nobility and chiefest
families to be the greatest Scholars and most renowned in
this kind. But two reasons hath made it a thing foolishly
odious in this Age. The one, that so many base companions
are the greatest Writers. The other, that our English Gene-
vian Purity hath quite debarred us of honest recreation: yet
the great Pillar, as they make him [*i.e.* JEAN CALVIN], of
that Cause hath shewed us as much wit and learning in this
kind as any other before or since.

Furthermore for all students, I will say thus much; that
the base conceit which men generally have of their wants is
such, as I scarce term him a Scholar that hath not all the
accomplyments [*accomplishments*] of a Gentleman; nor sufficiently wise that will not take opportunity in some sort to
shew it. For I can say thus much, that the University
wherein I lived [*evidently Cambridge*], and so I think the
other [*Oxford*], hath so many wise, excellent, sufficient,
men as, setting their learning aside wherein they are most
excellent, yet in all habiliments of a Gentleman they are
equal to any besides. This would that worthy SYDNEY oft
confess; and [Sir JOHN] HARINGTON's *ARIOSTO* (which,
Madam, was respected so much by you) sheweth that his
abode was in King's College [Cambridge]. Yet now it is
grown to this pass, that Learning is lightly respected; upon
a persuasion that it is to be found everywhere: a thing
untrue and unpossible.

Now in that I have written Love Sonnets; if any man
measure my affection by my style, let him say, I am in love.
No great matter! For if our purest Divines have not been

so, why are so many married? I mislike not that, nor I
would not have them mislike this. For a man may be in
love, and not marry; and yet wise: but he cannot marry
and not be in love, but be a mere fool.

Now for the manner. We will dispute that in some other
place; yet take this by the way: though I am so liberal to
grant thus much—a man may write of Love and not be in
love; as well as of husbandry and not go to the plough; or
of witches and be none; or of holiness and be flat profane.

But, wise and kind Lady, not to trouble your ears with
this idle discourse, let this suffice. I found favours undeserved in such manner as my rude ability wants means to
recompence; and therefore in the mean time I request you
to accept this. If I had not so wondered at your admirable
and rare virtues that my heart was surcharged with the
exceeding measure of your worthiness, I had not written.
You are happy every way, and so reputed. Live so, and I
wish so you may live long! Excuse me, favour me: and, if I
live (for I loath to admire without thankfulness), ere long it
shall be known what favours I received from wise Sir
RICHARD; to whom in all kind affects I rest bound.

For the Reader, if he look for my letters to crave his
favour; he is far deceived. For if he mislike anything, I am
sorry he took the pains to read: but if he do, let him dis-
praise; I much care not. For praise is not but as men
please, and it is no chief felicity. For I have heard some
men, and of late, for Sermons at Paul's Cross and for other
pains, so commended by all, excepting some few Cynics that
commend none that do well, that you would have thought
England would have striven for their speedy preferment:
but, like a wonder, it last but nine days; and all is quiet and
forgotten. The best is, they are young men and may live to
be preferred at another time. So what am I worse if men
mislike and use terms? I can say as much by them. For
our great men, I am sure, they want leisure to read: and if
they had; yet, for the most part, the worst speak worst.

Well let the Printer look he grow not a beggar by such
bargains, the Reader that he lose not his labour, and for
mine that is past! And whoso wisely, after an afternoon's
sleep, gapes, and saith, "O how young men spend their time
idly!"; first, let him spend his time better than to sleep:
secondly, he knows not my age. I feared a hot ague; and,
with TASSO, I was content to let my Wit blood.

But leaving these to their dogged humour; and wishing
your Ladyship all happiness, I humbly take my leave

From my chamber. September 4, 1593.

To the Reader.

 HAD thought, courteous and gentle Reader, not to have troubled thy patience with these lines: but that, in the neglect thereof, I should either scorn thee, as careless of thine opinion, a thing savouring of a proud humour; or despair to obtain thy favour, which I am loath to conceive of thy good nature.

If I were known, I would entreat in the best manner; and speak for him whom thou knewest. But being not known, thou speakest not against me; and therefore I much care not. For this kind of poetry wherein I wrote, I did it only to try my humour. And for the matter of Love, it may be I am so devoted to some one into whose hands these may light by chance, that she may say, which thou now sayest "That surely he is in love:" which if she do, then have I the full recompence of my labour; and the Poems have dealt sufficiently for the discharge of their own duty.

This Age is learnedly wise, and faultless in this kind of making their wits known: thinking so basely of our bare English, wherein thousands have travailed with such ill luck, that they deem themselves barbarous and the island barren, unless they have borrowed from Italy, Spain, and France their best and choicest conceits. For my own part, I am of this mind that our nation is so exquisite (neither would I overweeningly seem to flatter our home-spun stuff, or

diminish the credit of our brave travellers) that neither
Italy, Spain, nor France can go beyond us for exact invention.   For if anything be odious amongst us, it is the
exile of our old manners, and some base-born phrases
stuft up with such new terms, as a man may sooner feel
us to flatter by our incrouching eloquence than suspect it
from the ear.

And for the matter of Love, where every man takes upon
himself to court exactly; I could justly grace (if it be a
grace to be excellent in that kind) the Inns of Court, and
some Gentlemen like[wise] Students in both Universities:
whose learning and bringing up together with their fine
natures make so sweet a harmony as, without partiality, the
most injurious will prefer them before all others; and therefore they only are fitted to write of Love.

For others, for the most part, are men of mean reach,
whose debased minds prey upon every bad dish.   Men unfit
to know what Love means; deluded fondly with their own
conceit, misdeeming so divine a fancy; taking it to be the
contentment of themselves, the shame of others, the wrong of
virtue; and the refiner of the tongue, boasting of some few
favours.   These and such like errors (errors hateful to an
upright mind) commonly by learnless heads are reputed for
Love's Kingdom.   But vain men, naturally led; deluded
themselves, [they] deceive others.

For Love is a goddess (pardon me though I speak like a
Poet) not respecting the contentment of him that loves but
the virtues of the beloved, satisfied with wondering, fed with
admiration, respecting nothing but his Lady's worthiness,
made as happy by love as by all favours, chaste by honour,
far from violence: respecting but one; and that one in such

kindness honesty truth constancy and honour, as were all the World offered to make a change, yet the boot were too small, and therefore bootless. This is Love, and far more than this; which I know a vulgar head, a base mind, an ordinary conceit, a common person will not, and cannot, have. Thus do I commend that love wherewith, in these Poems, I have honoured the worthy L I C I A.

But the love wherewith VENUS' son hath injuriously made spoil of thousands, is a cruel Tyrant: occasion of sighs, oracle of lies, enemy of pity, way of error, shape of inconstancy, temple of treason, faith without assurance, monarch of tears, murderer of ease, prison of hearts, monster of Nature, poisoned honey, impudent courtezan, furious bastard: and in one word, not Love.

Thus, Reader, take heed thou err not! Esteem Love as thou ought[est]!

If thou muse, What my LICIA is? Take her to be some DIANA, at the least chaste; or some MINERVA: no VENUS, fairer far. It may be she is Learning's Image, or some heavenly wonder: which the Precisest may not mislike. Perhaps under that name I have shadowed "[The Holy] Discipline." It may be, I mean that kind courtesy which I found at the Patroness of these Poems, it may be some College. It may be my conceit, and pretend nothing. Whatsoever it be; if thou like it, take it! and thank the worthy Lady MOLLINEUX, for whose sake thou hast it: worthy indeed, and so not only reputed by me in private affection of thankfulness; but so equally to be esteemed by all that know her.

For if I had not received of her and good Sir RICHARD, of kind and wise Master LEE, of eourteous Master HOUGH-

TON, all matchless, matched in one kindred, those unrequit-
able favours ; I had not thus idly toyed.

If thou mislike it ; yet she, or they, or both, or divine
LICIA shall patronize it : or if none ; I will, and can, do it
myself. Yet I wish thy favour. Do but say, Thou art content ; and I rest thine. If not, Farewell ! till we both meet.
September 8. 1593.

To LICIA,

the wise, kind, virtuous, and fair.

RIGHT matchless Star, the honour of
   the sky!
  From whose clear shine heaven's vault
   hath all his light.
  I send these Poems to your graceful
   eye.
Do you but take them, and they have their right.
 I build besides a Temple to your name,
Wherein my thoughts shall daily sing your praise;
And will erect an Altar for the same,
Which shall, your virtues and your honour raise.
 But heaven, the Temple of your honour is;
Whose brazen tops your worthy self made proud:
The ground an Altar, base for such a bliss,
With pity torn, because I sighed so loud.
 And since my skill no worship can impart;
 Make you an incense of my loving heart!

SONNET I.

AD, all alone, not long I musing sat
But that my thoughts compelled me to aspire.
A laurel garland in my hand I gat,
So the Muses I approached the nigher.
My suit was this, A Poet to become;
To drink with them, and from the heavens be fed.
PHŒBUS denied; and sware, "There was no room
Such to be Poets as fond Fancy led."
With that I mourned, and sat me down to weep.
VENUS she smiled, and smiling to me said,
"Come drink with me, and sit thee still and sleep!"
This voice I heard, and VENUS I obeyed.
That poison, Sweet, hath done me all this wrong;
For now of Love must needs be all my Song.

SONNET II.

EARY was LOVE, and sought to take his rest.
He made his choice upon a Virgin's lap;
And slyly crept from thence into her breast,
Where still he meant to sport him in his hap.
The Virgin frowned, like PHŒBUS in a cloud,
"Go pack, sir boy, here is no room for such!
My breast, no wanton foolish boys must shroud!"
This said, my Love did give the Wag a touch.
Then as the foot, that treads the stinging snake,
Hastes to be gone, for fear what may ensue:
So LOVE, my Love was forced for to forsake;
And, for more speed, without his arrows flew.
"Pardon!" he said, "for why you seemed to me,
My mother VENUS in her pride to be."

SONNET III.

He heavens beheld the beauty of my Queen;
And all amazed, to wonder thus began:
"Why dotes not JOVE, as erst we all have seen,
And shapes himself like to a seemly man?
Mean are the matches which he sought before;
Like bloomless buds, too base to make compare:
And she alone hath treasured Beauty's store;
In whom all gifts and princely graces are."
CUPID replied, "I posted with the sun
To view the Maids that lived in all those days:
And none there was that might not well be won,
But She; most hard, most cold, made of delays."
Heavens were deceived, and wrong they do esteem;
She hath no heat, although She living seem.

SONNET IV.

Ove and my Love did range the forest wild,
Mounted alike upon swift coursers both.
LOVE her encountered, though he was a child,
"Let's strive!" said he.   Whereat my Love
was wroth;
And scorned the boy, and checked him with a smile.
"I mounted am, and armèd with my spear.
Thou art too weak!   Thyself do not beguile!
I could thee conquer, if I naked [*unarmed*] were!"
With this LOVE wept, and then my Love replied:
"Kiss me, sweet boy, so!   Weep, my boy, no more!"
Thus did my Love, and thus her force she tried:
LOVE was made ice, that fire was before.
A kiss of hers (as I, poor soul, do prove)
Can make the hottest, freeze; and coldest love.

SONNET V.

OVE, with her hair, my Love by force hath tied;
To serve her lips, her eyes, her voice, her hand.
I smiled for joy when I the boy espied
To lie unchained, and live at her command.
She, if She look, or kiss, or sing, or smile;
CUPID withal doth smile, doth sing, doth kiss.
Lips, hands, voice, eyes, all hearts that may beguile;
Because She scorns, all hearts but only this.
VENUS for this in pride began to frown,
That CUPID, born a god, inthralled should be:
She, in disdain, her pretty son threw down;
And in his place, with love she chainèd me.
So now, sweet Love, tho' I myself be thrall;
Not her a goddess, but thyself, I call.

SONNET VI.

Y Love, amazed, did blush herself to see,
Pictured by Art, all naked as she was.
" How could the Painter know so much by me,
Or Art effect what he hath brought to pass?
It is not like, he naked me hath seen;
Or stood so nigh for to observe so much."
No, Sweet, his eyes so near have never been;
Nor could his hands by Art have cunning such:
I showed my heart, wherein you printed were;
You, naked you, as here you painted are.
In that, my Love, your picture I must wear;
And show 't to all, unless you have more care:
Then take my heart, and place it with your own!
So shall you naked never more be known.

SONNET VII.

EATH, in a rage, assaulted once my heart
With love of her, my love that doth deny.
I scorned his force, and wished him to depart,
I heartless was, and therefore *could* not die.
　I live in her.　In her I placed my life.
She guides my soul, and her I honour must.
Nor is this life; but yet a living strife:
A thing unmeet, and yet a thing most just.
　CUPID, enraged, did fly to make me love;
My heart lay guarded with those burning eyes,
The sparks whereof denied him to remove:
So conquered now, he like a captive lies.
　　Thus two at once by love are both undone:
　　My heart not loved; and armless VENUS' son.

SONNET VIII.

ARD are the rocks, the marble, and the steel,
The ancient oak with wind and weather tosst;
But you, my Love, far harder do I feel
Than flint, or these, or is the winter's frost.
　My tears too weak, your heart they cannot move;
My sighs, that rock, like wind it cannot rent;
Too tiger-like, you swear you cannot love:
But tears and sighs you fruitless back have sent.
　The frost too hard, not melted with my flame;
I cinders am, and yet you feel no heat:
Surpass not these, sweet Love, for very shame!
But let my tears, my vows, my sighs entreat!
　　Then shall I say, as I by trial find,
　　These all are hard; but you, my Love, are kind.

SONNET IX.

OVE was laid down, all weary, fast asleep;
    Whereas my Love his armour took away.
    The boy awaked, and straight began to weep;
    But stood amazed, and knew not what to say.
" Weep not, my boy," said VENUS to her son,
" Thy weapons none can wield but thou alone.
LICIA the Fair, this harm to thee hath done;
I saw her here, and presently was gone.
    She will restore them, for she hath no need
To take thy weapons, where thy valour lies.
For men to wound, the Fates have her decreed
With favour, hands, with beauty, and with eyes."
    No, VENUS, no!   She scorns them, credit me!
    But robbed thy son, that none might care for thee!

SONNET X

PAINTER drew the image of the boy,
    Swift LOVE, with wings, all naked, and yet blind;
    With bow and arrows bent for to destroy.
    I blamed his skill; and fault I thus did find:
" A needless task I see thy cunning take:
Misled by love, thy fancy thee betrayed.
Love is no boy, nor blind, as men him make;
Nor weapons wears, whereof to be afraid:
    But if thou Love wilt paint with greatest skill;
A Love, a Maid, a goddess, and a Queen!
Wonder and view at LICIA's picture still!
For other Love, the World hath never seen.
    For She alone, all hope, all comfort, gives:
    Men's hearts, souls all, led by her favour, live."

SONNET XI.

N Ida Vale three Queens, the Shepherd saw;
    Queens of esteem, divine, they were all three.
    A sight of worth, but I a wonder show:
    Their virtues all in one alone to be.
   LICIA the Fair surpassing VENUS's pride,
(The matchless Queen, commander of the gods,
When, drawn with doves, she in her pomp doth ride)
Hath far more beauty and more grace by odds:
   JUNO, JOVE's wife, unmeet to make compare;
I grant a goddess, but not half so mild:
MINERVA wise, a virtue; but not rare.
Yet these are mean, if that my Love but smiled.
   She them surpasseth, when their prides are full,
   As far as they surpass the meanest trull.

SONNET XII.

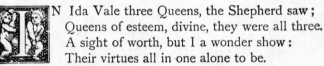

WISH sometimes, although a worthless thing,
    Spurred by ambition, glad for to aspire,
    Myself a Monarch, or some mighty King:
    And then my thoughts do wish for to be higher.
   But when I view what winds the cedars toss,
What storms men feel that covet for renown;
I blame myself that I have wished my loss:
And scorn a Kingdom, though it give a Crown.
   A' LICIA thou, the wonder of my thought,
My heart's content, procurer of my bliss;
For whom, a Crown I do esteem as nought:
And Asia's wealth, too mean to buy a kiss.
   Kiss me, sweet Love! this favour do for me;
   Then Crowns and Kingdoms shall I scorn for thee.

SONNET XIII.

NAMOURED JOVE, commanding, did entreat
CUPID to wound my Love : which he denied,
And swore he could not, for she wanted heat ;
And would not love, as he full oft had tried.
JOVE, in a rage, impatient this to hear,
Replied with threats, " I'll make you to obey ! "
Whereat the boy did fly away for fear
To LICIA's eyes, where safe entrenched he lay.
Then JOVE, he scorned ; and dared him to his face :
For now more safe than in the heavens he dwelled ;
Nor could JOVE's wrath do wrong to such a place,
Where Grace and Honour have their kingdom held.
Thus, in the pride and beauty of her eyes,
The silly boy, the greatest god defies.

SONNET XIV.

Y Love lay sleeping where birds music made,
Shutting her eyes, disdainful of the light :
The heat was great ; but greater was the shade
Which her defended from his burning sight.
This CUPID saw, and came a kiss to take ;
Sucking sweet nectar from her sugared breath.
She felt the touch, and blushed, and did awake.
Seeing 'twas LOVE, which she did think was DEATH,
She cut his wings, and caused him to stay ;
Making a vow, he should not thence depart
Unless to her, the wanton boy could pay
The truest, kindest, and most loving heart.
His feathers still She used for a fan ;
Till, by exchange, my heart his feathers wan.

SONNET XV.

STOOD amazed, and saw my LICIA shine
Fairer than PHŒBUS in his brightest pride;
Set forth in colours by a hand divine,
Where naught was wanting but a soul to guide.
It was a picture that I could descry,
Yet made with art so as it seemed to live;
Surpassing fair, and yet it had no eye:
Whereof my senses could no reason give.
With that the Painter bid me not to muse,
" Her eyes are shut; but I deserve no blame:
For if she saw, in faith, it could not choose
But that the work had wholly been aflame."
Then burn me, Sweet, with brightness of your eyes;
That, Phœnix-like. from thence I may arise.

SONNET XVI.

" GRANT, fairest kind, a kiss unto thy friend!"
A blush replied; and yet a kiss I had.
It is not heaven that can such nectar send;
Whereat my senses, all amazed, were glad.
This done, She fled as one that was afraid;
And I desired to kiss, by kissing more.
My Love, she frowned; and I my kissing stayed:
Yet wished to kiss her as I did before.
Then as the vine, the propping elm doth clasp,
Loth to depart, till both together die;
So fold me, Sweet; until my latest gasp!
That in thy arms, to death I kissed, may lie.
Thus whilst I live, for kisses I must call:
Still kiss me, Sweet, or kiss me not at all!

SONNET XVII.

S are the sands, fair LICIA, on the shore ;
Or coloured flowers, garlands of the Spring ;
Or as the frosts not seen nor felt before ;
Or as the fruits that Autumn forth doth bring ;
As twinkling stars, the tinsel of the night ;
Or as the fish that gallop in the seas ;
As airs, each part that still escapes our sight :
So are my Sighs, controllers of my ease.
Yet these are such as needs must have an end,
For things finite, none else hath Nature done :
Only the sighs which from my heart I send
Will never cease, but where they first began.
Accept them, Sweet, as incense due to thee !
For you immortal made them so to be.

SONNET XVIII.

 SWEAR, fair LICIA, still for to be thine ;
By heart, by eyes, by what I hold most dear !
Thou checkedst mine oath, and said, "These
were not mine ;
And that I had no right by them to swear."
Then by my sighs, my passions, and my tears,
My vows, my prayers, my sorrow, and my love,
My grief, my joy, my hope, and hopeless fears ·
My heart is thine, and never shall remove !
These are not thine, though sent unto thy view ;
All else I grant, by right they are thine own.
Let these suffice, that what I swear is true ;
And more than this, if that it could be known.
So shall all these, though troubles, ease my grief,
If that they serve to work in thee belief.

SONNET XIX.

HAT time, fair LICIA, when I stole a kiss
From off those lips where CUPID lovely laid,
I quaked for cold : and found the cause was this :
My Life which loved, for love behind me stayed.
I sent my Heart, my Life for to recall,
But that was held, not able to return :
And both detained, as captives were in thrall,
And judged by her, that both by sighs should burn.
Fair, burn them both ! for that they were so bold ;
But let the altar be within thy heart !
And I shall live, because my life you hold ;
You that give life to every living part.
A flame I took when as I stole the kiss :
Take you my life ! yet can I live with this.

SONNET XX.

IRST did I fear, when first my love began ;
Possessed in fits by watchful jealousy,
I sought to keep what I by favour wan,
And brooked no partner in my love to be.
But tyrant Sickness fed upon my Love,
And spread his ensigns dyed with colour white ;
Then was Suspicion glad for to remove ;
And loving much did fear to lose her quite.
Erect, fair Sweet, the colours thou didst wear !
Dislodge thy griefs, the short'ners of content !
For now of life, not love, is all my fear :
Lest life and love be both together spent.
Live but, fair Love, and banish thy disease !
And love, kind Heart, both when, and whom, thou please !

SONNET XXI.

ICIA, my Love, was sitting in a grove;
    Tuning her smiles unto the chirping songs:
    But straight she spied where two together strove,
    Each one complaining of the other's wrongs.
CUPID did cry, lamenting of the harm,
" JOVE's Messenger, thou wrong'st me too too far !
Use thou thy rod ! rely upon thy charm !
Think not by speech, my force thou can'st debar ! "
    " A rod, sir boy, were fitter for a child !
My weapons oft, and tongue, and mind you took :
And in my wrong, at my distress thou smiled ;
And scorn to grace me with a loving look."
    Speak you, Sweet Love, for you did all the wrong !
    That broke his arrows, and did bind his tongue.

SONNET XXII.

"MIGHT have died before my life began ;
    When as my father, for his country's good,
    The Persians' favour and the Sophy wan :
    But yet with danger of his dearest blood."
    Thy father, Sweet, whom danger did beset,
Escapèd all : and for no other end
But only this, that you he might beget :
Whom heavens decreed into the world to send.
    Then, father, thank thy daughter for thy life !
And Neptune praise, that yielded so to thee,
To calm the tempest, when the storms were rife ;
And that thy daughter should a VENUS be.
    I call thee VENUS, Sweet ! but be not wroth ;
    Thou art more chaste, yet seas did favour both.

SONNET XXIII.

Y Love was masked, and armèd with a fan ;
To see the sun so careless of his light :
Which stood and gazed ; and gazing, waxèd wan
To see a star, himself that was more bright.
Some did surmise She hid her from the sun ;
Of whom, in pride, She scorned for to be kissed :
And feared the harm by him to others done.
But these the reason of this wonder missed ;
Nor durst the sun, if that her face were bare,
In greatest pride presume to take a kiss :
But she, more kind, did show she had more care
Than with her eyes eclipse him of his bliss.
Unmask you, Sweet, and spare not ! dim the sun !
Your light's enough, although that his were done.

SONNET XXIV.

HEN as my Love lay sickly in her bed,
Pale Death did post, in hope to have a prey ;
But she so spotless made him, that he fled :
" Unmeet to die," he cried ; and could not stay.
Back he retired, and thus the heavens he told :
" All things that are, are subject unto me ;
Both towns, and men, and what the world doth hold :
But let fair LICIA still immortal be ! "
The heavens did grant. A goddess she was made,
Immortal, fair, unfit to suffer change.
So now she lives, and never more shall fade.
In earth, a goddess. What can be more strange ?
Then will I hope ! A goddess, and so near ;
She cannot choose, my sighs and prayers but hear.

SONNET XXV.

SEVEN are the Lights that wander in the skies:
And at these seven, I wonder in my Love.
To see the Moon how pale she doth arise;
Standing amazed, as though she durst not move:
    So is my Sweet, much paler than the snow;
Constant her looks, those looks that cannot change.
MERCURY the next, a god sweet-tongued we know;
But her sweet voice doth wonders speak more strange.
    The rising Sun doth boast him of his pride;
And yet my Love is far more fair than he.
The warlike MARS can wieldless weapons guide;
But yet that god is far more weak than She.
    The lovely VENUS seemeth to be fair;
But at her best, my Love is far more bright.
SATURN, for age, with groans doth dim the air;
Whereas my Love, with smiles doth give it light.
    Gaze at her brows, where heaven engrafted is;
Then sigh, and swear, There is no heaven but this.

SONNET XXVI.

LIVE, sweet Love, where as the gentle wind
Murmurs with sport, in midst of thickest boughs;
Where loving woodbine doth the harbour bind,
And chirping birds do echo forth my vows;
    Where strongest elm can scarce support the vine,
And sweetest flowers enamelled have the ground;
Where Muses dwell: and yet hereat repine
That on the earth so rare a place was found.
    But winds delight: I wish to be content.
I praise the woodbine: but I take no joy.
I moan the birds that music thus have spent.
As for the rest, they breed but mine annoy.
    Live thou, fair LICIA, in this place alone:
Then shall I joy, though all of these were gone.

SONNET XXVII.

HE crystal streams, wherein my Love did swim,
    Melted in tears, as partners of my woe;
    Her shine was such as did the fountain dim,
    The pearl-like fountain, whiter than the snow.
Then, like perfume resolvèd with a heat,
The fountain smoked, as if it thought to burn.
A wonder strange to see the cold so great,
And yet the fountain into smoke to turn.
    I searched the cause, and found it to be this:
She touched the water, and it burnt with love.
Now, by her means, it purchased hath that bliss
Which all diseases quickly can remove.
    Then if, by you, these streams thus blessèd be:
    Sweet, grant me love; and be not worse to me!

SONNET XXVIII.

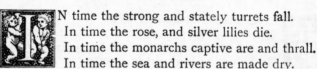N time the strong and stately turrets fall.
    In time the rose, and silver lilies die.
    In time the monarchs captive are and thrall.
    In time the sea and rivers are made dry.
The hardest flint in time doth melt asunder.
Still living fame, in time doth fade away.
The mountains proud, we see in time come under:
And earth, for aye, we see in time decay.
    The sun in time forgets for to retire
From out the East, where he was wont to rise.
The basest thoughts, we see in time aspire.
And greedy minds, in time do wealth despise.
    Thus all, sweet Fair, in time must have an end:
    Except thy beauty, virtues, and thy friend.

SONNET XXIX.

HEN as my LICIA sailèd in the seas,
Viewing with pride, god NEPTUNE's stately crown,
A calm she made, and brought the merchant ease;
The storm she stayed, and checked him with a
frown.
Love at the stern sat smiling, and did sing
To see how seas had learned for to obey;
And balls of fire into the waves did fling.
And still the boy, full wanton, thus did say:
"Both poles we burnt, whereon the world doth turn;
The round of heaven from earth unto the skies:
And now the seas, we both intend to burn;
I with my bow, and LICIA with her eyes."
Then since thy force, heavens, earth, nor seas can move;
I conquered, yield: and do confess I love.

SONNET XXX.

HEN as her lute is tunèd to her voice,
The air grows proud for honour of that sound;
And rocks do leap, to shew how they rejoice
That in the earth such music should be found.
When as her hair (more worth, more pale, than gold)
Like silver thread lies wafting in the air;
DIANA-like she looks, but yet more bold:
Cruel in chase, more chaste, and yet more fair.
When as she smiles, the cloud for envy breaks;
She JOVE in pride encounters with a check:
The sun doth shine for joy when as she speaks,
Thus heaven and earth do homage at her beck.
Yet all these graces, blots; not graces, are:
If you, my Love, of love do take no care.

SONNET XXXI.

EARS, months, days, hours, in sighs I sadly spend.
I black the night, wherein I sleepless toss.
I love my griefs, yet wish them at an end.
Thus time's expense increaseth but my loss.
I musing stand, and wonder at my Love;
That in so fair, should be a heart of steel.
And then I think, my fancy to remove:
But then more painful I my passions feel.
Thus must I love, sweet Fair, until I die;
And your unkindness doth my love increase:
I conquered am, I cannot it deny.
My life must end; yet shall my love not cease.
Then heavens, make LICIA fair most kind to me;
Or with my life, my love may finished be!

SONNET XXXII.

WROTE my sighs, and sent them to my Love.
I praised that Fair, that none enough could praise:
But plaints, nor praises, could fair LICIA move.
Above my reach, she did her virtues raise.
And thus replied, " False scrawl, untrue thou art!
To feign those sighs that nowhere can be found.
For half those praises came not from his heart;
Whose faith and love, as yet, was never found.
" Thy master's life, false scrawl, shall be thy doom!
Because he burns, I judge thee to the flame!
Both your attempts deserve no better room."
Thus, at her word, we ashes both became.
Believe me, Fair, and let my paper live!
Or be not fair, and so me freedom give.

SONNET XXXIII.

ALE are my looks, forsaken of my life :
Cinders, my bones ; consumèd with thy flame.
Floods are my tears, to end this burning strife ;
And yet I sigh, for to increase the same.
I mourn alone, because alone I burn :
Who doubts of this, then let him learn to love !
Her looks, cold ice into a flame can turn ;
As I distressèd in myself do prove.
Respect, fair LICIA, what my torments are !
Count but the tithe both of my sighs and tears !
See how my love doth still increase my care !
And care's increase, my life to nothing wears.
Send but a sigh, my flame for to increase :
Or lend a tear, and cause it so to cease.

SONNET XXXIV.

HEN as I wish, fair LICIA, for a kiss
From those sweet lips, where rose and lilies strive ;
Straight do mine Eyes repine at such a bliss,
And seek my Lips thereof for to deprive.
When as I seek to glut mine Eyes by sight ;
My Lips repine, and call mine Eyes away.
Thus both contend to have each other's right ;
And both conspire to work my full decay.
O force admired, of Beauty in her pride ;
In whose each part such strange effects there be,
That all my forces in themselves divide,
And make my senses plainly disagree.
If *all* were mine, this envy would be gone :
Then grant me *all*, fair Sweet ; or grant me none !

SONNET XXXV.

EAR how my Sighs are echoed by the wind !
See how my Tears are pitied by the rain !
Feel what a Flame possessèd hath my mind !
Taste but the Grief which I possess in vain !
Then if my Sighs, the blustering wind surpass ;
And wat'ry Tears, the drops of rain exceed ;
And if no Flame like mine nor is, nor was ;
Nor Grief like that whereon my soul doth feed :
Relent, fair LICIA ! when my Sighs do blow :
Yield at my Tears ! that flintlike drops consume :
Accept the Flame ! that doth my incense show :
Allow the Grief ! that is my heart's perfume :
  Thus Sighs, and Tears, Flame, Grief, shall plead for me ;
  So shall I pray, and you a goddess be.

SONNET XXXVI.

SPEAK, fair LICIA, what my torments be ;
But then my speech too partial do I find :
For hardly words can with those thoughts agree:
Those thoughts that swarm in such a troubled
    mind.
Then do I vow my tongue shall never speak,
Nor tell my grief that in my heart doth lie :
But, cannon-like, I, then surcharged, do break.
And so my silence worse than speech I try.
  Thus speech, or none, they both do breed my care :
I live dismayed and kill my heart with grief.
In all respects my case alike doth fare.
To him that wants ; and dares not ask relief.
  Then you, fair LICIA, Sovereign of my heart,
  Read to yourself my anguish and my smart !

SONNET XXXVII.

SWEET, I protest, and seal it with an oath,
    I never saw that so my thoughts did please :
    And yet content, displeased I see them wroth
    To love so much, and cannot have their ease.
I told my thoughts, " My Sovereign made a pause :
Disposed to grant, but willing to delay."
They then repined, for that they knew no cause ;
And swore they wished She flatly would say " Nay."
    Thus hath my love, my thoughts with treason filled ;
And 'gainst my Sovereign taught them to repine :
So thus my treason, all my thoughts hath killed ;
And made fair LICIA say, She is not mine.
    But thoughts too rash, my heart doth now repent :
    And, as you please, they swear they are content.

SONNET XXXVIII.

FAIR matchless Nymph, respect but what I crave !
    My thoughts are true, and honour is my love.
    I fainting die, whom yet a smile might save.
    You gave the wound, and can the hurt remove.
Those eyes, like stars that twinkle in the night ;
And cheeks, like rubies pale in lilies dyed ;
Those ebon [*ivory*] hands that darting have such might :
That in my soul, my love and life divide.
    Accept the Passions of a man possesst !
Let love be loved, and grant me leave to live !
Disperse those clouds that darkened have my rest ;
And let your heaven, a sunlike smile but give !
    Then shall I praise that heaven for such a sun ;
    That saved my life, when as my grief begun.

SONNET XXXIX.

Y grief began, fair Saint, when first I saw
Love, in those eyes, sit ruling with disdain ;
Whose sweet commands did keep a world in awe :
And caused them serve, your favour to obtain.
I stood as one enchanted with a frown ;
Yet smiled to see all creatures serve those eyes :
Where each with sighs paid tribute to that crown ;
And thought them gracèd by your dumb replies.
But I, ambitious, could not be content
Till that my service, more than sighs made known ;
And for that end, my heart to you I sent,
To say and swear that, Fair ! it is your own.
Then greater graces, LICIA, do impart !
Not dumb replies, unto a speaking heart.

SONNET XL.

A Sonnet made upon the Two Twins, daughters of the
Lady MOLLINEUX ; both passing like, and exceeding[ly] fair.

OETS did feign that heavens a VENUS had ;
Matchless herself, and CUPID was her son.
Men sued to these, and of their smiles were glad ;
By whom so many famous were undone.
Now CUPID mourns that he hath lost his might,
And that these Two so comely are to see ;
And VENUS frowns, because they have her right :
Yet both so like that both shall blameless be.
With heaven's Two Twins for godhead these may strive ;
And rule a World with least part of a frown :
Fairer than these Two Twins are not alive ;
Both conquering Queens, and both deserve a Crown.
My thoughts presage, which time to come shall try,
That thousands conquered, for their love shall die.

SONNET XLI.

F, aged CHARON, when my life shall end,
   I pass thy ferry and my waftage pay,
   Thy oars shall fail thy boat, and mast shall rend;
   And through the deep shall be a dry footway.
For why? My heart with sighs doth breathe such flame
That air and water both incensèd be:
The boundless ocean from whose mouth they came
(For from my heat not heaven itself is free!).
   Then since to me my loss can be no gain;
Avoid thy harm, and fly what I foretell!
Make thou my Love with me for to be slain;
That I with her, and both with thee, may dwell.
   Thy fact thus, CHARON, both of us shall bless:
   Thou save thy boat, and I my Love possess.

SONNET XLII.

OR if alone thou think to waft my Love,
   Her cold is such as can the sea command;
   And frozen ice shall let [*hinder*] thy boat to move.
   Nor can thy forces row it from the land.
   But if thou, friendly, both at once shall take;
Thyself mayest rest! For why? My sighs will blow.
Our cold and heat so sweet a thaw shall make
As that thy boat, without thy help, shall row.
   Then will I sit and glut me on those eyes
Wherewith my life, my eyes could never fill.
Thus from thy boat that comfort shall arise,
The want whereof my life and hope did kill.
   Together placed, so thou her scorn shalt cross:
   Where if we part, thy boat must suffer loss.

SONNET XLIII.

RE those two stars, her eyes, my life's light, gone?
By which my soul was freeèd from all dark:
And am I left distressed to live alone,
Where none my tears and mournful tale shall
mark?
Ah, Sun! why shine thy looks, thy looks like gold;
When, horseman brave, thou risest in the East?
Ah, CYNTHIA pale, to whom my griefs I told!
Why do you both rejoice both man and beast?
And I alone, alone that dark possess
By LICIA's absence, brighter than the Sun:
Whose smiling light did ease my sad distress,
And broke the clouds when tears like rain begun.
Heavens grant that light, and so me waking keep:
Or shut my eyes, and rock me fast asleep!

SONNET XLIV.

RUEL fair Love! I justly do complain
Of too much rigour, and thy heart unkind;
That, for mine eyes, thou hast my body slain:
And would not grant that I should favour find.
I looked, fair Love! and you my Love looked fair.
I sighed for love, and you for sport did smile.
Your smiles were such as did perfume the air;
And this perfumèd, did my heart beguile.
Thus I confess the fault was in mine eyes,
Begun with sighs, and endèd with a flame.
I, for your love, did all the world despise;
And in these Poems honoured have your name.
Then let your love so with my fault dispense,
That all my parts feel not mine eyes' offence.

SONNET XLV.

HERE shone a Comet, and it was full West.
  My thought presagèd what it did portend:
  I found it threatened, to my heart unrest;
  And might, in time, my joys and comfort end.
I further sought, and found it was a Sun;
Which day, nor night, did never use to set.
It constant stood, when heavens did restless run;
And did their virtues and their forces let.
  The World did muse, and wonder what it meant:
A Sun to shine, and in the West to rise.
To search the truth, I strength and spirits spent.
At length I found it was my LICIA's eyes.
    Now, never after, soul shall live in dark,
    That hath the hap, this western Sun to mark.

SONNET XLVI.

IF he be dead in whom no heart remains,
  Or lifeless be in whom no life is found;
  If he do pine, that never comfort gains;
  And be distressed that hath his deadly wound:
Then must I die, whose heart elsewhere is clad;
And lifeless pass the greedy worms to feed:
Then must I pine, that never comfort had;
And be distressed, whose wound with tears doth bleed
  Which if I do, why do I not wax cold?
Why rest I not like one that wants a heart?
Why move I still like him that life doth hold;
And sense enjoy both of my joy and smart?
    Like NIOBE Queen, which, made a stone, did weep:
    LICIA my heart, dead and alive, doth keep.

SONNET XLVII.

IKE MEMNON's rock, touched with the rising sun,
Which yields a sound, and echoes forth a voice :
But when it 's drowned in western seas is dumb ;
And drowsy-like, leaves off to make a noise.
So I, my Love, enlightened with your shine,
A Poet's skill within my soul I shroud ;
Not rude, like that which finer wits decline ;
But such as Muses, to the best allowed.
But when your figure and your shape is gone ;
I speechless am, like as I was before :
Or if I write, my verse is filled with moan ;
And blurred with tears, by falling in such store.
Then muse not, LICIA, if my Muse be slack :
For when I wrote, I did thy beauty lack.

SONNET XLVIII.

SAW, sweet LICIA, when the Spider ran
Within your house, to weave a worthless web ;
You present were, and feared her with your fan :
So that, amazèd, speedily she fled.
She, in your house, such sweet perfumes did smell ;
And heard the Muses with their notes refined :
Thus, filled with envy, could no longer dwell ;
But straight returned, and at your house repined.
"Then tell me, Spider, why of late I saw
Thee lose thy poison, and thy bowels gone ?
Did these enchant and keep thy limbs in awe,
And made thy forces to be small or none ?
No, no ! Thou didst, by chance, my LICIA see ;
Who, for her look, MINERVA seemed to be."

SONNET XLIX.

F that I die, fair LICIA, with disdain ;
Or heartless live, surprisèd with thy wrong :
The heavens and earth shall accent both my pain,
And curse the time so cruel and so long.
If you be kind, my Queen, as you are fair ;
And aid my thoughts that still for conquest strive :
Then will I sing, and never more despair,
And praise your kindness whilst I am alive.
Till then I pay the tribute of my tears,
To move thy mercy and thy constant truth.
Respect, fair Love, how these with sorrow wear
The truest heart ; unless it find some ruth.
    Then grace me, Sweet, and with thy favour raise me ;
    So shall I live, and all the World shall praise thee.

SONNET L.

' LICIA sigh ! and say, Thou art my own.
Nay, Be my own ! as you full oft have said.
So shall your truth unto the World be known :
And I, resolved ; where now I am afraid.
And if my tongue eternize can your praise,
Or silly speech increase your worthy fame ;
If aught I can, to heaven your worth can raise,
The Age to come shall wonder at the same.
In this respect, your love, sweet Love, I told ;
My faith and truth I vowed should be for ever.
You were the cause, if that I were too bold ;
Then pardon this my fault, or love me never
    But if you frown, I wish that none believe me :
    For, slain with sighs, I'll die before I'll grieve thee

SONNET LI.

HEN first the Sun, whom all my senses serve,
Began to shine upon this earthly round;
The heavens for her, all graces did reserve;
That, PANDOR'-like, with all she might abound.
APOLLO placed his brightness in her eyes,
His skill presaging, and his music sweet.
MARS gave his force. All force she now defies.
VENUS, her smiles; wherewith she MARS did meet.
Python, a voice. DIANA made her chaste.
CERES gave plenty. CUPID lent his bow;
THETIS, her feet. There PALLAS wisdom placed.
With these, she, Queen-like, kept a World in awe.
Yet all these honours deemèd are but pelf:
For she is much more worthy, of herself.

SONNET LII.

SUGARED talk! wherewith my thoughts do live.
O brows! Love's trophy, and my senses' shrine.
O charming smiles! that death or life can give.
O heavenly kisses! from a mouth divine.
O wreaths! too strong, and trammels made of hair!
O pearls! enclosèd in an ebon [*ivory*] pale.
O rose and lilies! in a field most fair,
Where modest white doth make the red seem pale.
O voice! whose accents live within my heart.
O heavenly hand! that more than ATLAS holds.
O sighs perfumed! that can release my smart.
O happy they! whom in her arms she folds.
Now if you ask, Where dwelleth all this bliss?
Seek out my Love! and she will tell you this.

An Ode.

LOVE, I repent me that I thought
 My sighs and languish dearly bought:
 For sighs and languish both did prove
 That he that languished sighed for love.
 Cruel rigour, foe to State,
 Looks disdainful, fraught with hate,
I did blame: but had no cause
(Love hath eyes, but hath no laws).
  She was sad, and could not choose
To see me sigh, and sit and muse.
We both did love, and both did doubt [*fear*]
Lest any should our love find out.
Our hearts did speak by sighs most hidden;
This means was left: all else forbidden.
  I did frown, her love to try
She did sigh, and straight did cry.
Both of us did signs believe
Yet either grievèd friend to grieve.
I did look, and then did smile:
She left sighing all that while.
Both were glad to see that change;
Things in love that are not strange. ‾
  Suspicion, foolish foe to Reason,
Caused me seek to find some treason
I.did court another Dame.
(False in love, it is a shame!)

She was sorry this to view,
Thinking faith was proved untrue.

   Then she swore, She would not love
One, whom false She once did prove.

   I did vow I never meant
From promise made, for to relent.

   The more I said, the worse she thought :
My oaths and vows were deemed as nought.
" False ! " She said, " how can it be,
To court another ; yet love me ?
Crowns and Love no partners brook :
If she be liked, I am forsook !
Farewell, False ! and love her still !
Your chance was good, but mine was ill.
No harm to you : but this I crave,
That your new Love may you deceive !
And jest with you, as you have done :
For light 's the love that 's quickly won."

   " Kind and fair Sweet, once believe me !
Jest I did ; but not to grieve thee.
Court I did, but did not love.
Words, and sighs, and what I spent
In show to her ; to you were meant.
Fond [*foolish*] I was, your love to cross
(Jesting love oft brings this loss).
Forget this fault ! and love your friend,
Which vows his truth unto the end ! "

   " Content," She said, " if this you keep."
   Thus both did kiss, and both did weep.
For women long they cannot chide :
As I, by proof, in this have tried.

A Dialogue betwixt two Sea Nymphs, DORIS and GALATEA, concerning POLYPHEMUS.

Briefly translated out of LUCIAN.

HE Sea Nymphs late did play them on the
  shore,
  And smiled to see such sport was new
   begun :
  A strife in love, the like not heard before ;
  Two Nymphs contend, Which had the
   conquest won ?
DORIS the fair, with GALATE did chide.
She liked her choice, and to her taunts replied.

DORIS.

Thy Love, fair Nymph ! that courts thee on this plain,
As shepherds say, and all the World can tell,
 Is that foul rude Sicilian CYCLOP-swain.
A shame, sweet Nymph, that he with thee should mell [*mix*]!

GALATEA.

Smile not, fair DORIS ! though he foul do seem.
Let pass thy words that savour of disgrace !
He's worth my love, and so I him esteem.
Renowned by birth, and comes of NEPTUNE's race.
 NEPTUNE, that doth the glassy ocean tame ;
 NEPTUNE, by birth from mighty JOVE which came.

DORIS.

I grant an honour to be NEPTUNE's child ;
A grace to be so near with JOVE allied :
But yet, sweet Nymph ! with this be not beguiled;
Where Nature's graces are by looks descried.
So foul, so rough, so ugly-like a Clown ;
And worse than this, a Monster with one eye.
    Foul is not gracèd, though it wear a Crown !
    But fair is Beauty.   None can that deny.

GALATEA.

Nor is he foul, or shapeless, as you say
Or worse : for that he clownish seems to be.
Rough, Saytr-like, the better he will play :
And manly looks the fitter are for me.
His frowning smiles are gracèd by his beard :
His eye-light, sun-like, shrouded is in one.
    This me contents ; and others makes afeard.
    He sees enough, and therefore wanteth none. With one eye.

DORIS.

Nay, then I see, sweet Nymph : thou art in love ;
And loving, doat'st ; and doating, dost commend
    Foul to be Fair.   This oft do Lovers prove.
    I wish him fairer, or thy love an end !

GALATEA.

DORIS, I love not : yet I hardly bear
Disgraceful terms, which you have spoke in scorn.
You are not loved : and that 's the cause I fear.
For why, my Love of JOVE himself was born.

Feeding his sheep of late, amidst this plain.
When as we Nymphs did sport us on the shore :
He scorned you all, my love for to obtain.
That grieved your hearts.   I knew as much before.
   Nay, smile not Nymphs!   The truth I only tell.
   For few can brook that others should excel.

DORIS.

Should I envy that Blind did you that spite ;
Or that your shape doth please so foul a Groom ?
The Shepherd thought of milk.   You looked so white.
The Clown did err, and foolish was his doom.
   Your look was pale, and so his stomach fed :
   But far from fair, where white doth want his red.

GALATEA.

Though pale my look ; yet he my love did crave ;
And lovely You, unliked, unloved, I view.
It 's better far, one base, than none, to have.
Your fair is foul, to whom there's none will sue.
   My Love doth tune his love unto his harp :
   His shape is rude ; but yet his wit is sharp.

DORIS.

Leave off, sweet Nymph! to grace a worthless Clown
He itched with love ; and then did sing, or say.
The noise was such as all the Nymphs did frown,
And well suspected that some ass did bray.
The woods did chide, to hear this ugly sound :
The prating ECHO scorned for to repeat.
This grisly voice did fear the hollow ground,
Whilst Art-less fingers did his harp-strings beat.

Two bear whelps in his arms this Monster bore :
With these new puppies did this Wanton play !
Their skins were rough ; but yet your loves were more.
He fouler was and far more fierce than they.
    I cannot choose, sweet Nymph ! to think, but smile,
    That some of us thou fearest, will thee beguile.

GALATEA.

Scorn not my Love ! until it can be known
That you have one that 's better, of your own.

DORIS.

I have no Love : nor, if I had, would boast :
Yet wooed have been by such as well might speed.
But him to love, the Shame of all the coast !
So ugly foul, as yet, I have no need.
    Now thus we learn what foolish love can do ?
    To think him fair, that 's foul and ugly too.

To hear this talk I sat behind an oak ;
And marked their words and penned them as they spoke

Ad Lectorem, distichon
cujusdam de Autore.

Lascivi quæres fuerit cur carminis Autor :
Carmine lascivus, mente pudicus erat.

A Lover's Maze.

[It will be seen that Three of these Stanzas go together, rhyming in their first words: *True, True, New.—Sweet, Sweet, Meet*, &c.]

TRUE are my thoughts: my thoughts that are untrue.
Blind are my eyes: my eyes that are not blind.
New is my love: my love that is not new.
Kind is that Fair: that Fair that is not kind.
 Thus eyes and thoughts, that fairest Fair, my love;
 Blind and untrue, unkind, unconstant prove.

True are my thoughts: because they never flit.
Untrue my thoughts: because they me betrayed.
Blind are my eyes: because in clouds I sit.
Not blind my eyes: because I looks obeyed.
 Thus eyes and thoughts, my dearest Fair, may view
 In sight, in love, nor blind, nor yet untrue.

New is my love: because it never dies.
Old is my love: because it ever lives.
Kind is that Fair: because it hate denies.
Unkind that Fair: because no hope it gives.
 Thus new my love, and still that Fair unkind,
 Renews my love; and I no favour find.

Sweet are my dreams: my dreams that are not sweet.
Long are the nights: the nights that are not long.
Meet are the pangs: these pangs that are unmeet.
Wronged is my heart: my heart that hath no wrong.
 Thus dreams and night, my heart, my pangs, and all,
 In taste, in length, conspire to work my fall.

Sweet are my dreams :   because my Love they show.
Unsweet my dreams :   because but dreams they are.
Long are the nights :   because no help I know.
Meet are the nights :   because they end my care.
   Thus dreams and nights, wherein my Love takes sport,
   Are sweet, unsweet ; are long, and yet too short.

Meet are my pangs :   because I was too bold.
Unmeet my pangs :   because I loved so well.
Wronged was my heart :   because my grief it told.
Not wronged. For why ?   My grief it could not tell.
   Thus you, my Love, unkindly cause this smart ;
   That will not love to ease my pangs and heart.

Proud is her look :   her look that is not proud.
Done all my days :   my days that are not done.
Loud are my sighs :   my sighs that are not loud.
Begun my death :   my death not yet begun.
   Thus looks and days, and sighs and death, might move
   So kind, so fair, to give consent to love.

Proud is her look :   because she scorns to see.
Not proud her look :   for none dare say so much.
Done are my days :   because they hapless be.
Not done my days :   because I wish them such.
   Thus looks and days increase this loving strife ;
   Not proud, not done, nor dead, nor giving life.

Loud are my sighs :   because they pierce the sky.
Not loud my sighs :   because they are not heard.
My death begun :   because I heartless cry.
But not begun :   because I am debarred.
   Thus sighs and death my heart no comfort give :
   Both life deny, and both do make me live.

Bold are her smiles: her smiles that are not bold.
Wise are her words;   those words that are not wise.
Cold are her lips: those lips that are not cold.
Ice are those hands: those hands that are not ice.
  Thus smiles and words, her lips, her hands, and She
  Bold, wise, cold, ice, love's cruel torments, be.

Bold are her smiles: because they anger slay.
Not bold her smiles: because they blush so oft.
Wise are her words: because they wonders say.
Not wise her words :   because they are not soft.
  Thus smiles and words, so cruel and so bold,
  So blushing wise, my thoughts in prison hold.

Cold are her lips: because they breathe no heat.
Not cold her lips: because my heart they burn.
Ice are her hands: because the snow 's so great.
Not ice her hands: that all to ashes turn.
  Thus lips and hands, cold ice, my sorrow bred ;
  Hands, warm white snow; and lips, cold cherry red.

Small was her waist: the waist that was not small.
Gold was her hair: the hair that was not gold.
Tall was her shape: the shape that was not tall.
Folding the arms: the arms that did not fold.
  Thus hair and shape, those folding arms and waist,
  Did make me love ; and loving made me waste.

Small was her *waist: because I could it span.
Not small her waste: because she wasted all.
Gold was her hair: because a crown it wan.
Not gold her hair: because it was more pale.
  Thus smallest *waist, the greatest waste doth [* *Spelt* waste
     make ;   *in the original*
  And finest hair, most fast a lover take.   *edition.*]

Tall was her shape:	because she touched the sky.
Not tall her shape:	because she comely was.
Folding her arms:	because she hearts could tie,
Not folded arms:	because all bands they pass.

    Thus shape, and arms, with love my heart did fly;
    That hers I am, and must be till I die.

Sad was her joy:	her joy that was not sad.
Short was her stay:	her stay that was not short.
Glad was her speech:	her speech that was not glad.
Sporting those toys:	those toys that were not sport.

    Thus was my heart, with joy, speech, toys, and stay,
    Possessed with love; and so stolen quite away.

Sad was her joy:	because she did suspect.
Not sad her joy:	because her joy she had.
Short was her stay:	because to small effect.
Long was her stay:	because I was so sad.

    Thus joy and stay both crossed a lover's sport;
    The one was sad, the other too too short.

Glad was her speech:	because she spake her mind.
Not glad her speech:	because afraid to speak.
Sporting her toys:	because my love was kind.
Not toys in sport:	because my heart they break.

    Thus speech and toys my love began in jest:
    Sweet, yield to love! and make thy servant blest!

      Tread you the Maze, sweet Love, that I have run:
      Mark but the steps, which I imprinted have.
      End but your love, whereas my thoughts begun:
      So shall I joy, and you a Servant have.
        If not, sweet Love, then this my suit deny:
        So shall you live, and so your Servant die.

An Elegy.

OWN in a bed, and on a bed of down ;.
LOVE, She, and I to sleep together lay.
She, like a wanton, kissed me with a frown,
"Sleep, sleep!" she said; but meant to steal away
I could not choose but kiss, but wake, but smile,
To see how She thought us two to beguile.

She feigned a sleep.   I waked her with a kiss.
A kiss to me she gave, to make me sleep.
" If I did wrong, sweet Love, my fault was this ;
In that I did not you thus waking keep.
Then kiss me, Sweet! that so I sleep may take ;
Or let me kiss, to keep you still awake ! "

The night drew on, and needs she must be gone.
She wakèd LOVE, and bid him learn to wait.
She sighed, She said, to leave me there alone :
And bid LOVE stay ; but practise no deceit.
LOVE wept for grief, and sighing made great moan:
And could not sleep, nor stay, if she were gone.

" Then stay, sweet Love!" A kiss with that I gave.
She could not stay ; but gave my kiss again.
A kiss was all that I could get or crave :
And, with a kiss, She bound me to remain.
" A' LICIA !" still I in my dreams did cry,
" Come, LICIA, come! or else my heart will die."

ELEGY II.

1. DISTANCE of place, my Love and me did part;
    Yet both did swear, We never would remove!
    In sign thereof, I bade her take my heart;
    Which did, and doth, and cannot choose but,
        love.
  Thus did we part, in hope to meet again;
  Where both did vow most constant to remain.

2.   A she there was that passed betwixt us both;
  By whom each knew how other's cause did fare:
  For men to trust men in their love are loath.
  Thus had we both of love a Lover's care.
    Haply he seeks his sorrows to renew,
    That for his love, doth make another sue.

3. By her a kiss, a kiss to me She sent;
  A kiss for price more worth than purest gold.
  She gave it her.   To me the kiss was meant.
  A she to kiss: what harm if she were bold?
    Happy those lips, that had so sweet a kiss!
    For heaven itself scarce yields so sweet a bliss.

4.   This modest she, blushing for shame of this,
  Or loath to part from that she liked so well,
  Did play false play; and gave me not the kiss:
  Yet my Love's kindness could not choose but tell.
    Then blame me not, that kissing, sighed and swore,
    "I kissed but her, whom you had kissed before!"

5.   "Sweet, love me more! and blame me not, sweet Love!
  I kissed those lips: yet, harmless, I do vow:
  Scarce would my lips from off those lips remove;
  For still, methought, sweet Fair, I kissèd you.
    And thus kind love, the sun of all my bliss,
    Was both begun, and ended, in a kiss.

6.   "Then send me more; but send them by your friend!
      Kiss none but her! nor her, nor none at all.
      Beware by whom such treasures you do send!
      I must them lose, except I for them call.
          And love me, Dear! and still still kissing be!
          Both like and love but none, sweet Love! but me!

ELEGY III.

I.   IF sad Complaint would shew a Lover's pain;
          Or Tears express the torments of my heart:
          If melting Sighs would ruth and pity gain;
          Or true Laments but ease a Lover's smart:

2.   Then should my Plaints the thunder's noise surmount;
        And Tears, like seas, should flow from out my eyes.
        Then Sighs, like air, should far exceed all count;
        And true Laments with sorrow dim the skies.

3.   But Plaints and Tears, Laments and Sighs I spend:
        Yet greater torments do my heart destroy.
        I could all these from out my heart still send;
        If, after these, I might my Love enjoy.

4.   But heavens conspire; and heavens I must obey:
        That seeking love, I still must want my ease.
        For greatest joys are tempered with delay:
        Things soon obtained do least of all us please.

5.   My thoughts repine, and think the time too long.
        My love impatient wisheth to obtain.
        I blame the heavens, that do me all this wrong:
        To make me loved; and will not ease my pain.

6.   No pain like this, to love and not enjoy.
No grief like this, to mourn and not be heard.
No time so long as that which breeds annoy.
No hell like this, to love and be deferred.

7.   But heaven shall stand, and earth inconstant fly ;
The sun shall freeze, and ice inconstant burn ;
The mountains flow, and all the earth be dry :
Ere time shall force my loving thoughts to turn.

8.   " Do you resolve, sweet Love ! to do the same :
Say that you do, and seal it with a kiss !
Then shall our truths [*troths*] the heavens' unkindness
    blame ;
That cannot hurt, yet shew their spite in this.

9.   " The silly Prentice, bound for many years,
Doth hope that time his service will release ;
The town besieged, that lives in midst of fears,
Doth hope in time the cruel wars will cease ;

10.   " The toiling Ploughman sings in hope to reap ;
The tossèd bark expecteth for a shore ;
The boy at school to be at play doth leap,
And straight forgets the fear he had before :

11. " If those, by hope, do joy in their distress ;
And constant are, in hope to conquer time :
Then let not hope in us, sweet Friend ! be less ;
And cause our love to wither in the prime.

" Let us conspire, and time will have an end ;
So both of us in time shall have a friend."

FINIS.

DIANA,

OR,

The excellent conceitful Sonnets
of *H. C.* Augmented with divers
Quatorzains of honourable
and learned personages.

DIVIDED INTO VIII. DECADES.

Vincitur a facibus, qui jacet ipse faces.

AT LONDON,
Printed by *Iames Roberts* for
Richard Smith.
1584.

THE PRINTER

to the Reader.

OBSCURED wonders, Gentlemen! visited me in TURNUS's armour; and I, in regard of ÆNEAS's honour, have unclouded them unto the world. You are that universe! You, that ÆNEAS! If you find PALLAS's girdle, murder them! if not, environed with barbarism, save them! and eternity will praise you.

Vale.

Unto Her Majesty's sacred honourable Maids.

ETERNAL TWINS ! that conquer Death and Time,
Perpetual advocates in heaven and earth !
Fair, chaste, immaculate, and all divine ;
Glorious alone, before the first man's birth :
 Your twofold CHARITES ! celestial lights !
Bow your sun-rising eyes, planets of joy,
Upon these Orphan Poems ! in whose rights
CONCEIT first claimed his birthright to enjoy.
 If pitiful, you shun the Song of Death ;
Or fear the stain of love's life-dropping blood ;
O know then, you are pure ; and purer faith
Shall still keep white the flower, the fruit, and bud.
 LOVE moveth all things. You that love, shall move
All things in him, and he in you shall love.

RICHARD SMITH.

THE FIRST DECADE.

SONNET I.

Esolved to love, unworthy to obtain,
    I do no favour crave; but, humble wise,
    To thee my sighs in verse I sacrifice,
    Only some pity, and no help to gain.
Hear then! and as my heart shall aye
        remain   [eyes;
    A patient object to thy lightning
A patient ear bring thou to thund'ring cries!
Fear not the crack! when I the blow sustain.
So as thine eye bred mine ambitious thought;
    So shall thine ear make proud my voice for joy.
Lo, Dear! what wonders great by thee are wrought,
    When I but little favours do enjoy.
The voice is made the ear for to rejoice:
And your ear giveth pleasure to my voice.

SONNET II.

Lame not my heart for flying up too high!
    Sith thou art cause that it this flight begun:
    For earthly vapours drawn up by the sun,
    Comets begin, and night suns in the sky.
Mine humble heart, so with thy heavenly Eye
    Drawn up aloft, all low desires doth shun:
    Raise then me up! as thou my heart hast done,
    So during night, in heaven remain may I.
I say again, Blame not my high desire!
    Sith of us both the cause thereof depends:
    In thee doth shine, in me doth burn a fire;
    Fire draws up other, and itself ascends.
Thine eye a fire, and so draws up my love;
My love a fire, and so ascends above.

SONNET III.

Ly low, dear love! thy sun dost thou not see?
Take heed! do not so near his rays aspire!
Lest (for thy pride, inflamed with wreakful ire)
It burn thy wings, as it hath burnèd me.
Thou, haply, sayst, "Thy wings immortal be,
And so cannot consumèd be with fire:
The one is Hope, the other is Desire;
And that the heavens bestowed them both on thee."
A Muse's words made thee with Hope to fly;
An Angel's face Desire hath begot;
Thyself engendered by a goddess' eye:
Yet for all this, immortal thou art not!
Of heavenly eye though thou begotten art:
Yet art thou born but of a mortal heart!

SONNET IV.

Friend of mine, pitying my hopeless love,
Hoping, by killing hope, my love to stay:
"Let not," quoth he, "thy hope, thy heart betray!
Impossible it is her heart to move."
But sith resolvèd love cannot remove,
As long as thy divine perfections stay:
Thy godhead then, he sought to take away.
Dear! seek revenge, and him a liar prove!
Gods only do impossibilities.
"Impossible," saith he, "thy grace to gain."
Show then the power of thy divinities
By granting me thy favour to obtain!
So shall thy foe give to himself the lie;
A goddess thou shalt prove; and happy I!

SONNET V.

HINE eye, the glass where I behold my heart.
  Mine eye, the window through the which thine eye
  May see my heart; and there thyself espy
  In bloody colours, how thou painted art!
Thine eye, the pyle is of a murdering dart:
  Mine eye, the sight thou tak'st thy level by
  To hit my heart, and never shoots awry.
  Mine eye thus helps thine eye to work my smart.
Thine eye, a fire is both in heat and light;
  Mine eye, of tears a river doth become.
  O that the water of mine eye had might
  To quench the flames that from thine eye doth come!
Or that the fires kindled by thine eye,
  The flowing streams of mine eyes could make dry!

SONNET VI.

INE Eye with all the deadly sins is fraught.
  1. First *proud*, sith it presumed to look so high.
  A watchman being made, stood gazing by;
  2. And *idle*, took no heed till I was caught.
3. And *envious*, bears envy that by thought,
  Should in his absence, be to her so nigh.
  To kill my heart, mine eye let in her eye;
  4. And so consent gave to a *murder* wrought.
5. And *covetous*, it never would remove
  From her fair hair. Gold so doth please his sight!
  6. *Unchaste*, a baud between my heart and love.
  7. A *glutton* eye, with tears drunk every night.
These sins procurèd have a goddess' ire:
Wherefore my heart is damned in love's sweet fire.

SONNET VII.

FALSELY doth Envy of your praises blame
   My tongue, my pen, my heart of flattery:
   Because I said, " There was no sun but thee ! "
      It called my tongue " the partial trump of Fame."
And saith my pen hath flatterèd thy name,
   Because my pen did to my tongue agree ;
   And that my heart must needs a flatterer be,
      Which taught both tongue and pen to say the same.
No, no, I flatter not when thee I call
   The sun, sith that the sun was never such :
   But when the sun, thee I compared withal ;
      Doubtless the sun I flatterèd too much.
Witness mine eyes, I say the truth in this !
They have seen thee, and know that so it is.

SONNET VIII.

MUCH Sorrow in itself my love doth move,
   More my Despair to love a hopeless bliss ;
   My Folly most, to love whom sure to miss ;
      O help me, but this last grief to remove !
All pains, if you command, it joy shall prove ;
   And wisdom to seek joy.   Then say but this,
   " Because my pleasure in thy torment is ;
      I do command thee, without hope to love ! "
So when this thought my sorrow shall augment,
   That my own folly did procure my pain,
   Then shall I say, to give myself content,
      " Obedience only made me love in vain.
It was your will, and not my want of wit ;
I have the pain, bear you the blame of it ! "

SONNET IX.

MY LADY's presence makes the Roses red,
    Because to see her lips they blush for shame.
    The Lily's leaves, for envy, pale became;
    And her white hands in them this envy bred.
The Marigold the leaves abroad doth spread;
    Because the sun's and her power is the same.
    The Violet of purple colour came,
    Dyed in the blood she made my heart to shed.
In brief. All flowers from her their virtue take;
    From her sweet breath, their sweet smells do proceed;
    The living heat which her eyebeams doth make
    Warmeth the ground, and quickeneth the seed.
The rain, wherewith she watereth the flowers,
Falls from mine eyes, which she dissolves in showers.

SONNET X.

HERALDS at arms do three perfections quote,
    To wit, most fair, most rich, most glittering;
    So, when those three concur within one thing,
    Needs must that thing, of honour, be a note.
Lately, I did behold a rich fair coat,
    Which wishèd Fortune to mine eyes did bring.
    A Lordly coat, yet worthy of a King,
    In which one might all these perfections note.
A field of lilies, roses " proper " bare;
    Two stars "in chief"; the " crest " was waves cf gold.
    How glittering 'twas, might by the stars appeaɪ;
    The lilies made it fair for to behold.
And RICH it was, as by the gold appeareth:
But happy he that in his arms it weareth!

THE SECOND DECADE.

SONNET I.

IF TRUE love might true love's reward obtain,
    Dumb wonder only might speak of my joy;
    But too much worth hath made thee too much
    And told me, long ago, I sighed in vain.   [coy,
Not then vain hope of undeservèd gain
    Hath made me paint in verses mine annoy;
    But for thy pleasure, that thou might'st enjoy
    Thy beauty's praise, in glasses of my pain.
See then, thyself! (though me thou wilt not hear)
    By looking on my verse.   For pain in verse,
    Love doth in pain, beauty in love appear.
    So, if thou wouldst my verses' meaning see,
Expound them thus, when I my love rehearse,
"None loves like he!" that is, "None fair like me!"

SONNET II.

IT MAY be, LOVE my death doth not pretend,
    Although he shoots at me: but thinks it fit
    Thus to bewitch thee for thy benefit!
    Causing thy will to my wish to condescend.
For witches, which some murder do intend,
    Do make a picture, and do shoot at it;
    And in that part where they the picture hit,
    The party's self doth languish to his end.
So LOVE, too weak by force thy heart to taint,
    Within my heart thy heavenly shape doth paint;
    Suffering therein his arrows to abide,
    Only to th'end he might, by witches' art,
Within my heart, pierce through thy picture's side;
And through thy picture's side, might wound my heart.

SONNET III.

THE SUN, his journey ending in the west,
   Taketh his lodging up in THETIS' bed ;
   Though from our eyes his beams be banished,
   Yet with his light the Antipodes be blest.
Now when the sun-time brings my sun to rest,
   (Which me too oft of rest hath hinderèd)
   And whiter skin with white sheet coverèd,
   And softer cheek doth on soft pillow rest,
Then I (O sun of suns! and light of lights!)
   Wish me with those Antipodes to be,
   Which see and feel thy beams and heat by nights.
   Well, though the night both cold and darksome is,
Yet half the day's delight the night grants me.
I feel my sun's heat, though his light I miss.

SONNET IV.

LADY! in beauty and in favour rare,
   Of favour, not of due, I favour crave.
   Nature to thee beauty and favour gave ;
   Fair then thou art, and favour thou may'st spare !
Nor when on me bestowed your favours are,
   Less favour in your face you shall not have :
   If favour then a wounded soul may save ;
   Of murder's guilt, dear Lady, then beware!
My loss of life a million fold were less,
   Than the least loss should unto you befall :
   Yet grant this gift! which gift when I possess,
   Both I have life, and you no loss at all.
For by your favour only I do live;
And favour you may well both keep and give.

SONNET V.

Y REASON absent, did mine Eyes require
    To watch and ward, and such foes to descry
    As they should ne'er my heart approaching spy:
        But traitor Eyes, my heart's death did conspire
(Corrupted with HOPE's gifts) ; let in DESIRE
    To burn my heart : and sought no remedy,
    Though store of water were in either Eye,
    Which well employed, might well have quenched the fire.
REASON returned ; LOVE and FORTUNE made
    Judges, to judge mine Eyes to punishment.
        FORTUNE, sith they, by sight my heart betrayed ;
        From wishèd sight, adjudged them banishment !
LOVE, sith by fire murdered my heart was found ;
Adjudged them in tears for to be drowned !

SONNET VI.

ONDER it is, and pity is't, that she
    In whom all beauty's treasure we may find,
    That may enrich the body and the mind ;
        Towards the poor, should use no charity.
My love has gone a begging unto thee !
    And if that Beauty had not been more kind
    That Pity, long ere this, he had been pined :
    But Beauty is content his food to be.
O pity have ! when such poor orphans beg.
    LOVE (naked boy !) hath nothing on his back ;
    And though he wanteth neither arm nor leg,
    Yet maimed he is, sith he his sight doth lack.
And yet (though blind) he beauty can behold,
And yet (though naked) he feels more heat than cold.

SONNET VII.

PITY refusing my poor Love to feed,
   A beggar starved for want of help, he lies ;
   And at your mouth (the door of Beauty) cries,
      That thence some alms of sweet grants might
But as he waiteth for some almes deed,   [proceed !
   A cherry tree before the door he spies.
   " O Dear ! " quoth he, " two cherries may suffice,
   Two only may save life, in this my need ! "
But beggars, Can they nought but cherries eat ?
   Pardon my Love ! He is a goddess' son,
   And never feedeth but on dainty meat ;
   Else need he not to pine, as he hath done.
For only the sweet fruit of this sweet tree,
Can give food to my Love, and life to me.

SONNET VIII.

THE fowler hides, as closely as he may,
   The net, where caught the silly bird should be ;
   Lest he the threatening poison should but see,
   And so for fear be forced to fly away.
My Lady so, the while she doth assay
   In curled knots fast to entangle me ;
   Put on her veil, to th'end I should not flee
   The golden net, wherein I am a prey.
Alas, most Sweet ! what need is of a net
   To catch a bird, that is already ta'en ?
   Sith with your hand alone, you may it get ;
   For it desires to fly into the same.
What needs such art, my thoughts then to entrap ;
When, of themselves, they fly into your lap ?

SONNET IX.

SWEET hand! the sweet but cruel bow thou art!
 From whence at me five ivory arrows fly;
 So with five wounds at once I wounded lie,
 Bearing my breast the print of every dart.
Saint FRANCIS had the like; yet felt no smart,
 Where I in living torments never die.
 His wounds were in his hands and feet; where I
 All these five helpless wounds feel in my heart.
Now, as Saint FRANCIS, if a Saint am I,
 The bow that shot these shafts a relic is.
 I mean the hand, which is the reason why
 So many for devotion thee would kiss:
And some thy glove kiss, as a thing divine;
This arrows' quiver, and this relic's shrine.

SONNET X.

FAIR Sun! if you would have me praise your light,
 When night approacheth, wherefore do you fly?
 Time is so short, beauties so many be,
 As I have need to see them day and night;
That by continual view, my verses might
 Tell all the beams of your divinity:
 Which praise to you, and joy should be to me;
 You living by my verse, I by your sight!
I by your sight, and not you by my verse,
 Need mortal skill immortal praise rehearse?
 No, no, though eyes were blind, and verse were dumb,
 Your beauty should be seen, and your fame known.
For by the wind which from my sighs do come,
Your praises round about the world are blown.

THE THIRD DECADE.

S O N N E T I .

Ncivil Sickness! hast thou no regard!
But dost presume my Dearest to molest!
And without leave, dar'st enter in that breast,
Whereto sweet Love approach yet never dared?
Spare thou her health! which my life hath not spared.
  Too bitter such revenge of my unrest.
  Although with wrongs, my thought she hath opprest ;
  My wrongs seek not revenge, they crave reward.
Cease Sickness!   Cease in her then to remain !
  And come, and welcome!   Harbour thou in me !
  Whom love long since hath taught to suffer pain.
  So she which hath so oft my pain increased
(O God, that I might so revengèd be),
By my poor pain, might have her pain released.

[*The next Seven Sonnets, II. to VIII., are assigned to Sir PHILIP SIDNEY,
and are printed with his collection in Vol. I. at the pages indicated
below.*]

HE SCOURGE of life, and death's extreme disgrace,
[*See Vol. I. p.* 114.]

OE! WOE to me!   On me, return the smart!
[*See Vol. I. p.* 114.]

HOU PAIN! the only guest of loathed CONSTRAINT,
[*See Vol. I. p.* 115.]

ND HAVE I heard her say, "O cruel pain!"
[*See Vol. I. p.* 115.]

INCE shunning pain, I ease can never find ;
[*See Vol. I. p.* 109.]

HEN LOVE, puft up with rage of his disdain,
[*See Vol. I. p.* 110.]

N WONTED walks, since wonted fancies change ;
[*See Vol. I. p.* 120.]

SONNET IX.

WOE TO mine eyes! the organs of mine ill;
   Hate to my heart! for not concealing joy;
   A double curse upon my tongue be still!
   Whose babbling lost what else I might enjoy.
When first mine eyes did with thy beauty toy,
   They to my heart thy wondrous virtues told;
   Who, fearing lest thy beams should him destroy,
   Whate'er he knew, did to my tongue unfold.
My tell-tale tongue, in talking over bold,
   What they in private council did declare,
   To thee! in plain and public terms unrolled:
   And so by that, made thee more coyer far.
What in thy praise he spoke, that didst thou trust!
And yet my sorrows, thou dost hold unjust!

SONNET X.

OF AN Athenian young man have I read,
   Who on blind FORTUNE's picture doated so;
   That when he could not buy it to his bed,
   On it he gazing, died for very woe.
My Fortune's picture art thou, flinty Dame!
   That settest golden apples to my sight;
   But wilt, by no means, let me taste the same!
   To drown in sight of land, is double spite.
Of Fortune, as thou learn'dst to be unkind;
   So learn to be unconstant to disdain!
   The wittiest women are to sport inclined.
   Honour is Pride, and Pride is nought but Pain.
Let others boast of choosing for the best;
'Tis substances, not names must make us blest.

THE FOURTH DECADE

SONNET I.

NEEDS MUST I leave, and yet needs must I love!
In vain my wit doth tell in verse my woe:
Despair in me, disdain in thee, doth show
How by my wit I do my folly prove.
All this; my heart from love can never move.
  Love is not in my heart. No, Lady! No,
  My heart is love itself. Till I forego
  My heart, I never can my love remove.
How can I then leave love? I do intend
  Not to crave grace, but yet to wish it still;
  Not to praise thee, but Beauty to commend:
  And so, by Beauty's praise, praise thee I will!
For as my heart is Love, love not in me:
So Beauty thou, beauty is not in thee!

SONNET II.

SWEET SOVEREIGN! since so many minds remain
Obedient subjects at thy beauty's call!
So many hearts bound in thy hairs as thrall!
So many eyes die with one look's disdain!
Go, seek the honour that doth thee pertain!
  That the Fifth Monarchy may thee befall.
  Thou hast such means to conquer men withal,
  As all the world must yield, or else be slain.
To fight, thou needst no weapons but thine eyes!
  Thine hair hath gold enough to pay thy men!
  And for their food, thy beauty will suffice!
  For men and armour, Lady, care have none!
For one will sooner yield unto thee then
When he shall meet thee naked all alone.

SONNET III.

HEN YOUR perfections to my thoughts appear,
They say among themselves, " O happy we,
Which ever shall so rare an object see!"
But happy heart, if thoughts less happy were!
For their delights have cost my heart full dear,
In whom of love a thousand causes be;
And each cause breeds a thousand loves in me;
And each love more than thousand hearts can bear.
How can my heart so many loves then hold;
Which yet, by heaps, increase from day to day?
But like a ship that's o'ercharged with gold,
Must either sink, or hurl the gold away.
But hurl not love! Thou canst not, feeble heart!
In thine own blood, thou therefore drownèd art!

SONNET IV.

OOLS BE they, that inveigh 'gainst MAHOMET;
Who's but a moral of love's monarchy.
By a dull adamant, as straw by jet,
He in an iron chest was drawn on high.
In midst of Mecca's temple roof, some say,
He now hangs, without touch or stay at all.
That MAHOMET is She, to whom I pray;
May ne'er man pray so ineffectual!
Mine eyes, love's strange exhaling adamants,
Un'wares, to my heart's temple's height have wrought
The iron Idol that compassion wants;
Who my oft tears and travails sets at nought.
Iron hath been transformed to gold by art
Her face, limbs, flesh and all, gold; save her heart.

SONNET V.

EADY TO seek out death in my disgrace,
 My Mistress 'gan to smooth her gathered brows;
 Whereby I am reprievèd for a space.
  O Hope and Fear! who half your torments knows?
It is some mercy in a black-mouthed Judge
 To haste his prisoner's end, if he must die.
Dear! if all other favour you shall grudge,
 Do speedy execution with your eye!
With one sole look, you leave in me no soul.
 Count it a loss to lose a faithful slave!
Would God, that I might hear my last bell toll,
 So in your bosom I might dig my grave.
Doubtful delay is worse than any fever.
Or help me soon! or cast me off for ever!

SONNET VI.

ACH DAY, new proofs of new despair I find,
 That is, new deaths. No marvel then, though I
 Make exile my last help; to th'end mine eye
  Should not behold the death to me assigned.
Not that from death, absence might save my mind;
 But that it might take death more patiently:
Like him, the which by Judge condemned to die,
 To suffer with more ease, his eyes doth blind.
Your lips, in scarlet clad, my Judges be,
 Pronouncing sentence of eternal "No!"
DESPAIR, the hangman that tormenteth me:
 The death I suffer is the life I have.
For only life doth make me die in woe,
And only death I, for my pardon crave.

SONNET VII.

THE RICHEST relic Rome did ever view
  Was CÆSAR's tomb ; on which, with cunning hand,
  JOVE's triple honours, the three fair Graces, stand ;
  Telling his virtues, in their virtues true.
This Rome admired : but, dearest Dear! in you
  Dwelleth the wonder of the happiest land
  And all the world to NEPTUNE's furthest strand.
  For what Rome shap'd hath living life in you !
Thy naked beauty, bounteously displayed,
  Enricheth monarchies of hearts with love !
  Thine eyes to hear complaints are open laid !
  Thine eyes' kind looks requite all pains I prove !
That of my death, I dare not thee accuse ;
But pride in me, that baser chance refuse.

SONNET VIII.

"WHY THUS unjustly," say, my cruel fate !
  " Dost thou adjudge my luckless eyes and heart ;
  The one to live exiled from that sweet smart,
  Where th'other pines, imprisoned without date ? "
My luckless eyes must never more debate
  Of those bright beams, that eased my love apart :
  And yet my heart, bound to them with love's dart,
  Must there dwell ever, to bemoan my state.
O had mine eyes been suffered there to rest !
  Often they had my heart's unquiet eased :
  Or had my heart with banishment been blest !
  Mine eye with beauty never had been pleased.
But since these cross effects hath fortune wrought ;
Dwell, heart, with her ! Eyes, view her in my thought !

[*Sonnet IX. is assigned to Sir PHILIP SIDNEY, and is printed with his
collection at p.* 122, *Vol. I.*]

FT HAVE I mused, but now at length I find

SONNET X.

OPE, like the hyæna, coming to be old,
Alters his shape; is turned into Despair.
Pity my hoary hopes! Maid of Clear Mould!
Think not that frowns can ever make thee fair!
What harm is it to kiss, to laugh, to play?
Beauty's no blossom, if it be not used.
Sweet dalliance keeps the wrinkles long away:
Repentance follows them that have refused.
To bring you to the knowledge of your good
I seek, I sue. O try, and then believe!
Each image can be chaste that's carved of wood.
You show you live, when men you do relieve.
Iron with wearing shines. Rust wasteth treasure.
On earth, but love there is no other pleasure.

THE FIFTH DECADE.

SONNET I.

A ME, poor wretch! my prayer is turned to sin.
I say, "I love!" My Mistress says, "'Tis lust!"
Thus most we lose, where most we seek to win.
Wit will make wicked what is ne'er so just.
And yet I can supplant her false surmise.
  Lust is a fire that, for an hour or twain,
  Giveth a scorching blaze, and then he dies :
  Love, a continual furnace doth maintain.
A furnace !   Well, this a furnace may be called ;
  For it burns inward, yields a smothering flame,
  Sighs which, like boiled lead's smoking vapour, scald.
  I sigh apace, at echo of Sighs' name.
Long have I served.   No short blaze is my love.
Hid joys there are, that maids scorn till they prove.

SONNET II.

Do NOT now complain of my disgrace,
  O Cruel Fair One !   Fair with cruel crost :
  Nor of the hour, season, time, nor place ;
  Nor of my foil, for any freedom lost ;
Nor of my courage, by misfortune daunted ;
  Nor of my wit, by overweening struck ;
  Nor of my sense, by any sound enchanted ;
  Nor of the force of fiery pointed hook ;
Nor of the steel that sticks within my wound ;
  Nor of my thoughts, by worser thoughts defaced ;
  Nor of the life, I labour to confound :
  But I complain, that being thus disgraced,
Fired, feared, frantic, fettered, shot through, slain ;
My death is such, as I may not complain.

SONNET III.

IF EVER Sorrow spoke from soul that loves,
    As speaks a spirit in a man possest ;
    In me, her spirit speaks.   My soul it moves,
        Whose sigh-swoll'n words breed whirlwinds in my
            breast :
Or like the echo of a passing bell,
    Which sounding on the water, seems to howl ;
    So rings my heart a fearful heavy knell,
    And keeps all night in consort with the owl.
My cheeks with a thin ice of tears are clad,
    Mine eyes like morning stars are bleared and red :
    What resteth then, but I be raging mad,
        To see that She, my cares' chief conduit-head,
When all streams else help quench my burning heart,
Shuts up her springs ; and will no grace impart.

SONNET IV.

YOU SECRET vales ! you solitary fields !
    You shores forsaken ! and you sounding rocks !
    If ever groaning heart hath made you yield,
        Or words half spoke that sense in prison locks ;
Then, 'mongst night shadows, whisper out my death !
    That when myself hath sealed my lips from speaking,
    Each tell-tale echo with a weeping breath,
        May both record my truth and true love's breaking.
You pretty flowers ! that smile for summer's sake,
    Pull in your heads ! before my wat'ry eyes
    Do turn the meadows to a standing lake,
        By whose untimely floods, your glory dies !
For lo, mine heart, resolved to moistening air,
Feedeth mine eyes, which double tear for tear.

SONNET V.

HIS shadow to Narcissus well presented;
    How fair he was, by such attractive love!
    So if thou would'st thyself thy beauty prove,
        Vulgar breath-mirrors might have well contented,
And to their prayers eternally consented,
    Oaths, vows and sighs, if they belief might move:
    But more thou forc'st, making my pen approve
    Thy praise to all, least any had dissented.
When this hath wrought, thou which before wert known
    But unto some, of all art now required;
    And thine eyes' wonders wronged; because not shown
    The world, with daily orisons desired.
Thy chaste fair gifts, with learning's breath is blown.
And thus my pen hath made thy sweets admired.

SONNET VI.

I AM no model figure, or sign of Care;
    But his eternal heart's-consuming essence:
    In whom grief's commentaries written are,
        Drawing gross passion into pure quintessence.
Not thine eye's fire; but fire of thine eye's disdain,
    Fed by neglect of my continual grieving,
    Attracts the true life's spirit of my pain;
    And gives it thee; which gives me no relieving.
Within thine arms, sad elegies I sing.
    Unto thine eyes, a true heart love-torn lay I.
    Thou smell'st from me, the savours sorrows bring.
    My tears to taste my truth, to touch display I.
Lo thus, each sense, dear Fair One! I importune:
But being Care, thou flyest me as Ill Fortune!

SONNET VII.

BUT being CARE, thou flyest me as ILL FORTUNE!
    CARE the consuming canker of the mind!
    The discord that disorders sweet hearts' tune!
    Th'abortive bastard of a coward mind!
The lightfoot lackey that runs post by death,
    Bearing the letters which contain our end!
    The busy advocate that sells his breath,
    Denouncing worst to him, is most his friend!
O Dear! this care no interest holds in me:
    But holy CARE, the Guardiant of thy fair,
    Thine honour's Champion, and thy virtue's Fee;
    The zeal which thee from barbarous times shall bear.
This CARE am I.   This care my life hath taken.
Dear to my soul! then, leave me not forsaken!

SONNET VIII.

DEAR to my soul! then, leave me not forsaken!
    Fly not! My heart within thy bosom sleepeth!
    Even from myself and sense I have betaken
    Me unto thee (for whom my spirit weepeth).
And on the shore of that salt teary sea,
    Couched in a bed of unseen seeming pleasure,
    Where, in imaginary thoughts, thy fair self lay—
    But being wak'd, robbed of my life's best treasure,
I call the heavens, air, earth, and seas to hear
    My love! my truth! and black disdained estate!
    Beating the rocks with bellowings of despair;
    Which still with plaints, my words reverberate.
Sighing, "Alas, what shall become of me?"
Whilst ECHO cries, "What shall become of me?"

SONNET IX.

WHILST ECHO cries, " What shall become of me ? "
And desolate, my desolations pity :
Thou in thy beauty's carrack sitt'st, to see
My tragic downfall, and my funeral ditty.
No timbrel, but my heart thou play'st upon,
Whose strings are stretched unto the highest key.
The diapason, love. Love is the unison ;
In love, my life and labours waste away.
Only regardless, to the world thou leav'st me,
Whilst slain HOPES, turning from the feast of sorrow,
Unto DESPAIR, their King, which ne'er deceives me,
Captives my heart, (whose black night hates the morrow)
And he, in truth of my distressed cry,
Plants me a weeping star within mine eye.

SONNET X.

PROMETHEUS for stealing living fire
From heaven's king, was judged eternal death ;
In self-same flame, with unrelenting ire,
Bound fast to Caucasus' low foot beneath.
So I, for stealing living beauty's fire
Into my verse, that it may always live ;
And change his forms to shapes of my desire :
Thou beauty's Queen ! self sentence like dost give !
Bound to thy feet, in chains of love I lie ;
For to thine eyes, I never dare aspire :
And in thy beauty's brightness do I fry,
As poor PROMETHEUS in the scalding fire.
Which tears maintain, as oil the lamp revives ;
Only my succour in thy favour lies.

THE SIXTH DECADE.

SONNET I.

ONE sun unto my life's day gives true light.
  One moon dissolves my stormy night of woes.
  One star my fate and happy fortune shows.
  One saint I serve, one shrine with vows I dight.
One sun transfix'd, hath burnt my heart outright.
  One moon opposed, my love in darkness throws.
  One star hath bid my thoughts my wrongs disclose.
  Saints scorn poor swains, shrines do my vows no right.
Yet if my love be found a holy fire,
  Pure, unstained, without idolatry ;
  And she, nathless, in hate of my desire,
  Lives to repose her in my misery.
My sun ! my moon ! my star ! my saint ! my shrine !
Mine be the torment, but the guilt be thine !

SONNET II.

TO live in hell, and heaven to behold ;
  To welcome life, and die a living death ;
  To sweat with heat, and yet be freezing cold ;
  To grasp at stars, and lie the earth beneath ;
To tread a maze that never shall have end ;
  To burn in sighs, and starve in daily tears ;
  To climb a hill, and never to descend ;
  Giants to kill, and quake at childish fears ;
To pine for food, and watch th'Hesperian tree :
  To thirst for drink, and nectar still to draw ;
  To live accurs'd, whom men hold blest to be ;
  And weep those wrongs which never creature saw :
If this be love, if love in these be founded,
My heart is love, for these in it are grounded.

SONNET III.

A CARVER, having loved too long in vain,
    Hewed out the portraiture of VENUS' son
    In marble rock, upon the which did rain
    Small drizzling drops, that from a fount did run:
Imagining the drops would either wear
    His fury out, or quench his living flame;
    But when he saw it bootless did appear,
    He swore the water did augment the same.
So I, that seek in verse to carve thee out,
    Hoping thy beauty will my flame allay,
    Viewing my verse and poems all throughout,
    Find my will rather to my love obey.
That, with the Carver, I my work do blame,
Finding it still th'augmenter of my flame.

SONNET IV.

A STRONOMERS the heavens do divide
    Into eight Houses, where the god remains;
    All which in thy perfections do abide!
    For in thy feet, the Queen of Silence reigns;
About thy waist, JOVE's Messenger doth dwell,
    Inchanting me, as I thereat admire;
    And on thy dugs, the Queen of Love doth tell,
    Her godhead's power in scrolls of my desire;
Thy beauty is the world's eternal Sun;
    Thy favours force a coward's heart to dare,
    And in thy hairs, JOVE and his riches won;
    Thy frowns hold SATURN; thine eyes the Fixèd Stars.
Pardon me then, Divine! to love thee well;
Since thou art heaven: and I, in heaven would dwell.

S O N N E T V .

WEARY of love, my THOUGHTS of Love complained,
　　Till REASON told them, there was no such power ;
　　And bade me view fair beauty's richest flower,
　　　To see if there a naked boy remained.
Dear ! to thine eyes, eyes that my soul hath pained,
　　THOUGHTS turned them back, in that unhappy hour,
　　To see if Love kept there his royal bower :
　　For if not there, then no place him contained.
There was he not, nor boy, nor golden bow ;
　　Yet as thou turned thy chaste fair eye aside,
　　A flame of fire did from thine eyelids go,
　　　Which burnt my heart, through my sore wounded side :
Then with a sigh, REASON made THOUGHTS to cry,
" There is no god of love, save that thine eye ! "

S O N N E T V I .

FORGIVE me, Dear ! for thundering on thy name ;
　　Sure 'tis thyself that shows my love distrest.
　　For fire exhaled, in freezing clouds possest,
　　　Warring for way, makes all the heavens exclaim.
Thy beauty so, the brightest living flame,
　　Wrapt in my cloudy heart, by winter prest,
　　Scorning to dwell within so base a nest,
　　Thunders in me thy everlasting flame.
O that my heart might still contain that fire !
　　Or that the fire would always light my heart !
　　Then should'st thou not disdain my true desire,
　　　Or think I wronged thee, to reveal to my smart :
For as the fire through freezing clouds doth break ;
So, not myself, but thou in me would'st speak.

SONNET VII.

MY HEART, mine Eye accuseth of his death.
  Saying, " His wanton sight bred his unrest : "
  Mine Eye affirms, " My Heart's unconstant faith
  Hath been his bane, and all his joys represt."
My Heart avows, " Mine Eye let in the fire,
  Which burns him with an everliving light."
  Mine Eye replies, " My greedy Heart's desire
  Let in those floods, which drown him day and night."
Thus wars my Heart, which Reason doth maintain,
  And calls my Eye to combat if he dare.
  The whilst, my Soul, impatient of disdain,
  Wrings from his bondage unto death more near ;
Save that my love, still holdeth him in hand,
" A kingdom thus divided, cannot stand ! "

SONNET VIII.

UNHAPPY day ! unhappy month and season !
  When first proud love, my joys away adjourning,
  Poured into mine eye (to her eye turning)
  A deadly juice, unto my green thoughts geason.
Prisoner I am unto the eye I gaze on :
  Eternally my love's flame is in burning :
  A mortal shaft still wounds me in my mourning :
  Thus prisoned, burnt, and slain; the spirit, soul, and reason ;
What tides me then, since these pains which annoy me,
  In my despair, are evermore increasing ?
  The more I love, less is my pain's releasing ;
  That cursèd be the fortune which destroys me,
The hour, the month, the season, and the cause ;
When love first made me thrall to lovers' laws.

SONNET IX.

LOVE have I followed all too long, nought gaining;
   And sighed I have in vain to sweet what smarteth,
   But from his bow a fiery arrow parteth;
   Thinking that I should him resist, not plaining.
But cowardly my heart submiss remaining,
   Yields to receive what shaft thy fair eye darteth!
   Well do I see, thine eye my bale imparteth;
   And that save death, no hope I am detaining.
For what is he can alter fortune's sliding?
   One in his bed consumes his life away,
   Other in wars, another in the sea:
   The like effects in me have their abiding;
For heavens avowed my fortune should be such,
That I should die by loving far too much.

SONNET X.

MY GOD, my God, how much I love my goddess!
   Whose virtues rare, unto the heavens arise.
   My God, my God, how much I love her eyes!
   One shining bright, the other full of hardness.
My God, my God, how much I love her wisdom!
   Whose works may ravish heaven's richest " maker."
   Of whose eyes' joys, if I might be partaker;
   Then to my soul, a holy rest would come.
My God, how much I love to hear her speak!
   Whose hands I kiss, and ravished oft rekisseth;
   When she stands wotless, whom so much she blesseth.
   Say then, What mind this honest love would break;
Since her perfections pure, withouten blot,
Makes her beloved of them, she knoweth not?

THE SEVENTH DECADE.

SONNET I.

HE FIRST Created held a joyous bower,
 A flowering field, the world's sole wonderment,
 Hight Paradise; from whence a woman's power
 Enticed him fall to endless banishment.
This on the banks of Euphrates did stand,
 Till the first Mover, by His wondrous might,
 Planted it in thine eyes! thy face! thy hands!
From whence the world receives his fairest light.
Thy cheeks contains choice flowers; thy eyes, two suns;
 Thy hands, the fruit that no life blood can stain;
 And in thy breath, that heavenly music wons;
 Which, when thou speak'st, angels their voices strain.
As from the first, thy Sex exilèd me!
So to this next, let me be called by thee!

SONNET II.

AIR GRACE of Graces! Muse of Muses all!
 Thou Paradise! thou only heaven I know!
 What influence hath bred my hateful woe,
 That I from thee and them, am forced to fall?
Thou fallen from me, from thee I never shall,
 Although my fortunes thou hast brought so low;
 Yet shall my faith and service with thee go!
 For live I do, on heaven and thee to call.
Banish'd all grace, no Graces with me dwell;
 Compelled to muse, my Muses from me fly;
 Excluded heaven, what can remain but hell?
 Exiled from Paradise, in hate I lie,
Cursing my stars: albeit I find it true,
I lost all these, when I lost love and you.

SONNET III.

WHAT viewed I, Dear! when I, thine eyes beheld?
  Love in his glory?   No, him THYRSIS saw,
  And stood the boy! whilst he, his darts did draw;
  Whose painted pride to baser swains he telled.
Saw I two suns?   That sight is seen but seld.
  Yet can their brood that teach the holy law
  Gaze on their beams, and dread them not a straw;
  Where princely looks are by their eyes repelled.
What saw I then?   Doubtless it was, AMEN!
  Armed with strong thunder and a lightning's flame;
  Who, bridegroom like, with power was riding then,
  Meaning that none should see him when he came.
Yet did I gaze; and thereby caught the wound
Which burns my heart, and keeps my body sound.

SONNET IV.

WHEN tedious much, and over weary long,
  Cruel disdain, reflecting from her brow,
  Hath been the cause that I endured such wrong;
  And rest thus discontent and weary now.
Yet when posterity, in time to come,
  Shall find th'uncancelled tenour of her vow;
  And her disdain be then confest of some,
  How much unkind and long, I find it now.
O yet even then (though then, will be too late
  To comfort me; dead, many a day, ere then),
  They shall confess—I did not force her heart:
  And time shall make it known to other men—
That ne'er had her disdain made me despair,
Had she not been so excellently fair.

SONNET V.

AD SHE not been so excellently fair,
  My Muse had never mourned in lines of woe :
  But I did too too inestimable weigh her,
    And that's the cause I now lament me so.
Yet not for her contempt do I complain me
  (Complaints may ease the mind, but that is all) ;
  Therefore though she too constantly disdain me,
    I can but sigh and grieve, and so I shall.
Yet grieve I not, because I must grieve ever ;
  And yet, alas, waste tears away in vain.
  I am resolved truly to persèver,
    Though she persisteth in her old disdain.
But that which grieves me most, is that I see
Those which most fair, the most unkindest be.

SONNET VI.

HUS LONG imposed to everlasting plaining
  (Divinely constant to the worthiest Fair),
  And moved by eternally disdaining,
    Aye to persèver in unkind despair :
Because now, Silence, wearily confined
  In tedious dying, and a dumb restraint,
  Breaks forth in tears from mine unable mind
    To ease her passion by a poor complaint :
O do not therefore to thyself suggest !
  That I can grieve, to have immured so long
  Upon the matter of mine own unrest :
    Such grief is not the tenour of my song,
    That 'bide so zealously so bad a wrong.
My grief is this.   Unless I speak and plain me,
Thou will persèver ever to disdain me.

SONNET VII.

THOU wilt persèver ever to disdain me;
   And I shall then die; when thou will repent it:
   O do not therefore from complaint restrain me!
   And take my life from me, to me that lent it.
For whilst these accents, weepingly exprest
   In humble lines, of reverentest zeal,
   Have issue to complaint from mine unrest;
   They but thy beauty's wonder shall reveal.
And though the grieved Muse of some other lover,
   (Whose less devotions knew but woes like mine)
   Would rather seek occasion to discover
   How little pitiful, and how much unkind;
   They other (not so worthy) beauties find.
O, I not so; but seek, with humble prayer,
Means how to move th'unmercifullest Fair.

SONNET VIII.

AS DRAWS the golden Meteor of the day
   Exhaled matter, from the ground to heaven;
   And by his secret nature, there to stay
   The thing fast held, and yet of hold bereaven;
So by th'attractive excellence and might,
   Born to the power of thy transparent eyes,
   Drawn from myself, ravished with thy delight,
   Whose dumb conceits divinely Sirenise,
Lo, in suspense of fear and hope upholden,
   Diversely poised with passions that pain me:
   No resolution dares my thoughts embolden,
   Since 'tis not I, but thou that dost sustain me.
O if there's none but thou can work my woe;
Wilt thou be still unkind, and kill me so?

SONNET IX.

WILT thou be still unkind, and kill me so?
  Whose humbled vows, with sorrowful appeal,
  Do still persist; and did, so long ago,
    Intreat for pity, with so pure a zeal?
Suffice the world shall, for the world can say
  How much thy power hath power, and what it can;
  Never was victor-hand yet moved to slay
  The rendered captive, or the yielding man.
Then, O, why should thy woman-thought impose
  Death and disdain on him, that yields his breath;
  To free his soul from discontent and woes,
  And humble sacrifice to a certain death?
O since the world knows, what the power can do:
What were't for thee, to save and love me too?

SONNET X.

MEET not mine, by others' discontent.
  For none compares with me in true devotion;
  Yet though my tears and sighs to her be spent,
    Her cruel heart disdains what they do motion.
Yet though persisting in eternal hate,
  To aggravate the cause of my complaining,
  Her fury ne'er confineth with a date:
  I will not cease to love, for her disdaining.
Such puny thoughts of unresolvèd ground,
  Whose inaudacity dares but base conceit,
  In me and my love never shall be found:
  Those coward thoughts, unworthy minds await.
But those that love well, have not yet begun;
Persèver ever, and have never done!

THE EIGHTH DECADE.

SONNET I.

PERSÈVER ever, and have never done !
You weeping accent of my weary song !
O do not you eternal passions shun ;
But be you true, and everlasting long !
Say that she doth requite you with disdain ;
Yet fortified with hope, endure your fortune !
Though cruel now, she will be kind again ;
Such haps as those, such love's as yours importune !
Though she protests the faithfullest severity
Inexecrable beauty is inflicting ;
Kindness, in time, will pity your sincerity !
Though now it be your fortune's interdicting.
For some can say, whose loves have known like passion,
" Women are kind by kind, and coy for fashion."

SONNET II.

GIVE period to my matter of complaining,
Fair Wonder of our time's admiring eye !
And entertain no more thy long disdaining,
Or give me leave, at last, that I may die !
For who can live, perpetually secluded
From death to life, that loathes her discontent ?
Less by some hope seducingly deluded,
Such thoughts aspire to fortunate event ;
But I, that now have drawn mal-pleasant breath,
Under the burden of thy cruel hate ;
O, I must long, and linger after death ;
And yet I dare not give my life her date :
For if I die, and thou repent t'have slain me ;
'Twill grieve me more, than if thou didst disdain me.

SONNET III.

WILL grieve me more than if thou didst disdain me,
  That I should die ; and thou, because I die so :
  And yet to die, it should not know to pain me,
  If cruel Beauty were content to bid so.
Death, to my life ; life, to my long despair
  Prolonged by her ; given to my love and days :
  Are means to tell how truly she is fair,
  And I can die to testify her praise.
Yet not to die, though Fairness me despiseth,
  Is cause why in complaint I thus persèver ;
  Though Death me and my love imparadiseth,
  By interdicting me from her for ever.
I do not grieve that I am forced to die,
But die, to think upon the reason, " Why ? "

SONNET IV.

MY TEARS are true : though Others be divine,
  And sing of wars, and Troy's new rising frame ;
  Meeting heroic feet in every line,
  That tread high measures in the Scene of Fame,
And I (though disaccustoming my Muse,
  And sing but low songs, in an humble vein)
  May one day raise my style, as others use ;
  And turn *Elizon* to a higher strain.
When reintombing from oblivious ages,
  In better stanzas her surviving wonder :
  I may opposed against the monster-rages
  That part desert and excellence asunder :
That she, though coy, may yet survive to see,
Her beauty's wonder lives again in me.

SONNET V.

SOMETIMES in verse I praised, sometimes in verse I
    sigh't.
No more shall pen with love and beauty mell;
But to my heart alone, my heart shall tell
How unseen flames do burn it day and night.
Lest flames give light, light bring my love to sight,
    And my love prove my folly to excel.
    Wherefore my love burns like the fire of hell;
    Wherein is fire, and yet there is no light.
For if one never loved like me; then why
    Skill-less blames he the thing he doth not know?
    And he that so hath loved, should favour show;
    For he hath been a fool as well as I.
Thus shall henceforth more pain, more folly have:
And folly past, may justly pardon crave.

[H. Constable.
† 1588.

A calculation upon the birth of an Honour-able Lady's Daughter ; born in the year 1588, and on a Friday.

AIR by inheritance! whom born we see
  Both in the Wondrous Year, and on the
    day
  Wherein the fairest Planet beareth sway;
  The heavens to thee, this fortune doth
    decree!
  Thou of a world of hearts in time shall be
A Monarch great; and with one beauty's ray
So many hosts of hearts, thy face shall slay;
  As all the rest, for love, shall yield to thee!
But even as ALEXANDER, when he knew
  His father's conquests, wept; lest he should leave
No kingdom unto him for to subdue:
  So shall thy mother, thee of praise bereave!
So many hearts already she hath slain;
As few behind to conquer shall remain.

FINIS.

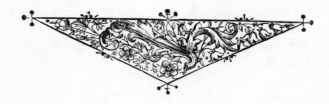

Samuel Daniel.

DELIA.

Ætas prima canat veneres, postrema tumultus.

[*From the Volume entitled DELIA and ROSAMOND augmented &c.* 1594.]

To the Right Honourable the Lady Mary, Countess of Pembroke.

WONDER of these! Glory of other times!
O Thou, whom Envy, ev'n, is forced t'admire!
Great Patroness of these my humble rhymes,
Which Thou, from out thy greatness, dost inspire!
Since only Thou hast deigned to raise them higher;
Vouchsafe now, to accept them as thine own!
Begotten by thy hand, and my desire;
Wherein my zeal, and thy great might is shown.
And seeing this unto the world is known;
O leave not, still, to grace thy work in me!
Let not the quickening seed be overthrown,
Of that which may be born to honour Thee!
Whereof, the travail I may challenge mine;
But yet the glory, Madam! must be thine!

Fifty-five Sonnets follow this Dedication, in the 1594 edition of Daniel's *DELIA and ROSAMUND AUGMENTED*. The edition was designed by the poet to be the final revision of his Sonnets to Delia, fifty of which had already appeared in a separate volume in 1592. One was now dropped and six were added. Twenty-two of the Sonnets included in the 1594 edition of Delia were originally published (in the case of three with verbal differences) among a series of twenty-eight forming an appendix to the 1591 quarto edition of Sidney's *ASTROPHEL and STELLA* (printed in this collection, vol. i. pp. 88-92 *supra*). Of these twenty-two poems, all of which appear in vol. i. pp. 88-92 *supra*, the three, which underwent much verbal change, are again reprinted here (see Nos. XIV., XLIII., and LV.), but the rest are now omitted. The place occupied by each of the nineteen omitted Sonnets is duly indicated, with a precise reference to the volume and page in which they may be found in our first volume.

TO DELIA.

SONNET I.

 Nto the boundless Ocean of thy beauty,
    Runs this poor river, charged with streams
        of zeal ;
    Returning Thee, the tribute of my
        duty,
    Which here my love, my youth, my plaints
        reveal.

Here, I unclasp the Book of my charged Soul ;
Where I have cast th'accounts of all my care :
Here, have I summed my sighs.   Here, I enrol
How they were spent for thee !   Look ! what they are !
Look on the dear expenses of my youth !
    And see how just I reckon with thine eyes !
    Examine well, thy beauty with my truth !
    And cross my cares, ere greater sums arise !
Read it, Sweet Maid ! though it be done but slightly !
Who can shew all his love, doth love but lightly.

Sonnet II.—'Go, wailing verse!'   See vol. i. p. 88 *supra.*
Sonnet III.—'If so it hap.'   See vol. i. p. 89 *supra.*

SONNET IV.

HESE plaintive verse[s], the Posts of my desire,
    Which haste for succour to her slow regard;
    Bear not report of any slender fire,
    Forging a grief, to win a fame's reward.
Nor are my passions limned for outward hue,
    For that no colours can depaint my sorrows:
    D E L I A herself, and all the world may view
    Best in my face, where cares hath tilled deep furrows.
No bays I seek, to deck my mourning brow,
    O clear-eyed Rector of the holy Hill!
    My humble accents bear the olive bough
    Of intercession to a tyrant's will.
These lines I use, t'unburden mine own heart ;
My love affects no fame, nor 'steems of art.

SONNET V.

HILST Youth and Error led my wandering mind,
    And set my thoughts, in heedless ways to range;
    All unawares, a goddess chaste I find,
    D I A N A-like, to work my sudden change.
For her, no sooner had mine eye bewrayed ;
    But with disdain to see me in that place,
    With fairest hand, the sweet unkindest maid
    Casts water-cold disdain upon my face :
Which turned my sport into a hart's despair,
    Which still is chased, while I have any breath,
    By mine own thoughts, set on me by my Fair.
    My thoughts, like hounds, pursue me to my death.
Those that I fostered, of mine own accord,
Are made by her, to murder thus their Lord.

SONNET VI.

AIR is my love, and cruel as she's fair:
> Her brow shades frowns, although her eyes are
>> sunny;
> Her smiles are lightening, though her pride despair;
> And her disdains are gall, her favours honey.
A modest maid, decked with a blush of honour,
> Whose feet do tread green paths of youth and love;
> The wonder of all eyes that look upon her:
> Sacred on earth, designed a saint above,
Chastity and Beauty, which were deadly foes,
> Live reconcilèd friends within her brow:
> And had she Pity, to conjoin with those;
> Then who had heard the plaints I utter now?
O had she not been fair, and thus unkind;
My Muse had slept, and none had known my mind!

SONNET VII.

HAD she not been fair, and thus unkind!
Then had no finger pointed at my lightness.
The world had never known what I do find,
> And clouds obscure had shaded still her brightness.
Then had no Censor's eye these lines surveyed,
> Nor graver brows have judged my Muse so vain:
> No sun, my blush and error had bewrayed;
> Nor yet the world had heard of such disdain.
Then had I walked with bold erectèd face;
> No downcast look had signified my miss:
> But my degraded hopes, with such disgrace,
> Did force me groan out griefs, and utter this.
For, being full, should I not then have spoken;
My sense, oppressed, had failed, and heart had broken.

SONNET VIII.

THou, poor Heart! sacrificed unto the fairest,
 Hast sent the incense of thy sighs to heaven!
 And still against her frowns, fresh vows repairest;
 And made thy passions with her beauty even.
And you, mine Eyes! the agents of my heart,
 Told the dumb message of my hidden grief:
 And oft, with careful tunes, with silent art,
 Did 'treat the cruel Fair to yield relief.
And you, my Verse! the advocates of love,
 Have followed hard the process of my case:
 And urged that title, which doth plainly prove
 My faith should win, if justice might have place.
Yet though I see, that nought we do can move her;
'Tis not disdain, must make me cease to love her.

Sonnet IX.—'If this be love.'   See vol. i. p. 99 *supra.*

SONNET X.

THEN love I, and draw this weary breath
 For her, the cruel Fair; within whose brow,
 I, written find, the sentence of my death,
 In unkind letters, wrought, she cares not how!
O thou that rul'st the confines of the night!
 Laughter-loving Goddess!   Worldly pleasures' Queen!
 Intenerate that heart! that sets so light
 The truest love that ever yet was seen:
And cause her leave to triumph, in this wise,
 Upon the prostrate spoil of that poor heart!
 That serves a Trophy to her conquering eyes,
 And must their glory to the world impart.
Once, let her know! sh' hath done enough to prove me;
And let her pity, if she cannot love me!

Sonnet XI.—'Tears, vows, and prayers.'   See vol. i. p. 90 *supra.*

SONNET XII.

M Y SPOTLESS love hovers, with purest wings,
  About the temple of the proudest frame;
  Where blaze those lights, fairest of earthly things,
  Which clear our clouded world with brightest flame.
M' ambitious thoughts, confinèd in her face,
  Affect no honour, but what she can give:
  My hopes do rest in limits of her grace;
  I weigh no comfort, unless she relieve.
For she, that can my heart imparadise,
  Holds in her fairest hand, what dearest is.
  My Fortune's Wheel 's the Circle of her Eyes;
  Whose rolling grace deign once a turn of bliss!
All my life's sweet consists in her alone ;
So much I love the most unloving one.

Sonnet XIII.—'Behold what hap.' See vol. i. p. 92 *supra.*

SONNET XIV.

[First printed, with verbal differences, in *Sonnets after Sidney's Astrophel.*
See *supra*, vol. i. p. 91.]

T HOSE snary locks are those same nets, my Dear!
  Wherewith my liberty, thou didst surprise !
  Love was the flame that fired me so near :
  The dart transpiercing were those crystal eyes.
Strong is the net, and fervent is the flame ;
  Deep is the wound, my sighs do well report.
  Yet I do love, adore, and praise the same
  That holds, that burns, that wounds in this sort ;
And list not seek to break, to quench, to heal
  The bond, the flame, the wound that festereth so,
  By knife, by liquor, or by salve to deal :
  So much I please to perish in my woe.
Yet lest long travails be above my strength ;
Good D E L I A ! Loose, quench, heal me, now at length !

Sonnet XV.—'If a true heart.' See vol. i. p. 95 *supra.*
Sonnet XVI.—'Happy in sleep.' See vol. i. p. 98 *supra.*

SONNET XVII.

[First printed in this edition.]

HY SHOULD I sing in verse?   Why should I frame
These sad neglected notes, for her dear sake ?
Why should I offer up unto her name,
   The sweetest sacrifice my youth can make?
Why should I strive to make her live for ever,
   That never deigns to give me joy to live?
   Why should m'afflicted Muse so much endeavour
   Such honour, unto cruelty to give?
If her defects have purchased her this fame;
   What should her virtues do? her smiles? her love?
   If this, her worst; how should her best inflame?
   What passions would her milder favours move ?
Favours, I think, would sense quite overcome;
And that makes happy lovers ever dumb.

Sonnet XVIII.—'Since the first look.' See vol. i. p. 96 *supra.*
Sonnet XIX.—'Restore thy tresses.' See vol. i. p. 94 *supra.*
Sonnet XX.—'If Beauty bright.' See vol. i. p. 98 *supra.*
Sonnet XXI.—'Come DEATH.' See vol. i. p. 99 *supra.*
Sonnet XXII.—'These sorrowing sighs.' See vol. i. p. 89 *supra.*

SONNET XXIII.

ALSE HOPE prolongs my ever certain grief,
   Traitor to me, and faithful to my Love.
A thousand times it promised me relief,
   Yet never any true effect I prove.
Oft, when I find in her no truth at all,
   I banish her, and blame her treachery:
   Yet, soon again, I must her back recall,
   As one that dies without her company.
Thus often, as I chase my Hope from me,
   Straightway, she hastes her unto DELIA's eyes:
   Fed with some pleasing look, there shall she be;
   And so sent back.   And thus my fortune lies.
Looks feed my Hope, Hope fosters me in vain;
Hopes are unsure, when certain is my Pain.

Sonnet XXIV.—'Look in my griefs!' See vol. i. p. 97 *supra.*
Sonnet XXV.—'Reign in my thoughts!' See vol. i. p. 93 *supra.*
Sonnet XXVI.—'Whilst by her eyes.' See vol. i. p. 97 *supra.*

SONNET XXVII.

[First printed in this edition.]

STILL in the trace of my tormented thought,
My ceaseless cares must march on to my death.
Thy least regard too dearly have I bought,
Who, to my comfort, never deign'st a breath !
Why should'st thou stop thine ears now to my cries ?
Whose eyes were open, ready to oppress me !
Why shutt'st thou not, the cause whence all did rise ?
Or hear me now, or seek how to redress me !
Injurious D E L I A ! Yet, I'll love thee still !
Whilst that I breathe in sorrow of my smart ;
I'll tell the world that I deserved but ill,
And blame myself, for to excuse thy heart !
Then judge ! who sins the greater of us twain :
I, in my love ; or thou, in thy disdain !

SONNET XXVIII.

[First printed in this edition.]

OFT do I marvel, whether D E L I A's eyes
Are eyes, or else two radiant stars that shine ?
For how could Nature ever thus devise
Of earth, on earth, a substance so divine ?
Stars, sure, they are ! Whose motions rule desires ;
And calm and tempest follow their aspects :
Their sweet appearing still such power inspires,
That makes the world admire so strange effects.
Yet whether fixed or wandering stars are they,
Whose influence rules the Orb of my poor heart ?
Fixed, sure, they are ! But wandering, make me stray
In endless errors ; whence I cannot part.
Stars, then, not eyes ! Move you, with milder view,
Your sweet aspect on him that honours you !

Sonnet XXIX.—'The star of my mishap.' See vol. i. p. 100 *supra.*

SONNET XXX.

[First printed in this edition.]

AND yet, I cannot reprehend the flight,
 Or blame th'attempt, presuming so to soar:
 The mounting venture, for a high delight,
 Did make the honour of the fall the more.
For who gets wealth, that puts not from the shore?
 Danger hath honour! great designs, their fame!
 Glory doth follow! courage goes before!
 And though th'event oft answers not the same;
Suffice that high attempts have never shame.
 The Mean-observer (whom base safety keeps)
 Lives without honour, dies without a name;
 And in eternal darkness ever sleeps.
And therefore, DELIA! 'tis to me, no blot;
To have attempted, though attained thee not!

Sonnet XXXI.—'Raising my hope.' See vol. i. p. 102 *supra*.
Sonnet XXXII.—'Why doth my mistress.' See vol. i. p. 91 *supra*.
Sonnet XXXIII.—'I once may see.' See vol. i. p. 101 *supra*.

SONNET XXXIV.

LOOK, DELIA! how we 'steem the half-blown rose,
 (The image of thy blush! and summer's honour)
 Whilst, in her tender green, she doth inclose
 The pure sweet beauty Time bestows upon her!
No sooner spreads her glory in the air,
 But straight her full-blown pride is in declining;
 She then is scorned, that late adorned the fair.
 So clouds thy beauty, after fairest shining!
No April can revive thy withered flowers,
 Whose blooming grace adorns thy glory now!
 Swift speedy Time, feathered with flying hours,
 Dissolves the beauty of the fairest brow.
O let not then such riches waste in vain!
But love! whilst that thou may'st be loved again!

SONNET XXXV.

BUt love! whilst that thou may'st be loved again!
Now, whilst thy May hath filled thy lap with flowers!
Now, whilst thy beauty bears without a stain!
   Now, use thy summer smiles, ere Winter lowers!
And whilst thou spread'st unto the rising sun,
   The fairest flower that ever saw the light;
   Now joy thy time, before thy sweet be done!
   And, DELIA! think thy morning must have night!
And that thy brightness sets at length to West;
   When thou wilt close up that, which now thou showest!
   And think the same becomes thy fading best,
   Which, then, shall hide it most, and cover lowest!
Men do not weigh the stalk, for that it was;
When once they find her flower, her glory pass.

SONNET XXXVI.

WHEN men shall find thy flower, thy glory pass:
And thou, with careful brow, sitting alone,
Receivèd hast this message, from thy glass;
   That tells the truth, and says that "All is gone!"
Fresh shalt thou see in me, the wounds thou madest;
   Though spent thy flame, in me the heat remaining.
   I that have loved thee thus before thou fadest,
   My faith shall wax, when thou art in thy waning!
The world shall find this miracle in me,
   That fire can burn, when all the matter 's spent.
   Then what my faith hath been, thyself shalt see!
   And that thou wast unkind, thou may'st repent!
Thou may'st repent, that thou hast scorned my tears,
When Winter snows upon thy golden hairs.

SONNET XXXVII.

HEN Winter snows upon thy golden hairs,
    And frost of Age hath nipped thy flowers near;
    When dark shall seem thy day, that never clears,
    And all lies withered that was held so dear:
Then take this picture, which I here present thee!
    Limned with a pencil, not all unworthy,
    Here, see the gifts that GOD and Nature lent thee!
    Here, read thy Self! and what I suffered for thee!
This may remain thy lasting monument,
    Which, happily, posterity may cherish :
    These colours, with thy fading, are not spent;
    These may remain, when thou and I shall perish.
If they remain, then thou shalt live thereby!
They will remain, and so thou canst not die!

SONNET XXXVIII.

THOU canst not die, whilst any zeal abound
    In feeling hearts, that can conceive these lines:
    Though thou, a LAURA, hast no PETRARCH found;
    In base attire, yet, clearly, Beauty shines.
And I, though born within a colder clime,
    Do feel mine inward heat as great (I know it).
    He never had more faith, although more rhyme:
    I love as well, though he could better show it.
But I may add one feather to thy fame,
    To help her flight throughout the fairest Isle;
    And if my pen could more enlarge thy name,
    Then should'st thou live in an immortal style.
For though that LAURA better limnèd be;
Suffice, thou shalt be loved as well as she!

SONNET XXXIX.

BE not grieved that these my papers should
Bewray unto the world, how fair thou art!
Or that my wits have shewed, the best they could,
    The chastest flame that ever warmèd heart.
Think not, sweet D E L I A! this shall be thy shame,
    My Muse should sound thy praise with mournful warble!
How many live, the glory of whose name
Shall rest in ice, while thine is graved in marble!
Thou may'st, in after ages, live esteemed!
    Unburied in these lines, reserved in pureness.
    These shall entomb those eyes, that have redeemed
    Me, from the vulgar; thee, from all obscureness.
Although my careful accents never moved thee!
Yet count it no disgrace, that I have loved thee!

SONNET XL.

ELIA! These eyes that so admireth thine!
    Have seen those walls the which ambition reared
    To check the world.   How they, entombed, have lain
    Within themselves: and on them ploughs have eared.
Yet found I, that no barbarous hand attained
    The spoil of Fame, deserved by virtuous men,
    Whose glorious actions, luckily, had gained
    Th'eternal annals of a happy pen.
Why then, though D E L I A fade! let that not move her!
    Though time do spoil her of the fairest veil
    That ever yet mortality did cover;
    Which must instar the Needle and the Rail.
That grace, that virtue, all that served t'in-woman,
Doth her, unto eternity assommon.

SONNET XLI.

FAIR and lovely Maid!   Look from the shore!
See thy LEANDER striving in these waves!
Poor soul! quite spent, whose force can do no more.
Now send forth hopes! (for now calm pity saves)
And waft him to thee, with those lovely eyes!
A happy convoy to a Holy Land.
Now show thy power! and where thy virtue lies!
To save thine own, stretch out the fairest hand!
Stretch out the fairest hand! a pledge of peace;
That hand that darts so right, and never misses!
I shall forget old wrongs.   My griefs shall cease.
And that which gave me wounds, I'll give it kisses.
O then, let th'ocean of my care find shore!
That thou be pleased, and I may sigh no more.

SONNET XLII.

READ in my face, a volume of despairs!
The wailing Iliads of my tragic woe;
Drawn with my blood, and printed with my cares,
Wrought by her hand that I have honoured so.
Who, whilst I burn, she sings at my soul's wrack,
Looking aloft from turret of her pride:
There, my Soul's Tyrant 'joys her in the sack
Of her own seat; whereof I made her guide.
There do these smokes, that from affliction rise,
Serve as an incense to a cruel Dame.
A sacrifice thrice-grateful to her eyes,
Because their power serves to exact the same.
Thus ruins She, to satisfy her will,
The Temple, where her name was honoured still.

SONNET XLIII.

[First printed, with verbal differences, in *Sonnets after Sidney's Astrophel* (1591).
See *supra*, vol. i. p. 95, where the sonnet opens ' My Cynthia hath.']

MY D ELIA hath the waters of mine eyes,
(The ready handmaids on her grace attending)
That never fall to ebb, but ever rise;
    For to their flow, she never grants an ending.
Th'ocean never did attend more duly
    Upon his Sovereign's course, the night's pale Queen;
Nor paid the impost of his waves more truly,
    Than mine unto her Deity have been.
Yet nought, the rock of that hard heart can move;
    Where beat these tears with zeal, and fury driveth:
And yet, I rather languish in her love,
    Than I would joy the fairest she that liveth.
I doubt to find such pleasure in my gaining;
As now I taste, in compass of complaining.

SONNET XLIV.

HOw long shall I, in mine affliction mourn?
A burden to myself, distressed in mind;
When shall my interdicted hopes return
    From out despair, wherein they live confined?
When shall her troubled brow, charged with disdain,
    Reveal the treasure which her smiles impart?
When shall my faith that happiness attain,
    To break the ice, that hath congealed her heart?
Unto herself, herself my love doth summon,
    (If love in her, hath any power to move):
And let her tell me, as she is a woman,
    Whether my faith hath not deserved her love?
I know she cannot! but must needs confess it;
Yet deigns not, with one simple sign t'express it.

SONNET XLV.

BEAUTY, sweet love! is like the morning dew;
 Whose short refresh upon the tender green,
 Cheers for a time, but till the sun doth show:
  And straight 'tis gone, as it had never been.
Soon doth it fade, that makes the fairest flourish;
 Short is the glory of the blushing rose:
 The hue which thou so carefully dost nourish;
 Yet which, at length, thou must be forced to lose.
When thou, surcharged with burden of thy years,
 Shalt bend thy wrinkles homeward to the earth;
 When Time hath made a passport for thy fears,
 Dated in age, the Kalends of our death:
But, ah! no more! This hath been often told;
And women grieve to think they must be old.

SONNET XLVI.

I MUST not grieve my love! whose eyes would read
 Lines of delight, whereon her youth might smile!
 Flowers have a time, before they come to seed;
  And she is young, and now must sport the while.
Ah, sport! sweet Maid! in season of these years;
 And learn to gather flowers before they wither!
 And where the sweetest blossom first appears;
 Let Love and Youth conduct thy pleasures thither!
Lighten forth smiles! to clear the clouded air,
 And calm the tempest which my sighs do raise!
 Pity and Smiles do best become the fair;
 Pity and Smiles shall yield thee lasting praise!
I hope to say, when all my griefs are gone,
" Happy the heart, that sighed for such a one!"

SONNET XLVII.

[First printed in this edition.]

At the Author's going into Italy.

WHITHER, poor Forsaken! wilt thou go?
To go from sorrow, and thine own distress;
When every place presents like face of woe,
    And no remove can make thy sorrows less!
Yet go, Forsaken! Leave these woods, these plains!
    Leave her and all! and all for her, that leaves
    Thee and thy love forlorn; and both disdains:
    And of both, wrongful deems, and ill conceives.
Seek out some place! and see if any place
    Can give the least release unto thy grief!
    Convey thee from the thought of thy disgrace!
    Steal from thy self! and be thy cares own thief!
But yet what comfort, shall I hereby gain?
Bearing the wound, I needs must feel the pain.

SONNET XLVIII.

❡ *This Sonnet was made at the Author's being in Italy.*

RAWN with th'attractive virtue of her eyes,
    My touched heart turns it to that happy coast;
    My joyful North! where all my fortune lies,
    The level of my hopes desirèd most.
There, where my DELIA, fairer than the sun,
    Decked with her youth, whereon the world doth smile,
    Joys in that honour, which her eyes have won:
    Th'eternal wonder of our happy isle.
Flourish, fair Albion!, Glory of the North!
    NEPTUNE's best darling! held between his arms:
    Divided from the world, as better worth;
    Kept for himself, defended from all harms!
Still let disarmèd peace deck her, and thee!
And Muse-foe MARS, abroad far fostered be!

SONNET XLIX.

CARE-charmer Sleep! Son of the sable Night!
Brother to Death! In silent darkness, born!
Relieve my anguish, and restore the light!
    With dark forgetting of my cares, return!
And let the day be time enough to mourn
    The shipwreck of my ill adventured youth!
    Let waking eyes suffice to wail their scorn,
    Without the torment of the night's untruth!
Cease, Dreams! th'imag'ry of our day desires,
    To model forth the passions of the morrow!
    Never let rising sun approve you liars!
    To add more grief to aggravate my sorrow.
Still let me sleep! embracing clouds in vain;
And never wake to feel the day's disdain.

SONNET L.

LET others sing of Knights and Palladins,
In agèd accents, and untimely words!
Paint shadows, in imaginary lines!
    Which well the reach of their high wits records:
But I must sing of Thee! and those fair eyes!
    Authentic shall my verse, in time to come,
    When yet the unborn shall say, " Lo, where she lies!
    Whose beauty made him speak, that else was dumb!"
These are the arks, the trophies I erect,
    That fortify thy name against old age;
    And these, thy sacred virtues must protect
    Against the dark, and Time's consuming rage.
Though th'error of my youth, they shall discover;
Suffice they shew I lived, and was thy lover!

SONNET LI.

[First printed in this edition].

A S TO the Roman, that would free his land,
   His error was his honour and renown;
   And more the fame of his mistaking hand,
   Than if he had the tyrant overthrown.
So, D E L I A !, hath mine error made me known,
   And my deceived attempt, deserved more fame:
   Than if I had the victory mine own,
   And thy hard heart had yielded up the same.
And so, likewise, renowned is thy blame!
   Thy cruelty! thy glory! O strange case!
   That errors should be graced, that merit shame;
   And sin of frowns bring honour to the face.
Yet, happy D E L I A !, that thou wast unkind;
But happier yet, if thou would'st change thy mind!

SONNET LII.

L IKE as the lute, that joys or else dislikes,
   As is his art that plays upon the same:
   So sounds my Muse, according as she strikes
   On my heart strings, high tuned unto her fame.
Her touch doth cause the warble of the sound,
   Which here I yield in lamentable wise,
   A wailing " descant " on the sweetest " ground,"
   Whose due reports give honour to her eyes.
Else harsh my style, untunable my Muse;
   Hoarse sounds the voice, that praiseth not her name!
   If any pleasing relish here I use;
   Then judge, the world! her beauty gives the same.
O happy " ground " that makes the music such!
And blessèd hand that gives so sweet a touch!

SONNET LIII.

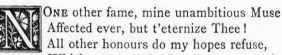

NONE other fame, mine unambitious Muse
    Affected ever, but t'eternize Thee!
    All other honours do my hopes refuse,
    Which meaner prized and momentary be.
For, GOD forbid! I should my papers blot
    With mercenary lines, with servile pen;
    Praising virtues in them that have them not,
    Basely attending on the hopes of men.
No! no! My Verse respects not Thames, nor Theatres;
    Nor seeks it to be known unto the great:
    But Avon, poor in fame, and poor in waters,
    Shall have my song, where D E L I A hath her seat.
Avon shall be my Thames, and She my Song;
    I'll sound her name, the river all along.

SONNET LIV.

UNHAPPY pen! and ill accepted papers!
    That intimate, in vain, my chaste desires:
    My chaste desires, the ever-burning tapers,
    Enkindled by her eyes' celestial fires.
Celestial fires! and unrespecting powers,
    That deign not view the glory of your might!
    In humble lines, the work of careful hours,
    The sacrifice I offer to her sight.
But since she scorns her own; this rests for me.
    I'll moan, myself; and hide the wrong I have:
    And so content me, that her frowns should be
    To m'infant style, the cradle and the grave.
What though myself no honour get thereby;
    Each birds sings to herself, and so will I!

SONNET LV.

[First printed, with verbal differences, in *Sonnets after Sidney's Astrophel* (1591).
See *supra*, vol. i. p. 101.]

LO HERE, the impost of a faith unfeigning,
　　That love hath paid, and her disdain extorted!
　Behold the message of my just complaining,
　　　That shews the world, how much my grief im-
　　　　ported!
These tributary plaints, fraught with desire,
　　I send those Eyes, the Cabinets of Love!
　The Paradise, whereto my hopes aspire,
　　From out this Hell, which mine afflictions prove.
Wherein I thus do live, cast down from mirth;
　　Pensive, alone, none but despair about me;
　My joys abortive, perished at their birth;
　　My cares long lived, and will not die without me.
This is my state! and DELIA's heart is such!
I say no more.　I fear, I said too much.

FINIS.

An Ode.

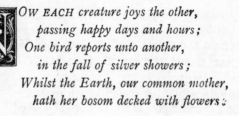

OW EACH creature joys the other,
 passing happy days and hours;
One bird reports unto another,
 in the fall of silver showers;
Whilst the Earth, our common mother,
 hath her bosom decked with flowers:

Whilst the greatest Torch of heaven,
 with bright rays, warms FLORA's lap;
Making nights and days both even,
 cheering plants with fresher sap :
My field, of flowers quite bereaven,
 wants refresh of better hap.

ECHO, daughter of the Air,
 babbling guest of rocks and hills,
Knows the name of my fierce Fair,
 and sounds the accents of my ills.
Each thing pities my despair;
 whilst that She, her lover kills.

Whilst that She, O cruel Maid!
 doth me and my love despise;
My life's flourish is decayed,
 that depended on her eyes:
But her will must be obeyed;
 and well, he ends! for love, who dies.

FINIS.

Sonnets

to the fairest

Coelia.

Parve, nec invideo, sine me liber ibis ad illam,
Hei mihi quod domino non licet ire tuo.—TRIST. I.

LONDON,
Printed by *Adam Islip*,
for W. P.
1594·

To the Reader.

COURTEOUS READER,

HEREAS I was fully determined to have concealed my Sonnets as things privy to myself; yet, of courtesy, having lent them to some, they were secretly committed to the Press and almost finished, before it came to my knowledge.

Wherefore making, as they say, Virtue of Necessity, I did deem it most convenient to prepose my Epistle, only to beseech you to account of them as of toys and amorous devices; and, ere long, I will impart unto the World another Poem, which shall be both more fruitful and ponderous.

In the mean while, I commit these, as a pledge, to your indifferent censures.

London, 1594.

W. PERCY.

COELIA.

SONNET I.

UDGED by my Goddess' doom to endless pain;
Lo, here I ope my Sorrow's Passion!
That every silly eye may view most plain
A Sentence given on no occasion.

   If that, by chance, they fall (most fortunate!)
Within those cruel hands that did enact it;
Say but "Alas, he was too Passionate!"
My doom is passed, nor can be now unactit."

   So mayst Thou see I was a spotless lover!
And grieve withal that, ere, thou dealt so sore!
Unto remorse, who goes about to move her,
Pursues the wingèd winds, and tills the shore!

   Lovely is her Semblance, hard is her Heart;
Wavering is her Mind, sure is her Dart!

SONNET II.

HAPPY hour, and yet unhappy hour!
  When first by chance I had my Goddess viewed;
  Then first I tasted of the sweetest sour
    Wherewith the cup of CYPRIA is embrued.
  For gazing firm without suspicion,
LOVE, cooped behind the chariot of her eye,
Justly to school my bold presumption,
Against my heart did let an arrow fly.
  " Fair Sir," quoth he, " to practise have you nought
But to be gazing on Divinity?
Before you part, your leare you shall be taught!"
With that, at once, he made his arrows hie.
  " Imperious God! I did it not to love her!
  Ah, stay thy hand! I did it but to prove her!"

SONNET III.

ROVE her! Ah, no! I did it but to love her!
  Then shoot amain, dread Liege! I stand unarmed.
  Although no hope that anything may move her;
    Some ease it is, to be by beauty charmed.
  Then quick, my Liege! then quick, and end thy game!
That all the World may see how thou hast plagued us;
Then cruel She shall view, unto her blame,
That "all men be not fickle," as they've termed us,
  May be, my words may win contrition!
If not my words, my sobs! if not my sobs,
My tears may move her to compassion!
If tears do fail, my tears, my words, my throbs:
  Ay me! ah no! tears, words, throbs, all in vain!
  She scorns my dole, and smileth at my pain!

S O N N E T I V.

HEAVENLY CŒLIA, as fair as virtuous!
The only Mirror of true Chastity!
Have I been 'gainst thy godhead impious,
That thus am guerdoned for my fealty?
   Have I not shed upon thine iv'ry shrine
Huge drops of tears with large eruptions?
Have I not offered, Evening, and at Prime,
My sighs, my *Psalms* of invocations?
   " What be men's sighs but cauls of guilefulness? "
" They shew, dear Love! true proofs of firmity! "
" What be your tears but mere ungraciousness? "
" Tears only plead for our simplicity ! "
   When all strike mute, She says " It is my duty ! "
   And claims as much as to her deity.

S O N N E T V.

AIR Queen of Cnidos! come, adorn my forehead!
And crown me with the laurel, Emperor!
Ió, thrice sing *Ió* about thy poet!
Lo, on my goddess, I am conqueror!
   For once, by chance, not sure or wittingly,
Upon my foot, her **ten**der foot alighted,
With that, she plucked it off full nimbly
As though the very touch had her affrighted.
   Dear Mistress! will you deal so cruelly,
To 'prive me of so small a benefit?
What! do you jerk it off so nimbly
As though, in very sooth, a snake had bit it!
   Yea, bit perhaps indeed! Ho, Muses, blab you!
   Not a word, Pieannets! or I will gag you!

SONNET VI.

OOD God! how senseless be we paramours,
So proudly on a Nothing for to vaunt it!
We cannot reap the meanest of all favours,
But, by-and-by, we think our suit is grantit!
     Had ye observed two Planets which then mounted,
Two certain signs of indignation;
Ye would have deemed rather both consented
To turn all hopes to desperation.
     Then can you waver so inconstantly
To shew first Love, and then Disdainfulness?
First for to bring a dram of courtesy,
Then mix it with an ounce of scornfulness?
          No, no, the doubt is answered! Certainly,
          She trod by chance; She trod not wittingly!

SONNET VII.

F IT be sin, so dearly for to love thee;
Come bind my hands! I am thy prisoner!
If yet a spark of pity may but move thee,
First sit, upon the cause, Commissioner!
     The same, well heard, may wrest incontinent,
Two floods from forth those rocks of adamant;
Which streaming down with force impatient
May melt the breast of my fierce RHADAMANT.
     Dearest Cruel, the cause, I see dislikes thee!
On us thy brows thou bends so direfully!
Enjoin me penance whatsoever likes thee;
Whate'er it be, I'll take it thankfully!
          Yet since, for love it is, I am thy Bondman;
          Good CŒLIA, use me like a Gentleman!

SONNET VIII.

TRIKE up, my Lute! and ease my heavy cares,
The only solace to my Passions :
Impart unto the airs, thy pleasing airs !
More sweet than heavenly consolations.

Rehearse the songs of forlorn amor'us
Driven to despair by dames tyrannical !
Of ALPHEUS' loss, of woes of TROILUS,
Of ROWLAND's rage, of IPHIS' funeral !

Ay me ! what warbles yields mine instrument !
The Basses shriek as though they were amiss !
The Means, no means, too sad the merriment !
No, no ! the music good, but thus it is

I loath both Means, merriment, Diapasons ;
So She and I may be but Unisons.

SONNET IX.

HILST others ween sole hopes to be a sa[l]ve,
Sole hopes I find to be my corrosive !
Whilst others found in hopes, an harbour have ;
From hopes, I feel a sea of sorrows rise !

For when mild hopes should ease my raging fires,
They fester more, in that they are but hopes ;
Then whilst I touch the foot of my Desires,
A storm of hate doth burst mine anchor ropes.

Were I but once resolved certainly,
Soon should I know which point my helm to steer ;
But She denies my suit most womanly,
As hidden documents for us to hear.

Lo, this the cause my hell forsakes me never.
"Tell me," dear Sweet, "thus shall I live for ever?"

SONNET X.

¶ *A Mystery.*

[Cf. Barnes's *Parthenophil*, vol. i. p. 200 *supra.*]

TO win the Fort, how oft have I assayed!
Wherein the heart of my fair Mistress lies.
What rams, what mines, what plots have I not laid!
Yet still am frighted from mine enterprise.
　　First from the leads of that proud citadel
Do foulder forth two fiery Culverins,
Under, two red coats keep the Larum Bell
For fear of close or open venturings;
　　Before the gates, Scorn, Fear, and Modesty
Do toss amain their pikes; but 'bove them all
Pudicity wields her staff most manfully,
Guarded with blocks, that keep me from the wall.
　　　Yet if this staff will ford me clear the way;
　　　In spite of all, I'll bear my Dame away!

SONNET XI.

To POLYXENA.

F ALL the women which of yore have been,
Alcest for virtue may be glorified;
For courage, Teuce; for features, Sparta's Queen;
For all in one, Polyxen deified.
　　If true it be, by old philosophy,
These souls to have, since destin, entered
To other bodies of like sympathy;
Thou art the last of these metampsychosed!
　　Thy courage wondrous! thy virtues peerless!
Thy features have the fairest ladies blamed!
Then (if thou scorn'st not such a Monarchess)
Henceforth, by reason good, thou shalt be named,
　　　Nor Teuce, nor Alcest, nor fair Helena;
　　　Thou shalt be named my dear Polyxena!

SONNET XII.

ŒLIA, of all sweet courtesies resolve me!
For wishèd grace, how must I now be doing?
Since OPS, the completest frame which did absolve
     thee,
Hath made each parcel to my sole undoing!

Those wires which should thy corps to mine unite,
Be rays to daze us from so near approach.
Thine eyne, which should my 'nighted sailors light,
Be shot to keep them off with foul reproach.

Those ruddy plums embrued with heavenly foods,
When I would suck them, turn to driest coral;
And when I couch between her lily buds,
They surge, like frothy water mounts above all.

     Surely, they were all made unto good uses;
     But She, them all untowardly abuses.

SONNET XIII.

ITH grievous thoughts and weighty care opprest,
One day, I went to VENUS's Fanacle;
Of Cyprian dreams, which did me sore molest,
To be resolved by certain Oracle.

No sooner was I past the temple's gate,
But from the shrine, where VENUS wont to stand,
I saw a Lady fair and delicate
Did beckon to me with her ivory hand.

Weening She was the Goddess of the Fane,
With cheerful looks I towards bent my pace:
Soon when I came, I found unto my bane,
A GORGON shadowed under VENUS' face;

     Whereat affright, when back I would be gone,
     I stood transformèd to a speechless stone.

SONNET XIV.

WHEN once I saw that no intreats would move her;
All means I sought to be deliverèd:
Against white CUPID and his golden Mother,
In high contempt, base words I utterèd:
When both, from clouds of her bright firmament,
With heavy griefs and strong disdain surmounted,
Upon my thoughts and me, did shoot revengement,
Whilst in our highest prides we were amounted.
Nor be they pleased to give us all these wounds,
To make me languish as a dying liver:
But from her orbs they fling their firebrands.
Thereby to quite consume both heart and liver.
Pardon, dread Powers! pardon my rash offence!
By Heaven's bright vail! 'twas 'gainst my conscience!

SONNET XV.

Echo.

[For similar 'Echo' poems, cf. vol. i. pp. 220-1, 272-6, and 301 *supra*, and vol. ii. 337 *infra*.]

WHAT is the Fair, to whom so long
      I plead ?   *Lead.*
    What is her face, so angel-like ?   *Angel-like.*
Then unto Saints in mind, Sh'is not unlike ?   *Unlike.*
What may be hoped of one so evil nat'red ?   *Hatred.*
    O then my woes how shall I ope best ?   *Hope best !*
Then She is flexible ?   *She is flexible.*
Fie, no, it is impossible !   *Possible.*
About her straight then only our best !   *You're best !*
    How must I first her loves to me approve ?   *Prove !*
How if She say I may not kiss her ?   *Kiss her !*
For all her bobs I must them bear, or miss her ?   *Yes, sir !*
Then will She yield at length to Love ?   *To love !*
    Even so ! *Even so !* By NARCISSE ! is it true ? *True !*
    Of thine honesty ? *I !* Adieu !   *Adieu !*

SONNET XVI.

WHAT may be thought of thine untowardness,
That movest still at every motion?
What may be hoped of so strange uncouthness,
That scorns all vows, scorns all devotion?
If I but sue, thou wouldst relieve mine anguish,
Two threatening arcs thou bendest rigorously!
Then if I swear thy love did make me languish,
Thou turn'st away, and smilest scornfully!
Then if I wish thou would'st not tyrannize;
Of Tyranny thou mak'st but a mockery!
And if I weep, my tears thou dost despise!
And if I stir, thou threatenest battery!
Frown on! smile on! mock me! despise me! threat me!
All shall not make me leave for to intreat thee!

SONNET XVII.

RELENT, my dear, yet unkind CŒLIA!
At length, relent, and give my sorrows end!
So shall I keep my long-wished holiday,
And set a trophy on a froward friend!
Nor tributes, nor imposts, nor other duties
Demand I will, as lawful Conqueror!
Duties, tributes, imposts unto thy beauties,
Myself will pay as yieldèd Servitor!
Then quick relent! thyself surrender us!
"Brave Sir, and why," quoth She, "must I relent?"
"Relent," cried I, "thyself doth conquer us!"
When eftsoons with my proper instrument
She cut me off, ay me! and answerèd,
"You cannot conquer, and be conquerèd."

SONNET XVIII.

" I CANNOT conquer and be conquerèd ! "
   Then whole myself I yield unto thy favour !
   Behold my thoughts float in an ocean, battered ;
     To be cast off, or wafted to thine harbour !
If of the fame, thou wilt then take acceptance,
Stretch out thy fairest hand, as flag of peace !
If not, no longer keep us in attendance ;
But all at once thy fiery shafts release !
   If thus I die, an honest cause of love
Will of my fates the rigour mitigate ;
Those gracious ey'n, which will a Tartar move,
Will prove my case the less unfortunate.
     Although my friends may rue my chance for aye,
     It will be said, " He died for CŒLIA ! "

SONNET XIX.

I T SHALL be said I died for CŒLIA !
   Then quick, thou grisly man of Erebus,
   Transport me hence unto PROSERPINA,
     To be adjudged as " wilful amorous."
To be hung up within the liquid air !
For all the sighs which I in vain have wasted :
To be through Lethe's waters cleansèd fair !
For those dark clouds which have my looks o'ercasted :
   To be condemned to everlasting fire !
Because at CUPID's fire, I wilful brent me,
And to be clad for deadly dumps in mire.
Among so many plagues which shall torment me,
     One solace I shall find, when I am over ;
     It will be known I died a constant lover !

SONNET XX.

ECEIVE these writs, my sweet and dearest Friend !
The lively patterns of my lifeless body ;
Where thou shalt find in ebon pictures penned,
How I was meek, but thou extremely bloody !
    I'll walk forlorn along the willow shades,
Alone, complaining of a ruthless Dame :
Where'er I pass, the rocks, the hills, the glades,
In piteous yells shall sound her cruel name !
    There will I wail the lot that Fortune sent me,
And make my moans unto the savage ears !
The remnant of the days which Nature lent me ;
I'll spend them all, concealed, in ceaseless tears !
    Since unkind Fates permit me not t'enjoy her ;
No more, burst eyes ! I mean for to annoy her !

FINIS.

To PARTHENOPHIL !

Upon his LAYA and PARTHENOPHE.

[*i.e.* inscribed to Barnabe Barnes, for whose poetical collection, *Parthenophil and Parthenophe,* see vol. i. p. 165 *seq. supra.* The reference at line 9 below seems to be to Barnes's Sestine 5, see vol. i. pp. 309-12.]

MADRIGAL.

HEN first I heard thy loves to LAYA,
I wished the gods to turn it to good hap !
Yet since I hear thy blessed flight away,
I joy thy chance, for fear of afterclap !
    Unwily man ! why couldst not keep thee there ?
But must with PARTHENOPH', thee 'gain entrap !
    I little rue thy well deserved tears !
The beast once 'scaped will ever shun the trap !
What tell'st thou me, "By spells, th' hast won thy Dear !"
Believe her, Friend ! no more than LAYA past !
Charmed Love endures but whilst the Charm doth last !

ZEPHERIA

Ogni di viene la sera.

Mysus et Hœmonia juvenis qui cus-
pide vulnus senserat, hac ipsa
cuspide sensit opem.

AT LONDON:
Printed by the Widow ORWIN, for N. L. and
JOHN BUSBY.
1594.

Alli veri figlioli delle Muse.

YE MODERN Laureates, famoused for your writ,
Who for your pregnance may in Delos dwell !
On your sweet lines, Eternity doth sit ;
Their brows ennobling with applause and laurel !
Triumph and Honour aye invest your writ !
Ye fet[ch] your pens from wing of singing swan,
When (sweetly warbling to herself) she floats
Adown Meander streams ; and like to organ,
Imparts, into her quills, melodious notes !
  Ye, from the Father of delicious phrases,
Borrow such Hymns as make your Mistress live
When Time is dead !   Nay, HERMES tunes the praises
Which ye, in Sonnets, to your Mistress give !
  Report, throughout our Western Isle doth ring,
The sweet tuned accents of your Delian sonnetry,
Which to Apollo's violin, ye sing !
O, then, your high strains drown his melody !
  From forth dead sleep of everlasting dark ;
Fame, with her trump's shrill summon, hath awaked
The Roman NASO, and the Tuscan PETRARCH,
Your spirit-ravishing lines to wonder at !
  O theme befitting high-Mused ASTROPHIL !

He, to your silvery Songs, lent sweetest touch !
Your Songs, the immortal spirit of your quill !
O, pardon ! for my artless pen too much
Doth dim your glories, through his infant skill.
    Though may I not, with you, the spoils divide
(Ye sacred Offspring of MNEMOSYNE !)
Of endless praise, which have your pens achieved
(Your pens the Trumps to Immortality !) ;
Yet be it lawful, that like maims I bide !
Like brunts and scars, in your Love's warfare !
And here, though in my homespun Verse, of them declare !

ZEPHERIA.

CANZON 1.

ULLED in a heavenly Charm of pleasing
Passions;
Many their well-thewed rhymes do fair
attemper
Unto their Amours! while another fashions
Love to his lines, and he on Fame doth
venture!
And some again, in mercenary writ,
Belch forth Desire, making Reward their mistress!
And though it chance some LAIS patron it,
At least, they sell her praises to the press!
The Muses' Nurse, I read, is EUPHEMIE;
And who but Honour makes his lines' reward,
Comes not, by my consent, within my pedigree!
'Mongst true-born sons, inherit may no bastard!
All in the humble accent of my Muse;
Whose wing may not aspire the pitch of Fame,
My griefs I here untomb! Sweet! them peruse!
Though low he fly, yet Honour is his game,
All while my pen quests on ZEPHERIA's name:
Whom, when it sprung thy wing, did thee relieve;
Now flown to mark, thus doth Desire thee retrieve!

CANZON 2.

Though be thou limned in these discoloured lines,
    (Delicious Model of my spirit's portrait!)
    Though be thou sable pencilled, these designs
    Shadow not beauty, but a sorrow's extract!
When I emprised, though in my love's affections,
The silver lustre of thy brow to unmask!
Though hath my Muse hyperbolised trajections;
Yet stands it, aye, deficient to such task.
    My slubb'ring pencil casts too gross a matter,
    Thy beauty's pure divinity to blaze!
For when my smoothèd tongue hath sought to flatter,
Thy Worth hath dearthed his words, for thy true praise!
    Then though my pencil glance here on thine eyes;
    Sweet! think thy Fair, it doth but portionise!

CANZON 3.

When, from the tower whence I derive love's heaven,
    Mine eyes (quick pursuivants!) the sight attached
    Of Thee, all splendent! I, as out of sweaven,
    Myself 'gan rouse, like one from sleep awaked.
Coveting eyes controlled my slowly gait,
And wood Desire to wing my feet for flight;
Yet unresolved, Fear did with eyes debate,
And said, " 'Twas but tra[ns]lucence of the light!"
    But when approached, where Thou thy stand didst take!
At gaze, I stood; like deer, when 'ghast, he spies
Some white in thick! Ah, then, the arrow strake
Through mine heart! sent from thy tiller eyes.
    Dead in thine aim, Thou seized what 'longed to thee!
    Mine heart, ZEPHERIA! then, became thy fee!

CANZON 4.

THEN, Desire! Father of Jouissance!
The Life of Love! the Death of dastard Fear!
The Kindest Nurse to true persèverance!
Mine heart inherited, with thy love's revere.
 Beauty! peculiar Parent of Conceit!
Prosperous Midwife to a travelling Muse!
The Sweet of life! NEPENTHE's eyes receipt!
Thee into me distilled, O Sweet, infuse!
 Love then (the spirit of a generous sprite!
An infant ever drawing Nature's breast!
The Sum of Life, that CHAOS did unnight!)
Dismissed mine heart from me, with thee to rest.
 And now incites me cry, " Double! or quit!
 Give back my heart, or take his body to it!"

CANZON 5.

NON, Fear (Sentinel of sad Discretion!
Strangling Repentance in his cradle age!
Care's Usher! Tenant to his own Oppression!)
Forced my thoughts' quest upon an idle rage.
 Enraged Passion (Scout to Love untrue!)
Commenting glosses on each smile and frown,
Christening the heavens and Erebus anew,
(Intolerable yoke to Love and Reason!
 Footstool to all affects! Beauty's sour handmaid!
The heart's hermaphrodite, passive in action!)
Hope now serenes his brow, anon dismayed,
A pleasing death, a life in pleased distraction.
 Thou on thy Mother, Fear! begot Despair;
 To whom, my Fate conveys me son and heir.

CANZON 6.

 Y FATE ! O not my fault ! hath me debarred
From forth thy favour's sunny sanctuary,
Unto the dear applause of thy regard,
Witness the world ! how I, my guest did marry !
    My tears, my sighs ; all have I summed in thee !
Conceit the total ! do not partialise !
And then accept of their infinity
As part of payment to exacting eyes !
    And yet thy Trophy to ennoble more,
My heart prepares anew to thesaurise
Sighs and love options such as it sent of yore,
Save number they ! faith only these englories !
    Yet though I thus enwealthy thy exchequer ;
    Seem it not strange, I live ZEPHERIA's debtor !

CANZON 7.

 ORE fair, but yet more cruel I thee deem
(Though by how much the more thou beauteous art,
So much of pity shouldst thou more esteem !) ;
Fairer than PHŒBE, yet a harder heart.
    Her when ACTŒON viewed with privy eye,
She doomed him but a death (a death he owed !),
While he pursued, before his dogs did fly.
Here was the worst of ill (good Queen !) she shewed.
    But when, a start, mine eye had thee espied
Though at discovert, yet stand I sentenced
Not to one death, to which I would have hied :
For since, unarmed, and to eye unfenced,
    Thy PHŒBE-fairer parts were mine eyes' prospective.
    O grief ! unto myself, disgraced I live !

CANZON 8.

ILLUMINATING Lamps!   Ye Orbs chrystallite!
Transparent mirrolds!   Globes divining beauty!
How have I joyed to wanton in your light?
Though was I slain by your artillery!
Ye blithsome Stars! like LEDA's lovely twins
(When clear they twinkle in the firmament),
Promise *esperance* to the seamen's wand'rings:
So have your shine made ripe mine heart's content.
Or as the light, which Sestyan HERO showed,
Arm-finned LEANDER to direct in waves,
When through the raging Hellespont he rowed,
Steering to Love's Port: so, by thine eyes' clear rays,
   Blest were my waves!   But since no light was found,
   Thy poor LEANDER in the deep is drowned!

CANZON 9.

WHEN as the Golden Waggoner had frayed
Black Winter's outrage, with his brighter shine;
And that in Mansion of the Twins he styed,
His team; then 'gan my heart to twine with thine!
Even when his gorgeous mantle he had spread,
Wherewith he wiped wept-tears from TELLUS' bosom;
Wantoning here with her, leaves THETIS' bed,
Like dainty midwife FLORA, to unwomb
   Sweet babes of TELLUS and HYPERION,   [(*sic*),
When ye full soomed in Winter's mew doon mooting,
O then, the seeds of Love, by thine eyes sown,
Down through mine eyes, within mine heart took rooting.
   This difference left 'twixt me and Nature's store;
   Her Spring returns!   My flower may spread no more!

CANZON 10.

How made I, then, attempt in courtly fashion,
 To gain the virgin conquest of thy love ?
 How did my sighs decipher inward Passion,
  When they to kind regard thy heart did move ?
When thou vouchsaf'st to grace the evening air,
How have I lain in ambush to betray thee ?
Our eyes have skirmished ! but my tongue would pray thee
To join thy Pity partner with thy Fair !
 Since that, how often have they sent wept Elegies
To beg remorse at thy obdurate heart !
How often hath my Muse in comic poesies,
To feed thy humour, played a comic part !
  But, now, the Pastime of my pen is silenced !
  To act in Tragic Vein, alone is licensed.

CANZON 11.

How wert thou pleasèd with my Pastoral Ode !
 Which late I sent thee; wherein I, thy Swain,
 In rural tune, on pipe did chaunt abroad
  Thee, for the loveliest Lass that traced the plain.
There, on thy head, I, FLORA's Chaplet placed !
There, did my pipe proclaim thee, Summer's Queen !
Each herdgroom, with that honour held thee graced !
When lawny white did chequer with thy green.
 There, did I bargain all my kids to thee !
My spotted lambkins, choicest of my fold !
So thou would'st sit and keep thy flock by me:
So much I joyed, thy beauty to behold.
 How many Cantons then, sent I to thee !
Who, though on two strings only raised their strain,
To wit, my Grief, and thy unmatched Beauty;
Yet well their harmony could please thy vein !
  Well could they please thee, and thou term them witty;
  But now as fortunes change, so change my Ditty !

CANZON 12.

HOw often have mine eyes (thine eye's apprentice
Bound by the Earnest of a sunny look),
Ta'en a judicial view of all thy graces!
Which here are registered in lasting book.
How oft have I, thy precious chain been fingering,
That ninefold circles thy delicious neck!
While they, the orb-like spheres of heaven resembling,
Thy face the Globe! which men clep Emperick.
How oft with wanton touches have I prest
Those breasts, more soft than silver down of swans;
When they by Alcidelian springs do rest!
Of which pure substance are thy lily hands.
But now, though eyes ne see, nor arms embrace thee;
Who yet shall let, in thought, me chief to place thee?

CANZON 13.

PROUD in thy love, how many have I cited,
Impartial, thee to view! whose eyes have lavished
Sweet beauteous objects oft have men delighted,
But thou, above delight, their sense hast ravished!
They, amorous artists, Thee pronounced Love's Queen!
And unto thy supremacy did swear,
" VENUS, at Paphos keep! no more be seen!"
Now CUPID, after Thee, his shafts shall bear!
How have I spent my spirit of Invention
In penning amorous stanzas to thy beauty?
But heavenly graces may not brook dimension;
No more may thine! for infinite they be.
But now, in harsh tune, I, of amours sing,
My pipe for them, grows hoarse! but shrill, to plaining!

CANZON 14.

HOUGH like an exile from mine eyes divorced
In solitary dungeon of Refuse
I live, impatient that I live, perforced,
From thee, dear object of mine eyes, a recluse.
Yet that divine *Idea* of thy grace,
The life imagery of thy love's sweet *souvenance*,
Within mine heart shall reign in sovereign place ;
Nay, shall it ever portray other semblance ?
No ! never shall that face, so fair depainted
Within the love-limned tablet of mine heart,
Emblemished be ! defaced ! or unsainted !
Till death shall blot it, with his pencil dart.
Yet, then, in these limned lines ennobled more,
Thou shalt survive, richer accomplished than before !

CANZON 15.

E'ER were the silvery wings of my Desire
Tainted with thought of black impurity !
The modest blush that did my cheeks attire,
Was to thy virgin fears, statute security !
When to a favour's sweet promotion
My joyless thoughts, thou hast advancèd higher !
O then sigh's sacrifice of my love's devotion
I sent, repurified in holy fire !
My fears, how oft have I ingeminated !
(O black recite of passèd misery !)
Thy heart for to entender ! they have intimated
(Besides what thou hast seen !) what I have suffered for thee !
But see ! since eyes were aliens to thy beauty,
I sing mine own faith, and neglect love's duty !

CANZON 16,

Ow have I forfeited thy kind regard,
   That thy disdain should thus enage thy brow!
   Which, whilom, was the scripture and the card
      Whereon thou made thy game, and sealed thy vow
Which, whilom, thou, with laurel vatical,
Ennobled hast (high signal of renown!),
Marrying my voice with thine, hast said withal,
"Be thou alone, alonely thou, AMPHION!"
   O how hath black night welked up this day!
My wasted hopes, why are they turned to graze
In pastures of despair? ZEPHERIA say,
Wherein have I, on love committed trespass!
   O, if in justice, thou must needs acquit me,
   Reward me with thy love! Sweet, heal me with thy pity!

CANZON 17.

Ow shall I deck my Love in love's habiliment,
   And her embellish in a right depaint?
   Sith now is left, nor rose, nor hyacinth,
      Each one their beauties with their hue acquaint.
   The gold ceiling of thy brow's rich frame
Designs the proud pomp of thy face's architure.
Crystal transparent casements to the same,
Are thine eyes' sun, which do the world depure;
   Whose silvery canopy, gold-wire fringes.
Thy brow, the bowling place for CUPID's eye.
Love's true-love knots, and lily-lozenges,
Thy cheeks, depainten in an immortal dye.
   If well, thou limned art, now, by face imagery;
   Judge, how, by life, I then should pencil thee!

CANZON 18.

EXACTER, should it fortune I should pencil thee;
What glory may attend though on my skill?
Even such as him befalls, whose pen doth copy
The sweet invention of another's quill.
   My Muse yet never journeyed to the Indes,
Thy Fair to purple in Alchermyan dye,
All on the weak spread of his eyes' wings
Sufficeth that thou mount, though not so high!
   Yet should it hap, that, in a kind vouchsafe,
The feature of my pen some grace do win;
Thereof, ZEPHERIA all the honour hath!
The copying scribe may claim no right therein:
    But if more nice wits censure my lines crooked,
    Thus I excuse, "I wrote, my light removed!"

CANZON 19.

NO! NO, ZEPHERIA! Fame is too rich a prize
My all-unmeriting lines for to attend on!
The best applause of my Muse, on thine eyes
   Depends! It craves but smiles, his pains to
    guerdon!
  But thine, the glory of this weak emprise!
Well wot I, his demerit is but bare!
Duteous respect then, will not that I portionise
To me, in love's respect, equal like care.
  Lovely respective! equal thou this care!
And with thine heaven's calm smiles, mine heart imparadise!
Shine forth thy comfort's sun, my fears' Dismayer!
O well it fits lovers to sympathise!
    Hold thou the spoils of Fame, for thine inheritance!
    Thy love, to me is sweetest *chevisance*!

CANZON 20.

How often hath my pen (mine heart's Solicitor!)
    Instructed thee in Breviat of my case!
    While Fancy-pleading eyes (thy beauty's Visitor!)
    Have patterned to my quill, an angel's face.
How have my Sonnets (faithful Counsellors!)
Thee, without ceasing moved for Day of Hearing!
While they, my Plaintive Cause (my faith's Revealers!)
Thy long delay, my patience, in thine ear ring.
    How have I stood at bar of thine own conscience;
When in Requesting Court my suit I brought!
How have thy long adjournments slowed the sentence,
Which I (through much expense of tears) besought!
    Through many difficulties have I run,
    Ah, sooner·wert thou lost, I wis, than won!

CANZON 21.

And is it by immutable Decree
    (Immutable, yet cruel Ordnance!)
    Ordained (still forced, I cry, " O strange impiety!")
On True Love, to impose such tyrant penance?
    That We, unto each other shall surrender
The sealed indentures of our love compacted;
And that thereof we make such loyal tender
As best shall seem to them that so enacted!
    Then list, while I advertise once again,
" Though we yield up our charters so ensealed:
Yet see that thou safeguard my counterpane!
And I, in heart, shall keep thy bond uncancelled;
    And so hereafter (if, at least, you please!)
    We'll plead this Redelivery was by duress!"

CANZON 22.

IT WAS not long ago, since, like a wanton,
　Froward, displeased with that it loves, I wis,
　Improved, I did write to thee, a Canton,
　Wherein I seemed to turn LOVE out of service.
　　Well said I herein, that I did but " seem " it !
　Loath to depart, he still retained to me ;
　Although displeased, yet each one well might deem,
　He was my servant, while he wore my livery !
　　Pensively grieved with that, that I had done,
　I wrote a Sonnet, which, by syllable,
　Eat up the former, and withal craved pardon;
　Vowing a large amends, as time should able.
　　" But who beyond his power vows, offends !
　　Presumptuous as thou art ! to name Amends."

CANZON 23.

THY coral-coloured lips, how should I portray
　Unto the unmatchable pattern of their sweet !
　A draught of blessedness I stole away
　From them, when last I kissed.　I taste it yet !
So did that sug'ry touch my lips ensucket.
　　On them, MINERVA's honey birds do hive
　Mellifluous words; when so thou please to frame
　Thy speech to entertainment !　Thence I derive
　My heart's sole paradise, and my lips sweet game.
　　Ye are the coral gates of Temple's clarion,
　Whereout the PYTHIUS preached divinity !
　Unto thy voice bequeathed the good ARION,
　His silvery lyre !　Such Pœan melody
　　Thy voice, the organ pipe of angels quire
　　Trebles !　Yet, one kiss; and I'll raise them higher !

CANZON 24.

UNTO the Muses, I resign my scroll,
Who sing with voice unto the spheres proportionable.
Sing ye! O write ye of my love's pure soul!
Unbody it, in words inimitable!
In high sphere, then, see ye her name enrolled!
On her heart throne, sits the divine ASTRÆA;
Who doth the balance of her favours hold,
Which she imparts in justice and demerit.
For virgin purity, white GALATEA
Doth type the sanctity of her purer spirit.
She, the fourth Grace, height PASITHÆA,
Only recorded by our first born son;
Whom after long sleep, we shall now untomb
And her translate into ZEPHERIA.
Amidst the CHARITES, possess thy room!
THALIA in heart, zealous URANIA;
The soul's musician, sweet THELXIONE;
Daughter of Love and Admiration!
A veil immortal shall we put on thee,
And on thy head instar the Gnosian Crown!
ARIADNE doth herself undeify,
Yielding her coronal to thine installation!
Now live in starry stage of heaven, a deity!
And sing we, IO ZEPHERIA! all in a rown.
"Hold! take thy scroll! With wing of immortality,
    Thy Love is clad! Nay, ought may her unsanctify,
    But proud Disdain!" Thanks, sweet CALLIOPE!

CANZON 25.

ET not Disdain, thy soul unsanctify!
Disdain, the passport for a lover's vow!
Unsieging, where its seeks to fortify
 With deadly frowns, the canons of the brow!
 Let not Disdain (the Hearse of virgin Graces!
The Counterpoison to unchastity!
The Leaven that doth sour the sweetest faces!)
Stain thy new purchased immortality!
 'Mongst Delian nymphs, in Angels' University,
Thou, my ZEPHERIA, liv'st matriculated!
The daughters of ethereal JOVE, thy deity
On holy hill, have aye perpetuated!
  O then, retire thy brows' artillery!
  Love more! and more bliss yet, shall honour thee!

CANZON 26.

HEN we, in kind embracements, had agreed
To keep a royal banquet on our lips;
How soon, have we another feast decreed!
 And how, at parting, have we mourned by fits!
 Eftsoons, in absence, have we wailed much more,
Till those void hours of intermission
Were spent! That we might revel as before,
How have we bribèd Time for expedition!
 And when remitted to our former love-plays;
How have we, overweening in delight,
Accused the Father Sexton of the days
That, then, with eagle's wings, he took his flight!
  But now, Old Man! fly on, as swift as thought!
  Sith eyes from love, and hope from heart is wrought.

CANZON 27.

NE'ER from a lofty pitch, hath made more speed,
The feather-sailing Falcon to the lure ;
Nor fairer stooped, when he on fist would feed,
Than I, ZEPHERIA ! to thine eyes allure !
Ne'er from the deep, when winds declare a tempest,
Posts with more haste the little Halcion,
Nor faster hies him to some safer rest ;
Than I have fled, from thy death-threatening frown !
Ne'er did the sun's love-mate, the gold Hetropion
Smile more resplendent lustre on her Dear !
Nay, ever was his shine to her more welcome,
Than thine to me, when smiling was thy cheer !
But now, my sun ! it fits thou take thy set !
And veil thy face with frowns, as with a frontlet !

CANZON 28.

WHEN clear hath been thy brow, and free from wrinkle,
(Thy smoothèd brow, my soul's sole hierarchy !)
When sweetly hath appeared in cheek the dimple,
There LOVE enthroned sways powerful monarchy !
Glad have I, then, rich statues to his deity
Erected. Then, have I his altar hallowed !
His rights, I held, with high solemnity !
His Trophy decked, and it with rosebuds strewed !
I kissed thy cheek ! Then thou, with gold artillery,
Hast him engirt, tasselled with purple twine,
(Featly contrived to hang his quiver by)
Besides a crimson scarf to veil his eyne :
But, see ! No sooner was he gay apparelled,
But that, false Boy ! away from us he fled !

CANZON 29.

Ow many golden days! have I set free
From tedious travail in a sadder Muse,
While I, of amours have conferred with thee!
While I, long absence never need excuse!
   Sweet was Occasion! and for sweet inexplicable,
That eyes' invited guests unto thine eyes' fare;
When, by thy dainty leave, on coral table
I fed! O there, I sucked celestial air!
   Amidst these sug'ry junkets thirsty, I
Have thy delicious hand, with my lips pressed!
I drew for wine, but found 'twas Ambrosie:
O how my spirits inly that refreshed!
    Yet, ay me! since I relished this delight;
    I e'er more thirsted with a hotter appetite!

CANZON 30.

Hat! Shall I ne'er more see those Halcion days!
Those sunny Sabbaths! Days of Jubilee!
Wherein I carrolled merry Roundelays,
   Odes, and Love Songs? which, being viewed by thee,
Received allowance worthy better writ!
When we, on Shepherds' Holy Days have hied
Down to the flow'ry pastures (flowers, for thy treading fit!)
Holy the day, when thou it sanctified!
   When thou, ZEPHERIA, wouldst but deign to bless it,
How have I, jealous over PHŒBUS' rays,
Clouded thy Fair! Then, fearing he would guess it
By thy white brow, it have I cinct' with bays!
    But, woe is me! that I have fenced thy beauty!
    Sith other must enjoy it, and not I.

CANZON 31.

Y ET none shall equal me in my demerit,
  Though happier (may it fortune) he may court it!
  Nor shall more faithful love his suit inherit!
  Ne paint like Passion, though he shew more Wit!
Admit, he write! My quill hath done as much!
Admit, he sigh! That have I done, and more!
Admit, he weep! These eyes have wept even such:
Their tears, as hearty; and in greater store!
  Yet, nearer may he press, and swear "He dies!"
Jove (thinks he) smiles at lovers' jurament:
Prove him! Then shalt thou find he falsely lies!
Many so threaten death, that nil experiment!
  Repulsed, then will he sue to do thee service!
  Said not I well now, that "he falsely lies!"

CANZON 32.

N ATURE, I find, doth, once a year, hold market!
  A gaudy fair of brooches and of babies;
  And bounteously to all doth She impart it,
  Yet chiefly to true Lovers, and fair Ladies.
There, may you see her dappart Com'nalty
Clad, some in purple, some in scarlet dye;
Whiles she (rich Queen!), in all her royalty,
Commands them spread their chaffer to the eye.
  The buyer pays no impost, nor no fees;
But rather to invite with wealthier pleasure,
She booths her fair with shade of broad-branched trees,
Wherein (good Queen!) her care doth match her treasure.
  With wealth of more cost, Nature doth Thee beautify!
  Save, careless, she hath left no shelter 'gainst thine eye!

CANZON 33.

ITHER, chaste PHŒBE's Nymphs flocked in procession,
   Whose beauties attractive all eyes so exercised
   With mazed-admire, that, for some late transgression,
   Men weened heaven's angels were unparadised.
Such saints, heaven's paradise contains but few,
Their roseate beauties, Nature's wealth distained;
Compared their lustre, checked her verdant hue,
They even her purest quintessence engrained.
   Anemone there stood with Daffodilly!
The purple Hyacinth, and the musk Rose!
Red Amaranthus, and the milk-bred Lily!
I came in quest; yet would I none of those!
   Unto HYPERION's bride, my choice I knit!
   There, in her goldy leaves, my love is writ!

CANZON 34.

INCE from the full feed of thy favour's lease,
   My thoughts (O Time's accursed memory!)
   Were forced (such shift, alas, did ill them please!)
   To crop on sedge sour and unsavoury;
Since from their sweet refresh, all pinèd, they
Have spent a lustre in sad widowhood;
Since when Sorrow to them hath served in pay,
Outlaws to Hope, immured from every good;
   Since from thy brow, the pompous gallery
Wherein were storised to mine eye, sweet objects,
Embroidered all with rare imàgery;
Whose ivory floor enamelled azure frets:
   Mine eye (O woe the while!) hath been sequestered!
   My heart, his grief therefore, in face hath registered.

CANZON 35.

INCE from the flowered sweets of every blessedness,
  Which from thy beauties delicate peruse
  Incessantly doth flow, mine heart, like anch'ress
  Aye cloistered, lives to sad and cheerless Muse.
    If any smiling joy fortune to fawn on me,
Suggesting to my spirit sweet content :
Anon, I article with his felicity ;
And ere mine heart vouchsafes him entertainment,
  I him depose, on these Interrogatories.
First, " If he came from my ZEPHERIA ? "
Then, " If he may to light restore mine eyes,
Which long have dwelt in dark ? " If then, he say,
  " Nay ! but thy thoughts to unbend from off her beauties,
    I come ! " eftsoons, I strangle him while in his infancy.
    Better slay him, than he do thee to die !

CANZON 36.

UT if, with error and unjust suspect,
  Thou shalt the burden of my grievance aggravate !
  Laying unto my charge thy love's neglect
  (A load which patience cannot tolerate !)
    First, to be ATLAS to my own Desire,
Then, to depress me with unkind construction ;
While to mine own griefs may I scarce respire :
This is to heap Ossa on Pelion !
    O would the reach yet of unequal censure
Might here but date his partiality ;

Mistrust (who ne'er is ripe, till worst be thought on)
Hath my crime racked, yet to more high extensure.
　And now 'tis drawn to flat Apostasy
　(So straight beset ; best, I lay hold on pardon !)
Why then, sith better i'st a penitentiary
To save, than to expose to shame's confusion.
　　Thy face being veiled, this penance I award,
　　　"Clad in white sheet, thou stand in Paul's Church-
　　　　yard ! "

CANZON 37.

WHEN last mine eyes dislodgèd from thy beauty,
　Though served with Process of a parent's Writ :
A *Supersedeas* countermanding duty,
　Even then, I saw upon thy smiles to sit !
　Those smiles which me invited to a Party,
Disperpling clouds of faint respecting fear ;
Against the Summons which was served on me,
A larger privilege of dispense did bear.
　Thine eyes' edict, the Statute of Repeal,
Doth other duties wholly abrogate,
Save such as thee endear in hearty zeal,
Then be it far from me, that I should derogate
　From Nature's Law, enregistered in thee !
　So might my love incur a *Præmunire.*

CANZON 38.

ROM the revenue of thine eyes' Exchequer,
    My faith, his Subsidy did ne'er detract!
    Though in thy favour's book, I rest a debtor;
    Yet, 'mongst accountants who their faith have crackt,
My name thou findest not irrotulate!
I list not stand indebted to infame;
(Foul them befall who pay in counterfeit!
Be they recognised in black Book of Shame!)
    But if the Rent, which wont was of assize,
Thou shalt enhance, through pride and coy disdain!
Exacting double tribute to thine eyes;
And yet encroachest on my heart's domain:
    Needs must I wish (though 'gainst my foyalty),
    That thou unsceptered be of Nature's royalty!

CANZON 39.

ND now, thou winged Ambassador of Wonder!
    Liberal dispenser of reproachful act!
    Who never whisperest, but in a voice of thunder!
    Explor'st what secrecy would fain have darked!
" Tell my ZEPHERIA! (sith thou nill be silenced!)
My hopes on her calm smiles did them embark;
Whose sunny shine seemed to have licensed
From them, all fear of tempest, or of wreck.
    Now, on the shelf of her brows' proud disdain,
A harbour, where they looked for asile,
The pilot who, 'fore now, did expect rain,
His bark in seas are all ydrenched, alack the while!
    Tell if, at least, she all, through fear, excordiate,
    Command thee not to peace, ere thou exordiate!"

CANZON 40.

BUT if She shall attend what fortunes sequelled
The *naufrage* of my poor afflicted bark;
Then tell, but tell in words unsyllabled!
    In sighs' untunèd accents, move her to hark
    Unto the tenour of thy sadder process!
Say then, " His tears (his heart's intelligencers!)
Did intimate the griefs did him possess.
Crying, ZEPHERIA, unto thee! these messengers
    I send!   O these, my loves, my faith shall witness!
O these shall record loves and faith unfeignèd!
Look how my soul bathes in their innocency!
Whose dying confidence him designs unstained
Of guilty blush-note of impurity.
(O Death! Highway to Life, when Love is distained!) "
    This said, if cruel She, no grace vouchsafe:
    Dead, may her Gravestone be her Epitaph!

Troppo sperar inganna.

FINIS.

I D E A.

IN
SIXTY-THREE
SONNETS.

BY

MICHAEL DRAYTON,
ESQUIRE.

LONDON,
Printed for JOHN SMETHWICK.
1619.

Drayton's *Idea* Sonnets appeared in four distinct editions, the contents of each of which varied considerably, before the fifth and final edition of 1619, which is printed here, and contains in all sixty-four sonnets. *Eighteen* of the sonnets in the present collection appeared originally in the first edition of 1594, *twenty-one* in the second edition of 1599, *eight* in the third edition of 1602 (reprinted in 1603), *seven* in the edition of 1605 (reprinted three times, in 1608, 1610, and 1613). *Ten* sonnets only were printed in the 1619 edition for the first time. The edition in which each sonnet first saw the light is duly indicated in this reprint.

To the Reader of these Sonnets.

[First printed in 1599 (No. 2), and in all later editions.]

NTO these Loves, who but for Passion looks;
At this first sight, here let him lay them by!
And seek elsewhere in turning other books,
Which better may his labour satisfy.
No far-fetched Sigh shall ever wound my breast!
Love from mine eye, a Tear shall never wring!
No "Ah me!"s my whining sonnets drest!
A Libertine! fantasticly I sing!
My Verse is the true image of my Mind,
Ever in motion, still desiring change:
And as thus, to variety inclined;
So in all humours sportively I range!
My Muse is rightly of the English strain,
That cannot long one fashion entertain.

IDEA.

I.

[First printed in 1619.]

IKE an adventurous seafarer am **I**,
  Who hath some long and dangerous voyage
    been;
  And called to tell of his discovery,
  How far he sailed, what countries he had
    seen;
    Proceeding from the port whence he put
      forth,
Shews by his compass how his course he steered,
When East, when West, when South, and when by North,
As how the Pole, to every place was reared;
  What capes he doubled, of what continent,
The gulfs and straits that strangely he had past;
Where most becalmed, where with foul weather spent,
And on what rocks in peril to be **cast**:
  Thus in my Love, Time calls **me** to relate
  My tedious travels, and oft-varying fate.

2.

[First printed in 1599 (No. 51), and in all later editions.]

Y HEART was slain, and none but you and I?
Who should I think the murder should commit;
Since but yourself, there was no creature by
But only I, guiltless of murdering it?
　It slew itself? The verdict on the view
Do quit the dead, and me not accessory.
Well, well! I fear it will be proved of you!
Th'evidence so great a proof doth carry.
　But O see! See, we need inquire no further!
Upon your lips, the scarlet drops are found!
And in your eye, the Boy that did the murder!
Your cheeks yet pale, since first he gave the wound!
　　By this I see, however things be past,
　　Yet Heaven will still have murder out at last.

3.

[First printed in 1599 (No. 6), and in all later editions.]

AKING my pen, with words to cast my woe,
Duly to count the sum of all my cares;
I find, my griefs innumerable grow:
The reck'nings rise to millions of despairs.
　And thus dividing of my fatal hours:
The payments of my Love, I read and cross;
Subtracting, set my Sweets unto my Sours.
My Joys' arrearage leads me to my loss.
　And thus mine eyes a debtor to thine eye,
Which by extortion gaineth all their looks;
My heart hath paid such grievous usury,
That all their wealth lies in thy Beauty's books,
　　And all is Thine which hath been due to me;
　　And I a bankrupt, quite undone by Thee!

4.

[First printed in 1602 (No. 66), and in all later editions.]

RIGHT Star of Beauty! on whose Eyelids sit
A thousand nymph-like and enamoured Graces,
The Goddesses of Memory and Wit,
Which there in order take their several places.
   In whose dear Bosom, sweet delicious LOVE
Lays down his quiver, which he once did bear,
Since he that blessèd Paradise did prove ;
And leaves his mother's lap, to sport him there.
   Let others strive to entertain with words !
My soul is of a braver mettle made :
I hold that vile, which vulgar Wit affords,
In me 's that faith which Time cannot invade !
   Let what I praise, be still made good by you !
   Be you most worthy, whilst I am most true !

5.

[First printed in 1599 (No. 8), and in all later editions.]

NOTHING but "No!" and "I!", and "I!" and "No!".
"How falls it out so strangely ?" you reply.
I tell ye, Fair ! I'll not be answered so !   [*Ay.]
With this affirming "No!", denying "I!".
   I say "I love !" You slightly answer "I!".
I say "You love !" You pule me out a "No!".
I say "I die !" You echo me with "I!".
"Save me !" I cry ; you sigh me out a "No!".
   Must Woe and I have naught but "No!" and "I!"?
No "I!" am I, if I no more can have.
Answer no more ! With silence make reply,
And let me take myself what I do crave !
   Let "No!" and "I!" with I and you be so,
   Then answer "No!" and "I!", and "I!" and "No!".

6.

[First printed in 1619.]

Ow many paltry foolish painted Things,
That now in coaches trouble every street,
Shall be forgotten (whom no Poet sings)
Ere they be well wrapped in their winding sheet !
Where I, to thee Eternity shall give !
When nothing else remaineth of these days.
And Queens hereafter shall be glad to live
Upon the alms of thy superfluous praise.
Virgins and matrons, reading these my rhymes,
Shall be so much delighted with thy Story,
That they shall grieve they lived not in these Times,
To have seen Thee, their sex's only glory !
So shalt thou fly above the vulgar throng,
Still to survive in my immortal Song.

7.

[First printed in 1599 (No. 10), and in all later editions.]

Ove, in a humour, played the prodigal,
And bade my Senses to a solemn feast ;
Yet more to grace the company withal,
Invites my Heart to be the chiefest guest.
No other drink would serve this glutton's turn,
But precious Tears distilling from mine ey'n ;
Which with my Sighs this epicure doth burn,
Quaffing carouses in this costly wine :
Where, in his cups, o'ercome with foul excess,
Straightways he plays a swaggering ruffian's part,
And at the banquet, in his drunkenness,
Slew his dear friend, my kind and truest Heart.
A gentle warning, friends ! thus may you see,
What 'tis to keep a drunkard, company !

8.

[First printed in 1619.]

HERE's nothing grieve me, but that Age should haste,
    That in my days, I may not see the old!
    That where those two clear sparkling Eyes are placed,
    Only two loopholes, then I might behold!
That lovely archèd ivory-polished Brow
Defaced with wrinkles, that I might but see!
Thy dainty Hair, so curled and crispèd now,
Like grizzled moss upon some agèd tree!
Thy Cheek, now flush with roses, sunk and lean!
Thy Lips, with age as any wafer thin!
Thy pearly Teeth, out of thy head so clean,
That when thou feed'st, thy Nose shall touch thy Chin!
    These Lines that now scornst, which should delight thee:
    Then would I make thee read, but to despite thee!

9.

[First printed in 1602 (No. 12), and in all later editions.]

S OTHER men, so I myself, do muse
    Why in this sort I wrest Invention so?
    And why these giddy metaphors I use,
    Leaving the path the greater part do go?
I will resolve you! I am lunatic!
And ever this in madmen you shall find,
What they last thought of, when the brain grew sick,
In most distraction, they keep that in mind.
Thus talking idly, in this Bedlam fit,
Reason and I (you must conceive) are twain;
'Tis nine years now, since first I lost my Wit.
Bear with me then, though troubled be my brain!
    With diet and correction, men distraught,
    (Not too far past), may to their wits be brought.

10.

[First printed in 1599 (No. 12), and in all later editions.]

O NOTHING fitter can I thee compare,
Than to the son of some rich penny-father ;
Who having now brought on his end with care,
Leaves to his son, all he had heaped together.
This new rich Novice, lavish of his chest,
To one man gives! doth on another spend!
Then here he riots! yet, amongst the rest,
Haps to lend some to one true honest friend.
Thy Gifts, thou in obscurity dost waste!
False friends, thy Kindness! born but to deceive thee.
Thy Love that is on the unworthy placed!
Time hath thy Beauty, which with age will leave thee!
Only that little, which to me was lent,
I give thee back! when all the rest is spent.

11.

[First printed in 1599 (No. 12), and in all later editions.]

OU'RE not alone when You are still alone,
O God! from You that I could private be!
Since You one were, I never since was one ;
Since You in Me, my self since out of Me.
Transported from my Self into your Being,
Though either distant, present yet to either:
Senselessly with too much joy, each other seeing;
And only absent, when We are together.
Give me my self! and take your self again!
Devise some means but how I may forsake You!
So much is mine that doth with You remain,
That taking what is mine, with me I take You!
You do bewitch Me! O that I could fly
From my self You, or from your own self I !

12.

[First printed in 1599 (No. 14), and in all later editions.]

To the Soul.

THAT learned Father, which so firmly proves
The Soul of Man immortal and divine,
And doth the several Offices define :

Anima, Gives her that Name, as she the body moves.
Amor, Then is she Love, embracing Charity.
Animus, Moving a will in us, it is the Mind :
Mens, Retaining knowledge, still the same in kind.
Memoria, As intellectual, it is Memory.
Ratio, In judging, Reason only is her name.
Sensus, In speedy apprehension, it is Sense.
Conscientia, In right and wrong, they call her Conscience.
Spiritus, The Spirit, when it to GODward doth inflame.
These of the Soul, the several functions be,
Which my heart lightened by thy Love, doth
see.

13.

[First printed in 1594 (No. 21), and in all later editions.]

To the Shadow.

ETTERS and lines, we see are soon defaced.
Metals do waste and fret with canker's rust.
The diamond shall once consume to dust;
And freshest colours, with foul stains disgraced.
Paper and ink can paint but naked words.
To write with blood, of force offends the sight.
And if with tears, I find them all too light :
And sighs and signs, a silly hope afford :
O sweetest Shadow, how thou serv'st my turn !
Which still shalt be, as long as there is sun,
Nor whilst the world is, never shall be done ;
Whilst moon shall shine, or any fire shall burn :
That everything whence shadow doth proceed,
May in his shadow, my Love's story read.

14.

[First printed in 1602 (No. 17), and in all later editions.]

I F HE, from heaven that filched that living fire,
Condemned by JOVE to endless torment be !
I greatly marvel, how you still go free!
That far beyond PROMETHEUS did aspire.

 The fire he stole, although of heavenly kind,
Which from above he craftily did take,
Of liveless clods, us living men to make ;
He did bestow in temper of the mind.

 But you broke into heaven's immortal store,
Where Virtue, Honour, Wit, and Beauty lay !
Which taking thence, you have escaped away,
Yet stand as free as e'er you did before :

  Yet old PROMETHEUS punished for his rape !
  Thus poor thieves suffer, when the greater 'scape.

15.

[First printed in 1619.]

His Remedy for Love.

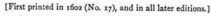INCE to obtain thee, nothing me will stead,
I have a Med'cine that shall cure my Love.
The powder of *her* Heart dried, when she is dead,
That gold nor honour ne'er had power to move ;

 Mixed with *her* Tears that ne'er her True Love
  crost,
Nor, at fifteen, ne'er longed to be a bride ;
Boiled with *her* Sighs, in giving up the ghost,
That for her late deceasèd husband died ;

 Into the same, then let a woman breathe,
That being chid, did never word reply ;
With one thrice-married's Prayers, that did bequeath
A legacy to stale virginity.

  If this receipt have not the power to win me ;
  Little I'll say, but think the Devil 's in me !

16.

[First printed in 1594 (No. 6), and in all later editions.]

An Allusion to the Phœnix.

MONGST all the creatures in this spacious round,
Of the birds' kind, the Phœnix is alone :
Which best by you, of living things is known ;
None like to that ! none like to you is found !
    Your Beauty is the hot and splend'rous sun.
The precious spices be your chaste Desire ;
Which being kindled by that heavenly fire,
Your life, so like the Phœnix 's begun.
    Yourself thus burnèd in that sacred flame,
With so rare sweetness all the heavens perfuming ;
Again increasing, as you are consuming,
Only by dying born the very same.
    And winged by Fame, you to the stars ascend !
So you, of time shall live beyond the end.

17.

[First printed in 1594 (No. 7), and in all later editions.]

To Time.

TAY, speedy Time ! behold, before thou pass
From Age to Age, what thou hast sought to see !
One in whom all the excellencies be,
In whom Heaven looks itself as in a glass.
    Time ! look thou too in this tralucent glass !
And thy youth past, in this pure mirror see !
As the World's Beauty in his infancy,
What it was then ; and thou, before it was.
    Pass on ! and to posterity tell this !
Yet see thou tell but truly, what hath been !
Say to our nephews, that thou once hast seen
In perfect human shape, all Heavenly Bliss !
    And bid them mourn, nay more, despair with thee,
(That she is gone) her like again to see !

18.

[First printed in 1594 (No. 8), and in all later editions.]

To the Celestial Numbers.

O THIS our World, to Learning, and to Heaven ;
Three Nines there are, to every one a Nine :
One number of the earth, the other both Divine,
One Woman now makes three odd numbers even.
   Nine Orders first, of Angels be in heaven ;
Nine Muses do, with Learning still frequent ;
These with the gods are ever resident.
Nine worthy Women, to the World were given.
   My worthy One, to these Nine Worthies addeth !
And my fair Muse, one Muse unto the Nine !
And my good Angel (in my soul, divine !),
With one more Order, these nine Orders gladdeth !
   My Muse, my Worthy, and my Angel then
Makes every One of these three Nines, a Ten.

19.

[First printed in 1599 (No. 2), and in all later editions.]

To Humour.

OU cannot love, my pretty Heart ! and why ?
There was a time you told me that you would ;
But now again, you will the same deny !
If it might please you, would to God you could !
   What, will you hate ? Nay, that you will not neither !
Nor love, nor hate ! how then ? What will you do ?
What, will you keep a mean then betwixt either ?
Or will you love me, and yet hate me too ?
   Yet serves not this ! What next, what other shift ?
You Will, and Will Not ; what a coil is here !
I see your craft ! Now, I perceive your drift !
And all this while, I was mistaken there.
   Your love and hate is this, I now do prove you !
You love in hate, by hate to make me love you.

20.

[First printed in 1599 (No. 22), and in all later editions.]

N EVIL Spirit (your Beauty) haunts me still,
　　Wherewith, alas, I have been long possesst ;
　　Which ceaseth not to attempt me to each ill,
　　Nor give me once, but one poor minute's rest.
　　　In me it speaks, whether I sleep or wake :
　　And when by means to drive it out I try,
　　With greater torments then it me doth take,
　　And tortures me in most extremitÿ.
　　　Before my face, it lays down my despairs,
　　And hastes me on unto a sudden death :
　　Now tempting me, to drown myself in tears ;
　　And then in sighing to give up my breath.
　　　　Thus am I still provoked to every evil,
　　　　By this good-wicked Spirit, sweet Angel-Devil.

21.

[First printed in 1619.]

WITLESS Gallant, a young wench that wooed
　　(Yet his dull spirit, her not one jot could move),
　　Intreated me, as e'er I wished his good,
　　To write him but one Sonnet to his Love.
　　　When I, as fast as e'er my pen could trot,
　　Poured out what first from quick Invention came ;
　　Nor never stood one word thereof to blot :
　　Much like his wit, that was to use the same.
　　　But with my verses, he his Mistress won ;
　　Who doated on the dolt beyond all measure.
　　But see !　For you, to heaven for phrase I run,
　　And ransack all APOLLO's golden treasure !
　　　　Yet by my froth, this Fool, his Love obtains :
　　　　And I lose you, for all my wit and pains !

22.

[First printed in 1602 (No. 25), and in all later editions.]

To Folly.

ITH fools and children, good discretion bears.
Then, honest people, bear with LOVE and me!
Nor older yet, nor wiser made by years,
Amongst the rest of fools and children be.
  LOVE, still a baby, plays with gauds and toys,
And like a wanton sports with every feather;
And idiots still are running after boys:
Then fools and children fittest to go together.
  He still as young as when he first was born;
No wiser I, than when as young as he:
You that behold us, laugh us not to scorn;
Give Nature thanks, you are not such as we!
    Yet fools and children sometimes tell in play,
    Some wise in shew, more fools indeed than they!

23.

[First printed in 1599 (No. 24), and in all later editions.]

OVE banished heaven, in earth was held in scorn;
Wand'ring abroad in need and beggary:
And wanting friends, though of a goddess born,
Yet craved the alms of such as passèd by.
I, like a man devout and charitable,
Clothèd the naked, lodged this wandering guest;
With sighs and tears still furnishing his table,
With what might make the miserable blest.
  But this Ungrateful! for my good desert,
Inticed my thoughts, against me to conspire;
Who gave consent to steal away my heart,
And set my breast (his lodging) on a fire.
    Well, well, my friends! when beggars grow thus bold;
    No marvel then, though Charity grow cold.

24.

[First printed in 1602 (No. 27), and in all later editions.]

HEAR some say, "This man is not in love!"
"Who! can he love? a likely thing!" they say.
"Read but his Verse, and it will easily prove!"
O, judge not rashly, gentle Sir, I pray!

    Because I loosely trifle in this sort,
As one that fain his sorrows would beguile:
You now suppose me, all this time, in sport;
And please yourself with this conceit the while.

    Ye shallow Censures! sometimes, see ye not,
In greatest perils, some men pleasant be;
Where Fame by death is only to be got,
They resolute! So stands the case with me.

      Where other men, in depth of Passion cry;
      I laugh at Fortune, as in jest to die!

25.

[First printed in 1599 (No. 25), and in all later editions.]

O, WHY should Nature niggardly restrain,
That foreign nations relish not our tongue?
Else should my Lines glide on the waves of Rhine,
And crown the Pyren's with my living Song.

    But bounded thus, to Scotland get you forth!
Thence take you wing unto the Orcades!
There let my Verse get glory in the north,
Making my sighs to thaw the frozen seas.

    And let the Bards within that Irish isle,
To whom my Muse with fiery wings shall pass,
Call back the stiff-necked rebels from exile,
And mollify the slaughtering Gallowglass!

      And when my flowing Numbers they rehearse,
      Let wolves and bears be charmèd with my Verse!

26.

[First printed in 1594 (No. 37), and in all later editions.]

To Despair.

 EVER love, where never Hope appears,
 Yet Hope draws on my never-hoping care;
 And my life's Hope would die but for Despair;
  My never-certain joy breeds ever certain fears.
 Uncertain dread gives wings unto my Hope;
Yet my Hope's wings are laden so with fear
As they cannot ascend to my Hope's sphere;
Though fear gives them more than a heavenly scope.
  Yet this large room is bounded with Despair,
So my Love is still fettered with vain Hope,
And liberty deprives him of his scope,
And thus am I imprisoned in the air.
  Then, sweet Despair, awhile hold up thy head!
  Or all my Hope, for sorrow, will be dead.

27.

[First printed in 1619.]

S NOT Love here, as 'tis in other climes?
 And differeth it, as do the several nations?
 Or hath it lost the virtue, with the Times?
  Or in this island altereth with the fashions?
  Or have our Passions lesser power than theirs,
Who had less Art, them lively to express?
Is Nature grown less powerful in their heirs,
Or in our fathers, did she more transgress?
  I am sure, my sighs come from a heart as true
As any man's that Memory can boast!
And my respects and services to you,
Equal with his, that loves his Mistress most!
  Or Nature must be partial in my cause,
  Or only You do violate her laws!

28.

[First printed in 1602 (No. 31), and in all later editions.]

O such as say, thy Love I overprize,
And do not stick to term my praises, folly;
Against these folks, that think themselves so wise,
I thus oppose my reason's forces wholly.

Though I give more than well affords my state,
In which expense, the most suppose me vain
(Which yields them nothing, at the easiest rate),
Yet, at this price, returns me treble gain.

They value not, unskilful how to use;
And I give much, because I gain thereby:
I that thus take, or they that thus refuse;
Whether are these deceivèd then, or I?

In everything, I hold this maxim still,
The circumstance doth make it good or ill.

29.

[First printed in 1599 (No. 29), and in all later editions.]

To the Senses.

Hen conquering Love did first my Heart assail;
Unto mine aid I summoned every Sense:
Doubting, if that proud tyrant should prevail,
My Heart should suffer for mine eyes' offence.

But he with beauty first corrupted Sight,
My Hearing bribed with her tongue's harmony,
My Taste by her sweet lips drawn with delight,
My Smelling won with her breath's spicery,

But when my Touching came to play his part
(The King of Senses, greater than the rest),
He yields Love up the keys unto my Heart;
And tells the others, how they should be blest.

And thus by those, of whom I hoped for aid;
To cruel Love, my soul was first betrayed.

30.

[First printed in 1594 (No. 5), and in all later editions.]

To the Vestals.

HOSE priests which first the Vestal Fire began,
Which might be borrowed from no earthly flame,
Devised a vessel to receive the sun,
Being stedfastly opposèd to the same :
    Where, with sweet wood, laid curiously by Art,
On which the sun might by reflection beat ;
Receiving strength for every secret part,
The fuel kindled with celestial heat.
    Thy blessèd Eyes, the sun which lights this fire !
My holy Thoughts, they be the Vestal Flame !
The precious odours be my chaste Desires !
My Breast's the vessel which includes the same !
    Thou art my VESTA ! Thou, my goddess art !
    Thy hallowed temple only is my Heart !

31.

[First printed in 1599 (No. 31), and in all later editions.]

To the Critics.

ETHINKS, I see some crooked Mimic jeer,
And tax my Muse with this fantastic grace ;
Turning my papers, asks, " What have we here ?"
Making withal some filthy antic face.
    I fear no censure, nor what thou canst say !
Nor shall my spirit, one jot of vigour lose !
Think'st thou, my Wit shall keep the packhorse way,
That every dudgen low Invention goes ?
    Since Sonnets thus in bundles are imprest,
And every drudge doth dull our satiate ear ;
Think'st thou, my Love shall in those rags be drest,
That every dowdy, every trull doth wear ?
    Up to my pitch, no common judgement flies !
    I scorn all earthly dung-bred scarabies !

32.

[First printed in 1594 (No. 24), and in all later editions.]

To the River Ankor.

UR floods' Queen, Thames, for ships and swans is
    crowned;
And stately Severn, for her shore is praised.
The crystal Trent, for fords and fish renowned;
And Avon's fame, to Albion's cliffs is raised,
    Carlegion Chester vaunts her holy Dee.
York, many wonders, of her Ouse can tell.
The Peak, her Dove, whose banks so fertile be:
And Kent will say, her Medway doth excel.
    Cotswold commends her Isis to the Tame.
Our northern borders boast of Tweed's fair flood.
Our western parts extol their Wilis' fame;
And the old Lea brags of the Danish blood.
    Arden's sweet Ankor, let thy glory be,
    That fair *IDEA* only lives by thee!

33.

[First printed in 1594 (No. 33), and in all later editions.]

To Imagination.

HILST yet mine Eyes do surfeit with delight,
  My woful Heart (imprisoned in my breast)
Wisheth to be transformèd to my sight,
That it, like those, by looking, might be blest.
    But whilst mine Eyes thus greedily do gaze,
Finding their objects over-soon depart;
These now the other's happiness do praise,
Wishing themselves, that they had been my Heart.
    That Eyes were Heart, or that the Heart were Eyes,
As covetous the other's use to have.
But finding Nature, their request denies,
This to each other mutually they crave.
    That since the one cannot the other be,
    That Eyes could think of that my Heart could see.

34.

[First printed in 1599 (No. 34), and in all later editions.]

To Admiration.

 ARVEL not, LOVE! though I thy power admire!
Ravished a world beyond the farthest thought,
And knowing more, than ever hath been taught,
That I am only starved in my Desire:
     Marvel not, LOVE! though I thy power admire!
Aiming at things exceeding all perfection;
To Wisdom's self to minister direction,
That I am only starved in my Desire:
     Marvel not, LOVE! though I thy power admire!
Though my Conceit I further seem to bend
Than possibly Invention can extend;
And yet am only starved in my Desire:
     If thou wilt wonder! here's the wonder, LOVE!
     That this to me doth yet no wonder prove.

35.

[First printed in 1594 (No. 12), and in all later editions.]

To Miracle.

 OME misbelieving and profane in Love,
When I do speak of miracles by thee,
May say, that thou art flatterèd by me;
Who only write, my skill in Verse to prove.
     See miracles! ye Unbelieving, see!
A dumb-born Muse made to express the mind!
A cripple Hand to write, yet lame by kind!
One by thy name, the other touching thee.
     Blind were mine eyes, till they were seen of thine;
And mine ears deaf, by thy fame healèd be:
My vices cured by virtues sprung from thee;
My hopes revived, which long in grave had lien.
     All unclean thoughts (foul spirits) cast out in me,
     Only by virtue that proceeds from thee.

36.

[First printed in 1619.]

CUPID *conjured.*

Hou purblind Boy! since thou hast been so slack
To wound her heart, whose eyes have wounded me;
And suffered her to glory in my wrack:
Thus to my aid, I lastly conjure thee!
　　By hellish Styx (by which the Thunderer swears)!
By thy fair Mother's unavoided power!
By HECATE's names! by PROSERPINE's sad tears,
When she was rapt to the infernal bower!
　　By thine own lovèd PSYCHE's! by the fires
Spent on thine altars, flaming up to heaven!
By all true lovers' sighs, vows, and desires!
By all the wounds that ever thou hast given!
　　I conjure thee, by all that I have named,
　　To make her love! or, CUPID, be thou damned!

37.

[First printed in 1602 (No. 41), and in all later editions.]

EAR! why should you command me to my rest,
When now the night doth summon all to sleep?
Methinks, this time becometh lovers best!
Night was ordained, together friends to keep.
　　How happy are all other living things,
Which, through the day, disjoined by several flight,
The quiet evening yet together brings,
And each returns unto his Love at night!
　　O thou that art so courteous else to all,
Why shouldst thou, Night! abuse me only thus!
That every creature to his kind dost call,
And yet 'tis thou dost only sever us?
　　Well could I wish, it would be ever day;
　　If, when night comes, you bid me go away!

38.

[First printed in 1594 (No. 31), and in all later editions.]

ITTING alone, Love bids me go and write!
Reason plucks back, commanding me to stay!
Boasting that She doth still direct the way,
Or else Love were unable to indite.
　　Love growing angry, vexèd at the spleen,
And scorning Reason's maimèd argument,
Straight taxeth Reason, wanting to invent
Where She with Love conversing hath not been.
　　Reason reproachèd with this coy disdain,
Despiteth Love, and laugheth at her folly:
And Love contemning Reason's reason wholly,
Thought it in weight too light by many a grain.
　　Reason put back, doth out of sight remove;
And Love alone picks reason out of love.

39.

[First printed in 1594 (No. 18), and in all later editions.]

OME, when in rhyme, they of their loves do tell;
With flames and lightnings their exordiums paint.
Some call on heaven, some invocate on hell,
And Fates and Furies, with their woes acquaint.
　　Elizium is too high a seat for me.
I will not come in Styx or Phlegethon.
The thrice-three Muses but too wanton be.
Like they that lust, I care not, I will none!
　　Spiteful ERINNYS frights me with her looks,
My manhood dares not, with foul ATE mell.
I quake to look on HECATE's charming books.
I still fear bugbears in APOLLO's cell.
　　I pass not for MINERVA! nor ASTREA!
　　Only I call on my divine *IDEA!*

40.

[First printed in 1594 (No. 44), and in all later editions.]

Y HEART the Anvil where my thoughts do beat;
My words the Hammers fashioning my Desire;
My breast the Forge including all the heat,
Love is the Fuel which maintains the fire.
   My sighs the Bellows which the flame increaseth,
Filling mine ears with noise and nightly groaning.
Toiling with pain, my labour never ceaseth;
In grievous Passions, my woes still bemoaning.
   My eyes with tears against the fire striving,
Whose scorching glede, my heart to cinders turneth:
But with those drops, the flame again reviving
Still more and more it, to my torment burneth.
   With SISYPHUS thus do I roll the stone,
   And turn the wheel with damnèd IXION.

41.

[First printed in 1594 (No. 43), and in all later editions.]

Love's Lunacy.

HY do I speak of joy, or write of love,
When my heart is the very den of horror;
And in my soul the pains of hell I prove,
With all his torments and infernal terror?
   What should I say?   What yet remains to do?
My brain is dry with weeping all too long.
My sighs be spent in uttering of my woe,
And I want words wherewith to tell my wrong.
   But still distracted in Love's lunacy,
And Bedlamlike, thus raving in my grief.
Now rail upon her hair, then on her eye,
Now call her "Goddess!" then I call her "Thief!"
   Now I deny her! then I do confess her!
   Now do I curse her! then again I bless her!

42.

[First printed in 1594 (No. 28), and in all later editions.]

OME men there be, which like my method well,
And much commend the strangeness of my vein.
Some say I have a passing pleasing strain,
Some say that in my humour I excel.
 Some, who not kindly relish my conceit,
They say, as poets do I use to feign,
And in bare words paint out my Passions' pain.
Thus sundry men, their sundry minds repeat.
 I pass not, I, how men affected be!
Nor who commends or discommends my Verse!
It pleaseth me, if I my woes rehearse!
And in my lines, if She, my love may see!
  Only my comfort still consists in this;
  Writing her praise, I cannot write amiss!

43.

[First printed in 1605 (No. 43), and in all later editions.]

HY should your fair eyes, with such sovereign grace,
Disperse their rays on every vulgar spirit,
Whilst I in darkness, in the self-same place,
Get not one glance to recompense my merit?
 So doth the plowman gaze the wandering star,
And only rest contented with the light;
That never learned what constellations are,
Beyond the bent of his unknowing sight.
 O why should Beauty (custom to obey),
To their gross sense apply herself so ill!
Would God! I were as ignorant as they!
When I am made unhappy by my skill!
  Only compelled on this poor good to boast,
  Heavens are not kind to them, that know them most!

44.

[First printed in 1599 (No. 43), and in all later editions.]

HILST thus my pen strives to eternize thee,
Age rules my lines with wrinkles in my face;
Where, in the Map of all my Misery,
Is modelled out the World of my disgrace:
Whilst in despite of tyrannizing Times,
MEDEAlike, I make thee young again!
Proudly thou scorn'st my world-outwearing rhymes,
And murder'st Virtue with thy coy disdain!
And though in youth, my youth untimely perish,
To keep Thee from oblivion and the grave;
Ensuing Ages yet my Rhymes shall cherish,
Where I entombed, my better part shall save;
And though this earthly body fade and die,
My Name shall mount upon Eternity!

45.

[First printed in 1599 (No. 44), and in all later editions.]

USES! which sadly sit about my chair,
Drowned in the tears extorted by my lines;
With heavy sighs, whilst thus I break the air,
Painting my Passions in these sad designs.
Since She disdains to bless my happy Verse,
The strong built Trophies to her living fame,
Ever henceforth my bosom be your hearse!
Wherein the World shall now entomb her name.
Enclose my music, you poor senseless walls!
Sith She is deaf and will not hear my moans,
Soften yourselves with every tear that falls!
Whilst I, like ORPHEUS, sing to trees and stones.
Which with my plaint seem yet with pity moved,
Kinder than She whom I so long have loved.

46.

[First printed in 1605 (No. 46), and in all later editions.]

PLAIN pathed Experience (th' unlearned's guide),
    Her simple followers evidently shews
    Sometimes what Schoolmen scarcely can decide,
    Nor yet wise Reason absolutely knows.
  In making trial of a murder wrought,
If the vile actors of the heinous deed
Near the dead body happily be brought,
Oft 't hath been proved, the breathless corse will bleed.
  She coming near, that my poor heart hath slain,
Long since departed (to the World no more),
Th' ancient wounds no longer can contain,
But fall to bleeding, as they did before.
    But what of this! Should She to death be led,
    It furthers Justice; but helps not the dead!

47.

[First printed in 1605 (No. 47), and in all later editions.]

IN PRIDE of Wit, when high desire of fame
    Gave life and courage to my lab'ring pen,
    And first the sound and virtue of my name
    Won grace and credit in the ears of men;
  With those, the thronged Theatres that press,
I in the Circuit for the laurel strove!
Where the full praise, I freely must confess,
In heat of blood, a modest mind might move.
  With shouts and claps at every little pause,
When the proud Round on every side hath rung;
Sadly I sit, unmoved with the applause,
As though to me it nothing did belong.
    No public glory vainly I pursue:
    All that I seek is to eternize you!

48.

[First printed in 1619.]

CUPID, I hate thee! which I'd have thee know!
A naked starveling ever mayst thou be!
Poor rogue! go pawn thy *fascia* and thy bow
For some poor rags, wherewith to cover thee!
Or if thou 'lt not, thy archery forbear!
To some base rustic do thyself prefer!
And when the corn 's sown, or grown into the ear;
Practice thy quiver, and turn crowkeeper!
Or being blind, as fittest for the trade,
Go hire thyself some bungling harper's boy!
They that are blind are minstrels often made!
So mayst thou live, to thy fair mother's joy!
    That whilst with MARS she holdeth her old way,
    Thou, her blind son, mayst sit by them and play.

49.

[First printed in 1599 (No. 46), and in all later editions.]

THOU leaden brain, which censur'st what I write,
And sayst my lines be dull, and do not move.
I marvel not thou feelst not my Delight,
Which never felt'st my fiery touch of Love!
But thou, whose pen hath like a packhorse served,
Whose stomach unto gall hath turned thy food,
Whose senses, like poor prisoners, hunger starved,
Whose grief hath parched thy body, dried thy blood.
Thou which hast scornèd life, and hated death;
And in a moment, mad, sober, glad, and sorry;
Thou which hast banned thy thoughts, and curst thy birth,
With thousand plagues more than in Purgatory:
    Thou, thus whose spirit, Love in his fire refines!
    Come thou and read, admire, applaud my Lines!

50.

[First printed in 1605 (No. 50), and in all later editions.]

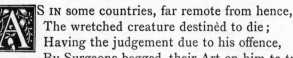

A S IN some countries, far remote from hence,
   The wretched creature destinèd to die;
   Having the judgement due to his offence,
     By Surgeons begged, their Art on him to try :
   Which on the living, work without remorse,
First make incision on each mastering vein,
Then staunch the bleeding, then transpierce the corse,
And with their balms recure the wounds again.
   Then poison, and with physic him restore;
Not that they fear the hopeless man to kill,
But their experience to increase the more.
Even so my Mistress works upon my ill,
   By curing me and killing me each hour,
   Only to shew her Beauty's sovereign power.

51.

[First printed in 1605 (No. 51), and in all later editions.]

CALLING to mind since first my Love begun,
   The uncertain Times, oft varying in their course;
   How things still unexpectedly have run,
     As it please the Fates, by their resistless force.
   Lastly, mine eyes amazèdly have seen
ESSEX's great fall ! TYRONE his peace to gain !
The quiet end of that long living Queen !
This King's fair Entrance ! and our peace with Spain !
   We and the Dutch at length ourselves to sever !
Thus the World doth and evermore shall reel :
Yet to my goddess am I constant ever !
Howe'er blind Fortune turn her giddy wheel,
   Though heaven and earth prove both to me untrue,
   Yet am I still inviolate to You !

52.

[First printed in 1619.]

WHAT dost thou mean, to cheat me of my heart?
   To take all mine, and give me none again?
   Or have thine eyes such magic, or that Art
   That what they get, they ever do retain?
Play not the Tyrant, but take some remorse!
Rebate thy spleen, if but for pity's sake!
Or cruel, if thou can'st not, let us scorse!
And for one piece of thine, my whole heart take!
   But what of pity, do I speak to thee!
Whose breast is proof against complaint or prayer:
Or can I think what my reward shall be
From that proud Beauty, which was my betrayer!
   What talk I of a heart, when thou hast none!
   Or if thou hast, it is a flinty one.

53.

[First printed in 1594 (No. 13), and in all later editions.]

Another to the river Ankor.

CLEAR Ankor, on whose silver-sanded shore,
   My soul-shrined Saint, my fair *IDEA* lives;
   O blessed brook! whose milk-white swans adore
   Thy crystal stream, refinèd by her eyes.
Where sweet myrrh-breathing ZEPHYR, in the Spring,
Gently distils his nectar-dropping showers:
Where nightingales in Arden sit and sing
Amongst the dainty dew-impearlèd flowers.
   Say thus, fair brook, when thou shalt see thy Queen,
" Lo, here thy shepherd spent his wandering years!
And in these shades, dear Nymph! he oft hath been!
And here to thee, he sacrificed his tears! "
   Fair Arden, thou my Tempe art alone!
   And thou, sweet Ankor, art my Helicon!

54.

[First printed in 1599 (No. 49), and in all later editions.]

Y ET read at last the Story of my Woe!
  The dreary abstracts of my endless cares,
  With my life's sorrow interlinèd so,
    Smoked with my sighs, and blotted with my tears.
  The sad Memorials of my Miseries!
Penned in the grief of mine afflicted ghost.
My Life's Complaint in doleful Elegies!
With so pure love as Time could never boast.
  Receive the incense which I offer here,
By my strong faith ascending to thy fame!
My zeal, my hope, my vows, my praise, my prayer,
My soul's oblations to thy sacred Name!
    Which Name, my Muse, to highest heavens shall raise,
    By chaste Desire, true Love, and virtuous Praise!

55.

[First printed in 1599 (No. 50), and in all later editions.]

M Y FAIR! if thou wilt register my Love,
  A world of volumes shall thereof arise!
  Preserve my Tears, and thou thyself shall prove
    A second Flood, down raining from mine eyes!
  Note but my Sighs, and thine eyes shall behold
The sunbeams smothered with immortal smoke!
And if by thee, my Prayers may be enrolled;
They, heaven and earth to pity shall provoke!
  Look thou into my breast, and thou shalt see
Chaste holy vows for my soul's sacrifice!
That soul, sweet Maid! which so hath honoured thee,
Erecting Trophies to thy sacred eyes.
    Those eyes to my heart shining ever bright,
    When darkness hath obscured each other light.

56.

[First printed in 1594 (No. 3), and in all later editions.]

An allusion to the Eaglets.

WHEN like an Eaglet, I first found my love,
 For that the virtue I thereof would know,
 Upon the nest I set it forth, to prove
 If it were of that kingly kind or no:
But it no sooner saw my sun appear,
But on her rays with open eyes it stood;
To shew that I had hatched it for the air,
And rightly came from that brave-mounting brood.
 And when the plumes were sunned with sweet Desire,
To prove the pinions, it ascends the skies!
Do what I could, it needsly would aspire
To my soul's sun, those two celestial Eyes.
 Thus from my breast, where it was bred alone,
 It after thee is, like an Eaglet flown.

57.

[First printed in 1605 (No. 57), and in all later editions.]

YOU best discerned of my mind's inward eyes,
 And yet your graces outwardly Divine,
 Whose dear remembrance in my bosom lies,
 Too rich a relic for so poor a shrine.
You, in whom Nature chose herself to view,
When she, her own perfection would admire;
Bestowing all her excellence on you,
At whose pure eyes, LOVE lights his hallowed fire;
 Even as a man that in some trance hath seen
More than his wondring utterance can unfold;
That, rapt in spirit, in better worlds hath been.
So must your praise distractedly be told!
 Most of all short, when I would shew you most,
 In your perfections so much am I lost.

58.

[First printed in 1605 (No. 58), and in all later editions.]

N FORMER times, such as had store of coin,
In wars at home, or when for conquests bound,
For fear that some their treasure should purloin,
Gave it, to keep, to Spirits within the ground :
  And to attend it, them as strongly tied,
Till they returned. Home when they never came,
Such as by Art to get the same have tried,
From the strong Spirit, by no means force the same.
  Nearer men come, that further flies away !
Striving to hold it strongly in the deep.
Even as this Spirit, so you alone do play
With those rich beauties, Heaven gives you to keep.
  Pity so left to the coldness of your blood,
  Not to avail you, nor do others good.

59.

[First printed in 1602 (No. 58), and in all later editions.]

To Proverbs.

S LOVE and I late harboured in one inn,
  With Proverbs thus each other entertain.
In Love there is no lack, thus I begin :
Fair words make fools, replieth he again.
  Who spares to speak, doth spare to speed, quoth I.
As well, saith he, *too forward as too slow.*
Fortune assists the boldest, I reply.
A hasty man, quoth he, *ne'er wanted woe !*
  Labour is light, where Love, quoth I, *doth pay.*
Saith he, *Light burden's heavy, if far born.*
Quoth I, *The Main lost, cast the By away !*
You have spun a fair thread, he replies in scorn.
  And having thus awhile each other thwarted,
  Fools as we met, so fools again we parted.

60.

[First printed in 1594 (No. 49), and in all later editions.]

EFINE my Weal, and tell the joys of heaven;
  Express my Woes, and shew the pains of hell!
  Declare what Fate unlucky stars have given!
    And ask a world upon my life to dwell!
  Make known the faith that Fortune could not move!
Compare my worth with others' base desert!
Let virtue be the touchstone of my Love!
  So may the heavens read wonders in my heart!
  Behold the clouds which have eclipsed my sun!
And view the crosses which my course do let!
Tell me, if ever since the world begun
So fair a rising, had so foul a set?
    And see, if TIME (if he would strive to prove)
    Can shew a Second to so pure a Love!

61.

[First printed in 1619.]

INCE there's no help, Come, let us kiss and part!
  Nay, I have done.   You get no more of me!
  And I am glad, yea, glad, with all my heart,
    That thus so cleanly, I my self can free.
  Shake hands for ever! Cancel all our vows!
And when we meet at any time again,
Be it not seen in either of our brows,
That we one jot of former love retain!
  Now at the last gasp of LOVE's latest breath.
When his pulse failing, Passion speechless lies;
When Faith is kneeling by his bed of death,
And Innocence is closing up his eyes:
    Now, if thou wouldst! when all have given him over,
    From death to life, thou might'st him yet recover!

62.

[First printed in 1594 (No. 50), and in all later editions.]

WHEN first I ended, then I first began;
Then more I travelled further from my rest.
Where most I lost, there most of all I wan;
Pined with hunger, rising from a feast.
Methinks, I fly, yet want I legs to go;
Wise in conceit, in act a very sot.
Ravished with joy amidst a hell of woe;
What most I seem that surest am I not.
I build my hopes, a world above the sky;
Yet with the mole I creep into the earth.
In plenty I am starved with penury;
And yet I surfeit in the greatest dearth.
I have, I want; despair, and yet desire:
Burned in a sea of ice, and drowned amidst a fire.

63.

[First printed in 1599 (No. 55), and in all later editions.]

TRUCE, gentle Love! a Parley now I crave!
Methinks, 'tis long since first these wars begun.
Nor thou, nor I, the better yet can have!
Bad is the match, where neither party won.
I offer free Conditions of fair Peace!
My heart for hostage that it shall remain.
Discharge our forces! Here, let malice cease!
So for my pledge, thou give me pledge again.
Or if no thing but death will serve thy turn,
Still thirsting for subversion of my State,
Do what thou canst! raze! massacre! and burn!
Let the World see the utmost of thy hate!
I send Defiance! since if overthrown,
Thou vanquishing, the conquest is mine own!

FINIS.

AMORETTI
AND
Epithalamion.
Written not long ſince by Edmunde *Spenſer*.

> Woodcut of
> the publisher's
> trade-mark
> with his motto:
> *Veritas tua et
> usque ad
> nubes.*

Printed for William *Ponſonby*. 1595.

SIR ROBERT NEEDHAM, KNIGHT.

IR, to gratulate your safe return from Ireland, I had nothing so ready, nor thought anything so meet, as these sweet conceited Sonnets, the deed of that well-deserving gentleman, Master Edmond Spenser: whose name sufficiently warranting the worthiness of the work, I do more confidently presume to publish it in his absence, under your name, to whom (in my poor opinion) the patronage thereof doth in some respects properly appertain. For, besides your judgment and delight in learned poesy, this gentle Muse, for her former perfection long wished for in England, now at the length crossing the seas in your happy company (though to yourself unknown) seemeth to make choice of you, as meetest to give her deserved countenance, after her return: entertain her, then, Right worshipful, in sort best beseeming your gentle mind, and her merit, and take in worth my goodwill herein, who seek no more but to show myself yours in all dutiful affection.

W. P.

To the Author.

ARK is the day, when Phœbus' face is shrouded,
 And weaker sights may wander soon astray :
 But, when they see his glorious rays unclouded,
 With steady steps they keep the perfect way :
So, while this Muse in foreign lands doth stay,
Invention weeps, and pens are cast aside ;
The time, like night, deprived of cheerful day ;
And few do write, but (ah!) too soon may slide.
Then, hie thee home, that art our perfect guide,
And with thy wit illustrate England's fame,
Daunting thereby our neighbours' ancient pride,
That do, for poesy, challenge chiefest name :
 So we that live, and ages that succeed,
 With great applause thy learned works shall read.

G. W. Senior.

H ! Colin, whether on the lowly plain,
 Piping to shepherds thy sweet roundelays :
 Or whether singing, in some lofty vein,
 Heroic deeds of past or present days ;
Or whether in thy lovely mistress' praise,
Thou list to exercise thy learned quill ;
Thy muse hath got such grace and power to please,
With rare invention, beautified by skill,
As who therein can ever joy their fill !
O ! therefore let that happy muse proceed
To climb the height of Virtue's sacred hill,
Where endless honour shall be made thy meed :
 Because no malice of succeeding days
 Can raze those records of thy lasting praise.

G. W. I.ᶜ

SONNET I.

APPY, ye leaves! when as those lily hands,
    Which hold my life in their dead-doing might,
    Shall handle you, and hold in love's soft bands,
    Like captives trembling at the victor's sight.
And happy lines! on which, with starry light,
Those lamping eyes will deign sometimes to look,
And read the sorrows of my dying spright,
Written with tears in heart's close-bleeding book.
And happy rhymes! bath'd in the sacred brook
Of Helicon, whence she derived is;
When ye behold that Angel's blessed look,
My soul's long-lacked food, my heaven's bliss;
    Leaves, lines, and rhymes, seek her to please alone,
    Whom if ye please, I care for other none!

SONNET II.

NQUIET thought! whom at the first I bred
    Of th' inward bale of my love-pined heart;
    And sithens have with sighs and sorrows fed,
    Till greater than my womb thou woxen art:
Break forth at length out of the inner part,
In which thou lurkest like to viper's brood;
And seek some succour both to ease my smart,
And also to sustain thyself with food.
But, if in presence of that fairest proud
Thou chance to come, fall lowly at her feet;
And, with meek humbless and afflicted mood,
Pardon for thee, and grace for me, entreat:
    Which if she grant, then live, and my love cherish:
    If not, die soon; and I with thee will perish.

SONNET III.

THE sovereign beauty which I do admire,
　　Witness the world how worthy to be praised!
　　The light whereof hath kindled heavenly fire
　　In my frail spirit, by her from baseness raised;
That, being now with her huge brightness dazed,
Base thing I can no more endure to view:
But, looking still on her, I stand amazed
At wondrous sight of so celestial hue.
So when my tongue would speak her praises due,
It stopped is with thought's astonishment;
And, when my pen would write her titles true,
It ravished is with fancy's wonderment:
　　Yet in my heart I then both speak and write
　　The wonder that my wit cannot endite.

SONNET IV.

NEW year, forth looking out of Janus' gate,
　　Doth seem to promise hope of new delight:
　　And, bidding th' old Adieu, his passed date
　　Bids all old thoughts to die in dumpish spright:
And, calling forth out of sad winter's night
Fresh Love, that long hath slept in cheerless bower,
Wills him awake, and soon about him dight
His wanton wings and darts of deadly power.
For lusty Spring now in his timely hour
Is ready to come forth, him to receive;
And warns the earth with divers-coloured flower
To deck herself, and her fair mantle weave.
　　Then you, fair flower! in whom fresh youth doth reign,
　　Prepare yourself new love to entertain.

SONNET V.

RUDELY thou wrongest my dear heart's desire,
In finding fault with her too portly pride:
The thing which I do most in her admire,
Is of the world unworthy most envied:
For in those lofty looks is close implied
Scorn of base things, and 'sdain of foul dishonour:
Threatening rash eyes which gaze on her so wide,
That loosely they ne dare to look upon her.
Such pride is praise; such portliness is honour;
That bolden'd innocence bears in her eyes;
And her fair countenance, like a goodly banner,
Spreads in defiance of all enemies.
  Was never in this world aught worthy tried,
  Without some spark of such self-pleasing pride.

SONNET VI.

BE NAUGHT dismayed that her unmoved mind
Doth still persist in her rebellious pride:
Such love, not like to lusts of baser kind,
The harder won, the firmer will abide.
The dureful oak, whose sap is not yet dried,
Is long ere it conceive the kindling fire;
But, when it once doth burn, it doth divide
Great heat, and makes his flames to heaven aspire.
So hard it is to kindle new desire
In gentle breast, that shall endure for ever:
Deep is the wound, that dints the parts entire
With chaste affects that naught but death can sever;
  Then think not long in taking little pain
  To knit the knot, that ever shall remain.

SONNET VII.

AIR eyes! the mirror of my mazed heart,
    What wondrous virtue is contained in you,
    The which both life and death forth from you
        dart,
Into the object of your mighty view?
For, when ye mildly look with lovely hue,
Then is my soul with life and love inspired:
But when ye lower, or look on me askew,
Then do I die, as one with lightning fired.
But, since that life is more than death desired,
Look ever lovely, as becomes you best;
That your bright beams, of my weak eyes admired,
May kindle living fire within my breast.
    Such life should be the honour of your light,
    Such death the sad ensample of your might.

SONNET VIII.

ORE than most fair, full of the living fire,
    Kindled above unto the Maker near;
    No eyes but joys, in which all powers conspire,
    That to the world naught else be counted dear;
Through your bright beams doth not the blinded guest
Shoot out his darts to base affections wound;
But Angels come to lead frail minds to rest
In chaste desires, on heavenly beauty bound.
You frame my thoughts, and fashion me within;
You stop my tongue, and teach my heart to speak;
You calm the storm that passion did begin,
Strong through your cause, but by your virtue weak.
    Dark is the world, where your light shined never;
    Well is he born, that may behold you ever.

SONNET IX.

ONG-while I sought to what I might compare
    Those powerful eyes, which lighten my dark
      spright ;
    Yet find I naught on earth, to which I dare
Resemble th' image of their goodly light.
Not to the Sun ; for they do shine by night ;
Nor to the Moon ; for they are changed never ;
Nor to the Stars ; for they have purer sight ;
Nor to the Fire ; for they consume not ever ;
Nor to the Lightning ; for they still perséver ;
Nor to the Diamond ; for they are more tender ;
Nor unto Crystal ; for nought may them sever ;
Nor unto Glass ; such baseness mought offend her.
    Then to the Maker self they likest be,
    Whose light doth lighten all that here we see.

SONNET X.

NRIGHTEOUS lord of love, what law is this,
    That me thou makest thus tormented be,
    The whiles she lordeth in licentious bliss
    Of her freewill, scorning both thee and me?
See ! how the tyranness doth joy to see
The huge massácres which her eyes do make ;
And humbled hearts brings captive unto thee,
That thou of them mayst mighty vengeance take,
But her proud heart do thou a little shake,
And that high look, with which she doth control
All this world's pride, bow to a baser make,
And all her faults in thy black book enroll :
    That I may laugh at her in equal sort,
    As she doth laugh at me, and makes my pain her sport.

SONNET XI.

AILY when I do seek and sue for peace,
And hostages do offer for my truth ;
She, cruel warrior, doth herself address
To battle, and the weary war renew'th ;
Ne will be moved with reason, or with ruth,
To grant small respite to my restless toil ;
But greedily her fell intent pursu'th,
Of my poor life to make unpitied spoil.
Yet my poor life, all sorrows to assoil,
I would her yield, her wrath to pacify :
But then she seeks, with torment and turmoil,
To force me live, and will not let me die.
    All pain hath end, and every war hath peace ;
    But mine, no price nor prayer may surcease.

SONNET XII.

NE day I sought with her heart-thrilling eyes
To make a truce, and terms to entertain :
All fearless then of so false enemies,
Which sought me to entrap in treason's train.
So, as I then disarmed did remain,
A wicked ambush which lay hidden long
In the close covert of her guileful eyen,
Thence breaking forth, did thick about me throng.
Too feeble I t' abide the brunt so strong,
Was forced to yield myself into their hands ;
Who, me captiving straight with rigorous wrong,
Have ever since me kept in cruel bands.
    So, Lady, now to you I do complain,
    Against your eyes, that justice I may gain.

SONNET XIII.

IN that proud port, which her so goodly graceth,
Whiles her fair face she rears up to the sky,
And to the ground her eye-lids low embaseth,
Most goodly temperature ye may descry;
Mild humbless, mixed with awful majesty.
For, looking on the earth whence she was born,
Her mind remember'th her mortality,
Whatso is fairest shall to earth return.
But that same lofty countenance seems to scorn
Base thing, and think how she to heaven may climb;
Treading down earth as loathsome and forlorn,
That hinders heavenly thoughts with drossy slime.
   Yet lowly still vouchsafe to look on me;
   Such lowliness shall make you lofty be.

SONNET XIV.

RETURN again, my forces late dismayed,
Unto the siege by you abandon'd quite.
Great shame it is to leave, like one afraid,
So fair a piece, for one repulse so light.
'Gainst such strong castles needeth greater might
Than those small forts which ye were wont belay:
Such haughty minds, enur'd to hardy fight,
Disdain to yield unto the first assay.
Bring therefore all the forces that ye may,
And lay incessant battery to her heart;
Plaints, prayers, vows, ruth, sorrow, and dismay;
Those engines can the proudest love convert:
   And, if those fail, fall down and die before her;
   So dying live, and living do adore her.

SONNET XV.

E tradeful Merchants, that, with weary toil,
　　Do seek most precious things to make your
　　　gain;
　　And both the Indias of their treasure spoil;
What needeth you to seek so far in vain?
For lo, my love doth in her self contain
All this world's riches that may far be found:
If sapphires, lo, her eyes be sapphires plain;
If rubies, lo, her lips be rubies sound;
If pearls, her teeth be pearls, both pure and round;
If ivory, her forehead ivory ween;
If gold, her locks are finest gold on ground;
If silver, her fair hands are silver sheen:
　　But that which fairest is, but few behold,
　　Her mind adorned with virtues manifold.

SONNET XVI.

NE day as I unwarily did gaze
　　On those fair eyes, my love's immortal light;
　　The whiles my 'stonish'd heart stood in amaze,
　　Through sweet illusion of her look's delight;
I mote perceive how, in her glancing sight,
Legions of loves with little wings did fly;
Darting their deadly arrows, fiery bright,
At every rash beholder passing by.
One of those archers closely I did spy,
Aiming his arrow at my very heart:
When suddenly, with twinkle of her eye,
The Damsel broke his misintended dart.
　　Had she not so done, sure I had been slain;
　　Yet as it was, I hardly scap'd with pain.

SONNET XVII.

HE glorious portrait of that Angel's face,
  Made to amaze weak men's confused skill,
  And this world's worthless glory to embase,
  What pen, what pencil, can express her fill?
For, though he colours could devise at will,
And eke his learned hand at pleasure guide,
Lest, trembling, it his workmanship should spill;
Yet many wondrous things there are beside:
The sweet eye-glances, that like arrows glide;
The charming smiles, that rob sense from the heart;
The lovely pleasance; and the lofty pride;
Cannot expressed be by any art.
 A greater craftsman's hand thereto doth need.
 That can express the life of things indeed.

SONNET XVIII.

HE rolling wheel that runneth often round,
  The hardest steel, in tract of time doth tear:
  And drizzling drops, that often do redound,
  The firmest flint doth in continuance wear:
Yet cannot I, with many a dropping tear
And long entreaty, soften her hard heart;
That she will once vouchsafe my plaint to hear,
Or look with pity on my painful smart;
But, when I plead, she bids me play my part;
And, when I weep, she says, "Tears are but water,"
And, when I sigh, she says, "I know the art";
And, when I wail, she turns her self to laughter.
 So do I weep, and wail, and plead in vain,
 Whiles she as steel and flint doth still remain.

II.   P   9

SONNET XIX.

HE merry cuckoo, messenger of spring,
His trumpet shrill hath thrice already sounded,
That warns all lovers wait upon their king,
Who now is coming forth with garland crowned.
With noise whereof the choir of birds resounded,
Their anthems sweet, devised of love's praise,
That all the woods their echoes back rebounded,
As if they knew the meaning of their lays.
But 'mongst them all, which did love's honour raise,
No word was heard of her that most it ought;
But she his precept proudly disobeys,
And doth his idle message set at naught.
  Therefore, O love, unless she turn to thee
  Ere cuckoo end, let her a rebel be!

SONNET XX.

N vain I seek and sue to her for grace,
And do mine humbled heart before her pour;
The whiles her foot she in my neck doth place,
And tread my life down in the lowly flower.
And yet the lion that is lord of power,
And reigneth over every beast in field,
In his most pride disdaineth to devour
The silly lamb that to his might doth yield.
But she, more cruel, and more savage wild,
Than either lion or the lioness,
Shames not to be with guiltless blood defiled,
But taketh glory in her cruelness.
  Fairer than fairest! let none ever say,
  That ye were blooded in a yielded prey.

SONNET XXI.

As it the work of nature or of art,
 Which tempered so the feature of her face,
 That pride and meekness, mixed by equal
 part,
Do both appear t'adorn her beauty's grace?
For with mild pleasance, which doth pride displace,
She to her love doth lookers' eyes allure;
And, with stern countenance, back again doth chase
Their looser looks that stir up lusts impure;
With such strange terms her eyes she doth inure,
That, with one look, she doth my life dismay;
And with another doth it straight recure;
Her smile me draws; her frown me drives away.
  Thus doth she train and teach me with her looks;
  Such art of eyes I never read in books!

SONNET XXII.

His holy season, fit to fast and pray,
 Men to devotion ought to be inclined:
 Therefore, I likewise, on so holy day,
 For my sweet saint some service fit will find.
Her temple fair is built within my mind,
In which her glorious image placed is,
On which my thoughts do day and night attend,
Like sacred priests that never think amiss!
There I to her, as th' author of my bliss,
Will build an altar to appease her ire;
And on the same my heart will sacrifice,
Burning in flames of pure and chaste desire:
  The which vouchsafe, O goddess, to accept,
  Amongst thy dearest relics to be kept.

SONNET XXIII.

ENELOPE, for her Ulysses' sake,
 Devis'd a web her wooers to deceive ;
 In which the work that she all day did make,
 The same at night she did again unreave :
Such subtle craft my damsel doth conceive,
Th' importune suit of my desire to shun :
For all that I in many days do weave,
In one short hour I find by her undone.
So, when I think to end that I begun,
I must begin and never bring to end :
For with one look she spills that long I spun ;
And with one word my whole year's work doth rend.
 Such labour like the spider's web I find,
 Whose fruitless work is broken with least wind.

SONNET XXIV.

HEN I behold that beauty's wonderment,
 And rare perfection of each goodly part ;
 Of nature's skill the only complement ;
 I honour and admire the Maker's art.
But when I feel the bitter, baleful smart,
Which her fair eyes unwares do work in me,
That death out of their shiny beams do dart ;
I think that I a new Pandora see,
Whom all the Gods in council did agree
Into this sinful world from heaven to send ;
That she to wicked men a scourge should be,
For all their faults with which they did offend.
 But, since ye are my scourge, I will entreat,
 That for my faults ye will me gently beat.

SONNET XXV.

Ow long shall this like dying life endure,
    And know no end of her own misery,
    But waste and wear away in terms unsure,
    'Twixt fear and hope depending doubtfully ?
Yet better were at once to let me die,
And shew the last ensample of your pride ;
Than to torment me thus with cruelty,
To prove your power, which I too well have tried.
But yet if in your hardened breast ye hide
A close intent at last to shew me grace ;
Then all the woes and wrecks which I abide,
As means of bliss I gladly will embrace ;
    And wish that more and greater they might be,
    That greater meed at last may turn to me.

SONNET XXVI.

WEET is the rose, but grows upon a briar ;
    Sweet is the juniper, but sharp his bough ;
    Sweet is the eglantine, but pricketh near ;
    Sweet is the fir-bloom, but his branch is
        rough ;
Sweet is the cypress, but his rind is tough ;
Sweet is the nut, but bitter is his pill ;
Sweet is the broom-flower, but yet sour enough ;
And sweet is moly, but his root is ill.
So every sweet with sour is tempered still,
That maketh it be coveted the more :
For easy things, that may be got at will,
Most sorts of men do set but little store.
    Why then should I account of little pain,
    That endless pleasure shall unto me gain !

SONNET XXVII.

AIR Proud! now tell me, why should fair be
    proud,
    Sith all world's glory is but dross unclean,
    And in the shade of death itself shall shroud,
However now thereof ye little ween!
That goodly idol, now so gay beseen,
Shall doff her flesh's borrow'd fair attire,
And be forgot as it had never been,
That many now much worship and admire!
Ne any then shall after it inquire,
Ne any mention shall thereof remain,
But what this verse, that never shall expire,
Shall to your purchase with her thankless pain!
    Fair! be no longer proud of that shall perish;
    But that, which shall you make immortal, cherish.

SONNET XXVIII.

HE laurel-leaf, which you this day do wear,
    Gives me great hope of your relenting mind:
    For since it is the badge which I do bear,
    Ye, bearing it, do seem to me inclin'd:
The power thereof, which oft in me I find,
Let it likewise your gentle breast inspire
With sweet infusion, and put you in mind
Of that proud maid, whom now those leaves attire,—
Proud Daphne, scorning Phœbus' lovely fire,
On the Thessalian shore from him did fly:
For which the gods, in their revengeful ire,
Did her transform into a laurel-tree.
    Then fly no more, fair Love, from Phœbus' chase,
    But in your breast his leaf and love embrace.

SONNET XXIX.

EE! how the stubborn damsel doth deprave
My simple meaning with disdainful scorn;
And by the bay, which I unto her gave,
Accounts myself her captive quite forlorn.
The bay (quoth she) is of the victors born,
Yielded them by the vanquish'd as their meeds,
And they therewith do poets' heads adorn,
To sing the glory of their famous deeds.
But sith she will the conquest challenge needs,
Let her accept me as her faithful thrall;
That her great triumph, which my skill exceeds,
I may in trump of fame blaze over all.
   Then would I deck her head with glorious bays,
   And fill the world with her victorious praise.

SONNET XXX.

Y LOVE is like to ice, and I to fire;
How comes it then that this her cold so great
Is not dissolv'd through my so hot desire,
But harder grows the more I her entreat?
Or how comes it that my exceeding heat
Is not delay'd by her heart-frozen cold;
But that I burn much more in boiling sweat,
And feel my flames augmented manifold!
What more miraculous thing may be told,
That fire, which all things melts, should harden ice;
And ice, which is congeal'd with senseless cold,
Should kindle fire by wonderful device!
   Such is the power of love in gentle mind,
   That it can alter all the course of kind.

SONNET XXXI.

AH! why hath nature to so hard a heart
Given so goodly gifts of beauty's grace!
Whose pride depraves each other better part,
And all those precious ornaments deface.
Sith to all other beasts of bloody race
A dreadful countenance she given hath;
That with their terror all the rest may chase,
And warn to shun the danger of their wrath.
But my proud one doth work the greater scathe,
Through sweet allurement of her lovely hue;
That she the better may in bloody bath
Of such poor thralls her cruel hands embrue.
  But, did she know how ill these two accord,
  Such cruelty she would have soon abhor'd.

SONNET XXXII.

THE painful smith, with force of fervent heat,
The hardest iron soon doth mollify;
That with his heavy sledge he can it beat,
And fashion to what he it list apply.
Yet cannot all these flames, in which I fry,
Her heart more hard than iron soft a whit;
Ne all the plaints and prayers, with which I
Do beat on th' anvil of her stubborn wit
But still, the more she fervent sees my fit,
The more she freezeth in her wilful pride;
And harder grows, the harder she is smit
With all the plaints which to her be applied.
  What then remains but I to ashes burn,
  And she to stones at length all frozen turn!

SONNET XXXIII.

REAT wrong I do, I can it not deny,
    To that most sacred Empress, my dear dread,
    Not finishing her Queen of Faery,
    That mote enlarge her living praises, dead.
But Lodwick, this of grace to me aread ;
Do ye not think th' accomplishment of it
Sufficient work for one man's simple head,
All were it, as the rest, but rudely writ ?
How then should I, without another wit,
Think ever to endure so tedious toil !
Sith that this one is toss'd with troublous fit
Of a proud love, that doth my spirit spoil.
    Cease then, till she vouchsafe to grant me rest ;
    Or lend you me another living breast.

SONNET XXXIV.

IKE as a ship, that through the ocean wide,
    By conduct of some star, doth make her way;
    When as a storm hath dim'd her trusty guide
    Out of her course doth wander far astray !
So I, whose star, that wont with her bright ray
Me to direct, with clouds is over-cast,
Do wander now, in darkness and dismay,
Through hidden perils round about me placed ;
Yet hope I well that, when this storm is past,
My Helice, the loadstar of my life,
Will shine again, and look on me at last,
With lovely light to clear my cloudy grief,
    Till then I wander careful, comfortless,
    In secret sorrow, and sad pensiveness.

SONNET XXXV.

Y HUNGRY eyes, through greedy covetise
　　Still to behold the object of their pain,
　　With no contentment can themselves suffice ;
　　But, having, pine ; and, having not, complain.
For, lacking it, they cannot life sustain ;
And, having it, they gaze on it the more ;
In their amazement like Narcissus vain,
Whose eyes him starv'd : so plenty makes me poor.
Yet are mine eyes so filled with the store
Of that fair sight, that nothing else they brook,
But loathe the things which they did like before,
And can no more endure on them to look.
　　All this world's glory seemeth vain to me,
　　And all their shows but shadows, saving she.

SONNET XXXVI.

ELL me, when shall these weary woes have end,
　　Or shall their ruthless torment never cease ;
　　But all my days in pining languor spend,
　　Without hope of assuagement or release ?
Is there no means for me to purchase peace,
Or make agreement with her thrilling eyes ;
But that their cruelty doth still increase,
And daily more augment my miseries ?
But, when ye have shown all extremities,
Then think how little glory ye have gained
By slaying him, whose life, though ye despise,
Might have your life in honour long maintained.
　　But by his death, which some perhaps will moan,
　　Ye shall condemned be of many a one.

SONNET XXXVII.

W HAT guile is this, that those her golden tresses
    She doth attire under a net of gold ;
    And with sly skill so cunningly them dresses,
    That which is gold, or hair, may scarce be told ?
Is it that men's frail eyes, which gaze too bold,
She may entangle in that golden snare ;
And, being caught, may craftily enfold
Their weaker hearts, which are not well aware ?
Take heed, therefore, mine eyes, how ye do stare
Henceforth too rashly on that guileful net,
In which, if ever ye entrapped are,
Out of her bands ye by no means shall get.
    Fondness it were for any, being free,
    To covet fetters, though they golden be !

SONNET XXXVIII.

A RION, when, through tempest's cruel wrack,
    He forth was thrown into the greedy seas ;
    Through the sweet music, which his harp did
        make,
Allur'd a dolphin him from death to ease.
But my rude music, which was wont to please
Some dainty ears, cannot, with any skill,
The dreadful tempest of her wrath appease,
Nor move the dolphin from her stubborn will,
But in her pride she doth perséver still,
All careless how my life for her decays :
Yet with one word she can it save or spill.
To spill were pity, but to save were praise !
    Choose rather to be praised for doing good,
    Than to be blam'd for spilling guiltless blood.

SONNET XXXIX.

WEET smile! the daughter of the Queen of Love,
    Expressing all thy mother's powerful art.
    With which she wonts to temper angry Jove,
    When all the gods he threats with thundering
        dart :
Sweet is thy virtue, as thy self sweet art.
For, when on me thou shined'st late in sadness,
A melting pleasance ran through every part,
And me revived with heart-robbing gladness,
Whilst rapt with joy resembling heavenly madness,
My soul was ravish'd quite as in a trance ;
And, feeling thence, no more her sorrow's sadness,
Fed on the fulness of that cheerful glance,
    More sweet than nectar, or ambrosial meat,
    Seem'd every bit which thenceforth I did eat.

SONNET XL.

ARK when she smiles with amiable cheer,
    And tell me whereto can ye liken it ;
    When on each eyelid sweetly do appear
    An hundred graces as in shade to sit.
Likest it seemeth, in my simple wit,
Unto the fair sunshine in summer's day ;
That, when a dreadful storm away is flit,
Through the broad world doth spread his goodly ray ;
At sight whereof, each bird that sits on spray,
And every beast that to his den was fled,
Comes forth afresh out of their late dismay,
And to the light lift up their drooping head.
    So my storm-beaten heart likewise is cheered
    With that sunshine, when cloudy looks are cleared.

SONNET XLI.

S IT her nature, or is it her will,
    To be so cruel to an humbled foe?
    If nature; then she may it mend with skill:
    If will; then she at will may will forego.
But if her nature and her will be so,
That she will plague the man that loves her most,
And take delight t' increase a wretch's woe;
Then all her nature's goodly gifts are lost:
And that same glorious beauty's idle boast
Is but a bait such wretches to beguile,
As, being long in her love's tempest toss'd,
She means at last to make her piteous spoil.
    O fairest fair! let never it be named,
    That so fair beauty was so foully shamed.

SONNET XLII.

HE love which me so cruelly tormenteth,
    So pleasing is in my extremest pain,
    That, all the more my sorrow it augmenteth,
    The more I love and do embrace my bane.
Ne do I wish (for wishing were but vain)
To be acquit fro my continual smart;
But joy, her thrall for ever to remain,
And yield for pledge my poor captivéd heart;
The which, that it from her may never start,
Let her, if please her, bind with adamant chain:
And from all wandering loves, which mote pervert
His safe assurance, strongly it restrain.
    Only let her abstain from cruelty,
    And do me not before my time to die.

SONNET XLIII.

HALL I then silent be, or shall I speak?
 And, if I speak, her wrath renew I shall;
 And, if I silent be, my heart will break,
 Or choked be with overflowing gall.
What tyranny is this, both my heart to thrall,
And eke my tongue with proud restraint to tie;
That neither I may speak nor think at all,
But like a stupid stock in silence die!
Yet I my heart with silence secretly
Will teach to speak, and my just cause to plead;
And eke mine eyes, with meek humility,
Love-learned letters to her eyes to read;
 Which her deep wit, that true heart's thought can spell,
 Will soon conceive, and learn to construe well.

SONNET XLIV.

HEN those renowned noble Peers of Greece,
 Through stubborn pride, amongst themselves
  did jar,
 Forgetful of the famous golden fleece;
Then Orpheus with his harp their strife did bar.
But this continual, cruel, civil war,
The which my self against my self do make;
Whilst my weak powers of passions warréd are;
No skill can stint, nor reason can aslake.
But, when in hand my tuneless harp I take,
Then do I more augment my foes' despite;
And grief renew, and passions do awake
To battle, fresh against my self to fight.
 'Mongst whom the more I seek to settle peace,
 The more I find their malice to increase.

SONNET XLV.

EAVE, lady! in your glass of crystal clean,
    Your goodly self for evermore to view:
    And in my self, my inward self, I mean,
    Most lively like behold your semblance true.
Within my heart, though hardly it can shew
Thing so divine to view of earthly eye,
The fair Idea of your celestial hue
And every part remains immortally:
And were it not that, through your cruelty,
With sorrow dimmed and deformed it were,
The goodly image of your visnomy,
Clearer than crystal, would therein appear.
    But, if yourself in me ye plain will see,
    Remove the cause by which your fair beams darkened be.

SONNET XLVI.

HEN my abode's prefixed time is spent,
    My cruel fair straight bids me wend my way:
    But then from heaven most hideous storms are
        sent,
As willing me against her will to stay.
Whom then shall I, or heaven or her, obey?
The heavens know best what is the best for me:
But as she will, whose will my life doth sway,
My lower heaven, so it perforce must be.
But ye high heavens, that all this sorrow see,
Sith all your tempests cannot hold me back,
Assuage your storms, or else both you, and she,
Will both together me too sorely wrack.
    Enough it is for one man to sustain
    The storms, which she alone on me doth rain.

SONNET XLVII.

RUST not the treason of those smiling looks,
  Until ye have their guileful trains well tried:
For they are like but unto golden hooks,
  That from the foolish fish their baits do hide:
So she with flattering smiles weak hearts doth guide
Unto her love, and tempt to their decay;
Whom, being caught, she kills with cruel pride,
And feeds at pleasure on the wretched prey:
Yet, even whilst her bloody hands them slay,
Her eyes look lovely, and upon them smile;
That they take pleasure in her cruel play,
And, dying, do themselves of pain beguile.
  O mighty charm! which makes men love their bane,
  And think they die with pleasure, live with pain.

SONNET XLVIII.

NNOCENT paper; whom too cruel hand
  Did make the matter to avenge her ire:
  And, ere she could thy cause well understand,
  Did sacrifice unto the greedy fire.
Well worthy thou to have found better hire,
Than so bad end for heretics ordained;
Yet heresy nor treason didst conspire,
But plead thy master's cause, unjustly pained.
Whom she, all careless of his grief, constrained
To utter forth the anguish of his heart:
And would not hear, when he to her complained
The piteous passion of his dying smart.
  Yet live for ever, though against her will,
  And speak her good, though she requite it ill.

SONNET XLIX.

AIR cruel! why are ye so fierce and cruel?
  Is it because your eyes have power to kill?
  Then know that mercy is the Mighty's jewel:
  And greater glory think, to save than spill.
But if it be your pleasure, and proud will,
To shew the power of your imperious eyes;
Then not on him that never thought you ill,
But bend your force against your enemies:
Let them feel th' utmost of your cruelties;
And kill with looks, as cockatrices do:
But him, that at your footstool humbled lies,
With merciful regard give mercy to.
  Such mercy shall you make admir'd to be;
  So shall you live, by giving life to me.

SONNET L.

ONG languishing in double malady
  Of my heart's wound, and of my body's grief;
  There came to me a leech, that would apply
  Fit medicines for my body's best relief.
Vain man, quoth I, that hast but little prief
In deep discovery of the mind's disease;
Is not the heart of all the body chief,
And rules the members as itself doth please?
Then, with some cordials, seek first to appease
The inward languor of my wounded heart,
And then my body shall have shortly ease:
But such sweet cordials pass physician's art.
  Then, my life's leech! do your skill reveal;
  And, with one salve, both heart and body heal.

II.   Q   9

SONNET LI.

O I not see that fairest images
    Of hardest marble are of purpose made,
    For that they should endure through many
        ages,
Ne let their famous monuments to fade?
Why then do I, untrained in lover's trade,
Her hardness blame, which I should more commend?
Sith never aught was excellent assayed
Which was not hard t' achieve and bring to end.
Ne aught so hard, but he, that would attend,
Mote soften it and to his will allure:
So do I hope her stubborn heart to bend,
And that it then more steadfast will endure:
    Only my pains will be the more to get her;
    But, having her, my joy will be the greater.

SONNET LII.

O OFT as homeward I from her depart,
    I go like one that, having lost the field,
    Is prisoner led away with heavy heart,
    Despoiled of warlike arms and knowen shield.
So do I now myself a prisoner yield
To sorrow and to solitary pain;
From presence of my dearest dear exiled,
Long-while alone in languor to remain.
There let no thought of joy, or pleasure vain,
Dare to approach, that may my solace breed;
But sudden dumps, and dreary sad disdain
Of all world's gladness, more my torment feed.
    So I her absence will my penance make,
    That of her presence I my meed may take.

SONNET LIII.

HE Panther, knowing that his spotted hide
    Doth please all beasts, but that his looks them
       fray ;
    Within a bush his dreadful head doth hide,
To let them gaze, whilst he on them may prey :
Right so my cruel fair with me doth play ;
For, with the goodly semblance of her hue,
She doth allure me to mine own decay,
And then no mercy will unto me shew.
Great shame it is, thing so divine in view,
Made for to be the world's most ornament,
To make the bait her gazers to embrue :
Good shames to be to ill an instrument !
    But mercy doth with beauty best agree,
    As in their Maker ye them best may see.

SONNET LIV.

F THIS world's theatre in which we stay,
    My love like the spectator, idly sits ;
    Beholding me, that all the pageants play,
    Disguising diversely my troubled wits.
Sometimes I joy when glad occasion fits,
And mask in mirth like to a comedy :
Soon after, when my joy to sorrow flits,
I wail, and make my woes a tragedy.
Yet she, beholding me with constant eye,
Delights not in my mirth, nor rues my smart :
But, when I laugh, she mocks ; and, when I cry,
She laughs, and hardens evermore her heart.
    What then can move her ? if nor mirth nor moan,
    She is no woman, but a senseless stone.

SONNET LV.

O OFT as I her beauty do behold,
And therewith do her cruelty compare,
I marvel of what substance was the mould,
The which her made at once so cruel fair.
Not earth ; for her high thoughts more heavenly are :
Not water ; for her love doth burn like fire :
Not air ; for she is not so light or rare :
Not fire ; for she doth freeze with faint desire.
Then needs another element inquire
Whereof she mote be made, that is, the sky.
For to the heaven her haughty looks aspire :
And eke her mind is pure immortal high.
    Then, sith to heaven ye likened are the best,
    Be like in mercy as in all the rest.

SONNET LVI.

AIR ye be sure, but cruel and unkind,
As is a tiger, that with greediness
Hunts after blood ; when he by chance doth
    find
A feeble beast, doth felly him oppress.
Fair be ye sure, but proud and pitiless,
As is a storm, that all things doth prostrate ;
Finding a tree alone all comfortless,
Beats on it strongly, it to ruinate.
Fair be ye sure, but hard and obstinate,
As is a rock amidst the raging floods ;
'Gainst which, a ship, of succour desolate,
Doth suffer wreck both of herself and goods.
    That ship, that tree, and that same beast, am I.
    Whom ye do wreck, do ruin, and destroy.

SONNET LVII.

WEET warrior! when shall I have peace with you
High time it is this war now ended were
Which I no longer can endure to sue,
Ne your incessant batt'ry more to bear:
So weak my powers, so sore my wounds, appear,
That wonder is how I should live a jot,
Seeing my heart through-lanced everywhere
With thousand arrows, which your eyes have shot:
Yet shoot ye sharply still, and spare me not,
But glory think to make these cruel stours,
Ye cruel one! what glory can be got,
In slaying him that would live gladly yours!
  Make peace therefore, and grant me timely grace,
  That all my wounds will heal in little space.

SONNET LVIII.

By her that is most assured to her self.

EAK is th' assurance that weak flesh reposeth
In her own power, and scorneth other's aid;
That soonest falls, when as she most supposeth
Herself assured, and is of naught afraid.
All flesh is frail, and all her strength unstayed,
Like a vain bubble blowen up with air;
Devouring time and changeful chance have prey'd
Her glory's pride that none may it repair.
Ne none so rich or wise, so strong or fair,
But faileth, trusting on his own assurance;
And he, that standeth on the highest stair,
Falls lowest; for on earth naught hath endurance.
  Why then do ye, proud fair, misdeem so far,
  That to yourself ye most assured are!

SONNET LIX.

HRICE happy she! that is so well assured
Unto herself, and settled so in heart,
That neither will for better be allured,
Ne feared with worse to any chance to start;
But, like a steady ship, doth strongly part
The raging waves, and keeps her course aright;
Ne aught for tempest doth from it depart,
Ne aught for fairer weather's false delight.
Such self-assurance need not fear the spite
Of grudging foes, ne favour seek of friends:
But, in the stay of her own steadfast might,
Neither to one herself nor other bends.
   Most happy she, that most assur'd doth rest;
   But he most happy, who such one loves best.

SONNET LX.

HEY, that in course of heavenly spheres are
   skilled,
   To every planet point his sundry year:
   In which her circle's voyage is fulfilled,
As Mars in threescore years doth run his sphere.
So, since the winged god his planet clear
Began in me to move, one year is spent:
The which doth longer unto me appear,
Than all those forty which my life out-went.
Then by that count, which lovers' books invent,
The sphere of Cupid forty years contains,
Which I have wasted in long languishment,
That seemed the longer for my greater pains.
   But let my love's fair Planet short her ways,
   This year ensuing, or else short my days.

SONNET LXI.

HE glorious image of the Maker's beauty,
  My sovereign saint, the idol of my thought,
  Dare not henceforth, above the bounds of duty,
  T' accuse of pride, or rashly blame for aught.
For being, as she is, divinely wrought,
And of the brood of Angels heavenly born;
And with the crew of blessed Saints upbrought,
Each of which did her with their gifts adorn;
The bud of joy, the blossom of the morn,
The beam of light, whom mortal eyes admire;
What reason is it then but she should scorn
Base things, that to her love too bold aspire?
  Such heavenly forms ought rather worshipped be,
  Than dare be lov'd by men of mean degree.

SONNET LXII.

HE weary year his race now having run,
  The new begins his compass'd course anew:
  With show of morning mild he hath begun,
  Betokening peace and plenty to ensue.
So let us, with this change of weather view,
Change eke our minds, and former lives amend:
The old year's sins forepast let us eschew,
And fly the faults with which we did offend.
Then shall the new year's joy forth freshly send,
Into the glooming world, his gladsome ray:
And all these storms, which now his beauty blend,
Shall turn to calms, and timely clear away.
  So, likewise, Love! cheer you your heavy spright,
  And change old year's annoy to new delight.

SONNET LXIII.

FTER long storms and tempests' sad assay,
  Which hardly I endured heretofore,
  In dread of death, and dangerous dismay,
  With which my silly bark was tossed sore:
I do at length descry the happy shore,
In which I hope ere long for to arrive:
Fair soil it seems from far, and fraught with store
Of all that dear and dainty is alive.
Most happy he! that can at last achieve
The joyous safety of so sweet a rest;
Whose least delight sufficeth to deprive
Remembrance of all pains which him oppressed.
  All pains are nothing in respect of this;
  All sorrows short that gain eternal bliss.

SONNET LXIV.

OMING to kiss her lips (such grace I found,)
  Me seemed, I smelt a garden of sweet flowers,
  That dainty odours from them threw around,
  For damsels fit to deck their lovers' bowers.
Her lips did smell like unto gillyflowers;
Her ruddy cheeks, like unto roses red;
Her snowy brows, like budded bellamoures;
Her lovely eyes, like pinks but newly spread;
Her goodly bosom, like a strawberry bed;
Her neck, like to a bunch of Columbines;
Her breast, like lilies, ere their leaves be shed;
Her nipples, like young blossomed jessamines:
  Such flagrant flowers do give most odorous smell;
  But her sweet odour did them all excel.

SONNET LXV.

HE doubt which ye misdeem, fair love, is vain,
     That fondly fear to lose your liberty;
     When, losing one, two liberties ye gain,
     And make him bond that bondage erst did fly.
Sweet be the bands, the which true love doth tie
Without constraint, or dread of any il l
The gentle bird feels no captivity
Within her cage; but sings, and feeds her fill.
There pride dare not approach, nor discord spill
The league 'twixt them, that loyal love hath bound:
But simple truth, and mutual good-will,
Seeks with sweet peace, to salve each other's wound:
     There faith doth fearless dwell in brazen tower,
     And spotless pleasure builds her sacred bower.

SONNET LXVI.

O ALL those happy blessings, which ye have
     With plenteous hand by heaven upon you
         thrown;
     This one disparagement they to you gave,
That ye your love lent to so mean a one.
Ye, whose high worth's surpassing paragon
Could not on earth have found one fit for mate,
Ne but in heaven matchable to none,
Why did ye stoop unto so lowly state?
But ye thereby much greater glory gat,
Than had ye sorted with a prince's peer:
For, now your light doth more itself dilate,
And, in my darkness, greater doth appear.
     Yet, since your light hath once illumined me,
     With my reflex yours shall increased be.

SONNET LXVII.

IKE as a huntsman after weary chase,
 Seeing the game from him escap'd away,
 Sits down to rest him in some shady place,
 With panting hounds beguiled of their prey:
So, after long pursuit and vain assay,
When I all weary had the chase forsook,
The gentle deer returned the self-same way,
Thinking to quench her thirst at the next brook:
There she, beholding me with milder look,
Sought not to fly, but fearless still did bide;
Till I in hand her yet half trembling took,
And with her own goodwill her firmly tied.
 Strange thing, me seemed, to see a beast so wild,
 So goodly won, with her own will beguil'd.

SONNET LXVIII.

OST glorious Lord of life! that, on this day,
 Did'st make thy triumph over death and sin;
 And, having harrow'd hell, did'st bring away
 Captivity thence captive, us to win:
This joyous day, dear Lord, with joy begin;
And grant that we, for whom thou diddest die,
Being with thy dear blood clean wash'd from sin,
May live for ever in felicity!
And that thy love we weighing worthily,
May likewise love thee for the same again;
And for thy sake, that all like deer did'st buy,
With love may one another entertain!
 So let us love, dear love, like as we ought:
 Love is the lesson which the Lord us taught.

SONNET LXIX.

HE famous warriors of antique world
    Used trophies to erect in stately wise;
    In which they would the records have enroll'd
    Of their great deeds and valorous emprize.
What trophy then shall I most fit devise,
In which I may record the memory
Of my love's conquest, peerless beauty's prize,
Adorn'd with honour, love, and chastity!
Even this verse, vow'd to eternity,
Shall be thereof immortal monument;
And tell her praise to all posterity,
That may admire such world's rare wonderment;
    The happy purchase of my glorious spoil,
    Gotten at last with labour and long toil.

SONNET LXX.

RESH Spring, the herald of love's mighty king,
    In whose coat-armour richly are displayed
    All sorts of flowers, the which on earth do spring,
    In goodly colours gloriously arrayed;
Go to my love, where she is careless laid,
Yet in her winter's bower not well awake;
Tell her the joyous time will not be stayed,
Unless she do him by the forelock take;
Bid her therefore herself soon ready make,
To wait on Love amongst his lovely crew;
Where every one, that misseth then her make,
Shall be by him amerced with penance due.
    Make haste, therefore, sweet love, whilst it is prime;
    For none can call again the passed time.

SONNET LXXI.

JOY to see how, in your drawen work,
   Yourself unto the bee ye do compare;
   And me unto the spider, that doth lurk
   In close await, to catch her unaware:
Right so yourself were caught in cunning snare
Of a dear foe, and thralled to his love;
In whose straight bands ye now captivéd are
So firmly, that ye never may remove.
But as your work is woven all above
With woodbine flowers and fragrant eglantine;
So sweet your prison you in time shall prove,
With many dear delights bedecked fine.
   And all thenceforth eternal peace shall see
   Between the spider and the gentle bee.

SONNET LXXII.

FT, when my spirit doth spread her bolder wings,
   In mind to mount up to the purest sky;
   It down is weighed with thought of earthly
      things,
And clogged with burden of mortality;
Where, when that sovereign beauty it doth spy,
Resembling heaven's glory in her light,
Drawn with sweet pleasure's bait, it back doth fly,
And unto heaven forgets her former flight.
There my frail fancy, fed with full delight,
Doth bathe in bliss, and mantleth most at ease;
Ne thinks of other heaven, but how it might
Her heart's desire with most contentment please.
   Heart need not wish none other happiness,
   But here on earth to have such heaven's bliss.

SONNET LXXIII.

EING myself captivéd here in care,
    My heart, whom none with servile bands can tie,
    But the fair tresses of your golden hair,
    Breaking his prison, forth to you doth fly.
Like as a bird, that in one's hand doth spy
Desired food, to it doth make his flight:
Even so my heart, that wont on your fair eye
To feed his fill, flies back unto your sight.
Do you him take, and in your bosom bright
Gently encage, that he may be your thrall:
Perhaps he there may learn, with rare delight,
To sing your name and praises over all:
    That it hereafter may you not repent,
    Him lodging in your bosom to have lent.

SONNET LXXIV.

OST happy letters! fram'd by skilful trade,
    With which that happy name was first design'd,
    The which three times thrice happy hath me
        made,
With gifts of body, fortune, and of mind.
The first my being to me gave by kind,
From mother's womb deriv'd by due descent:
The second is my sovereign Queen most kind
That honour and large riches to me lent:
The third, my love, my life's last ornament,
By whom my spirit out of dust was raised:
To speak her praise and glory excellent,
Of all alive most worthy to be praised.
    Ye three Elizabeths! for ever live,
    That three such graces did unto me give.

SONNET LXXV.

NE day I wrote her name upon the strand;
 But came the waves, and washed it away:
 Again, I wrote it with a second hand;
 But came the tide, and made my pains his prey.
Vain man, said she, that dost in vain assay
A mortal thing so to immortalize;
For I myself shall like to this decay,
And eke my name be wiped out likewise.
Not so, quoth I, let baser things devise
To die in dust, but you shall live by fame:
My verse your virtues rare shall eternize,
And in the heavens write your glorious name.
 Where, when as death shall all the world subaue,
 Our love shall live, and later life renew.

SONNET LXXVI.

AIR bosom! fraught with virtue's richest treasure
 The nest of love, the lodging of delight,
 The bower of bliss, the paradise of pleasure,
 The sacred harbour of that heavenly spright;
How was I ravish'd with your lovely sight,
And my frail thoughts too rashly led astray!
Whiles diving deep through amorous insight,
On the sweet spoil of beauty they did prey;
And twixt her paps (like early fruit in May,
Whose harvest seemed to hasten now apace),
They loosely did their wanton wings display,
And there to rest themselves did boldly place.
 Sweet thoughts! I envy your so happy rest,
 Which oft I wish'd, yet never was so blest.

SONNET LXXVII.

As it a dream, or did I see it plain;
 A goodly table of pure ivory,
 All spread with junkets, fit to entertain
 The greatest Prince with pompous royalty:
'Mongst which, there in a silver dish did lie
Two golden apples of unvalued price;
Far passing those which Hercules came by,
Or those which Atalanta did entice;
Exceeding sweet, yet void of sinful vice;
That many sought, yet none could ever taste;
Sweet fruit of pleasure, brought from Paradise
By Love himself, and in his garden placed.
 Her breast that table was, so richly spread;
 My thoughts the guests, which would thereon have fed.

SONNET LXXVIII.

Acking my love, I go from place to place,
 Like a young fawn, that late hath lost the hind;
 And seek each where, where last I saw her face,
 Whose image yet I carry fresh in mind.
I seek the fields with her late footing signed;
I seek her bower with her late presence deck'd;
Yet nor in field nor bower I her can find;
Yet field and bower are full of her aspect:
But, when mine eyes I thereunto direct,
They idly back return to me again:
And, when I hope to see their true object,
I find myself but fed with fancies vain.
 Cease then, mine eyes, to seek herself to see;
 And let my thoughts behold herself in me.

SONNET LXXIX.

MEN call you fair, and you do credit it,
    For that yourself ye daily such do see:
    But the true fair, that is the gentle wit,
    And virtuous mind, is much more praised of me:
For all the rest, however fair it be,
Shall turn to naught and lose that glorious hue;
But only that is permanent and free
From frail corruption, that doth flesh ensue.
That is true beauty: that doth argue you
To be divine, and born of heavenly seed;—
Deriv'd from that fair Spirit, from whom all true
And perfect beauty did at first proceed:
    He only fair, and what He fair hath made;
    All other fair, like flowers, untimely fade.

SONNET LXXX.

AFTER so long a race as I have run
    Through Faery land, which those six books
        compile,
    Give leave to rest me being half foredone,
And gather to myself new breath awhile.
Then, as a steed refreshed after toil,
Out of my prison I will break anew;
And stoutly will that second work assoil,
With strong endeavour and attention due.
Till then give leave to me, in pleasant mew
To sport my muse, and sing my love's sweet praise;
The contemplation of whose heavenly hue,
My spirit to a higher pitch will raise:
    But let her praises yet be low and mean,
    Fit for the handmaid of the Faery Queen.

SONNET LXXXI.

AIR is my love, when her fair golden hairs
With the loose wind waving ye chance to mark;
Fair, when the rose in her red cheeks appears;
Or in her eyes the fire of love doth spark.
Fair, when her breast, like a rich laden bark,
With precious merchandise she forth doth lay;
Fair, when that cloud of pride, which oft doth dark
Her goodly light, with smiles she drives away.
But fairest she, when so she doth display
The gate with pearls and rubies richly dight;
Through which her words so wise do make their way
To bear the message of her gentle spright.
　The rest be work of nature's wonderment:
　But this the work of heart's astonishment.

SONNET LXXXII.

OY of my life! full oft for loving you
I bless my lot, that was so lucky placed:
But then the more your own mishap I rue,
That are so much by so mean love embased;
For, had the equal heavens so much you graced
In this as in the rest, ye mote invent
Some heavenly wit, whose verse could have enchased
Your glorious name in golden monument.
But since ye deigned so goodly to relent
To me your thrall, in whom is little worth;
That little, that I am, shall all be spent
In setting your immortal praises forth:
　Whose lofty argument, uplifting me,
　Shall lift you up unto an high degree.

II,　　　　　　　　　　R　　　　　　　　　　9

SONNET LXXXIII.

[In all early editions, this sonnet is numbered LXXXIV., and the succeeding poems are
numbered LXXXV. *et seq*.   But the sonnet originally headed LXXXIII. is a repetition of
the sonnet already printed as number XXXV.   That sonnet is not repeated here, and the
numbering is altered accordingly.]

LET not one spark of filthy lustful fire
    Break out, that may her sacred peace molest;
    Ne one light glance of sensual desire
    Attempt to work her gentle mind's unrest:
But pure affections breed in spotless breast,
And modest thoughts breath'd from well-tempered sprites,
Go visit her in her chaste bower of rest
Accompanied with angel-like delights.
There fill yourself with those most joyous sights,
The which myself could never yet attain:
But speak no word to her of these sad plights,
Which her too constant stiffness doth constrain.
    Only behold her rare perfection,
    And bless your fortune's fair election.

SONNET LXXXIV.

THE world that cannot deem of worthy things,
    When I do praise her, say I do but flatter:
    So does the cuckoo, when the mavis sings,
    Begin his witless note apace to clatter.
But they that skill not of so heavenly matter,
All that they know not envy or admire;
Rather than envy, let them wonder at her,
But not to deem of her desert aspire.
Deep, in the closet of my parts entire,
Her worth is written with a golden quill,
That me with heavenly fury doth inspire,
And my glad mouth with her sweet praises fill:
    Which when as Fame in her shrill trump shall thunder,
    Let the world choose to envy or to wonder.

SONNET LXXXV.

ENOMOUS tongue tipp'd with vile adders' sting,
    Of that self kind with which the Furies fell
    Their snaky heads do comb, from which a
        spring
Of poisoned words and spiteful speeches well ;
Let all the plagues, and horrid pains, of hell
Upon thee fall for thine accursed hire
That with false forged lies, which thou didst tell,
In my true love did stir up coals of ire,
The sparks whereof let kindle thine own fire,
And, catching hold on thine own wicked head,
Consume thee quite, that didst with guile conspire
In my sweet peace such breaches to have bred !
    Shame be thy meed, and mischief thy reward,
    Due to thy self, that it for me prepared !

SONNET LXXXVI.

INCE I did leave the presence of my love,
    Many long weary days I have outworn ;
    And many nights, that slowly seemed to move
    Their sad protract from evening until morn.
For, when as day the heaven doth adorn,
I wish that night the noyous day would end :
And, when as night hath us of light forlorn,
I wish that day would shortly reascend.
Thus I the time with expectation spend,
And fain my grief with changes to beguile,
That further seems his term still to extend,
And maketh every minute seem a mile.
    So sorrow still doth seem too long to last ;
    But joyous hours do fly away too fast.

SONNET LXXXVII.

INCE I have lack'd the comfort of that light,
    The which was wont to lead my thoughts astray;
    I wander as in darkness of the night,
    Afraid of every danger's least dismay.
Ne aught I see, though in the clearest day,
When others gaze upon their shadows vain,
But th' only image of that heavenly ray,
Whereof some glance doth in mine eye remain.
Of which beholding the Idæa plain,
Through contemplation of my purest part,
With light thereof I do myself sustain,
And thereon feed my love-affamish'd heart:
    But, with such brightness whilst I fill my mind,
    I starve my body, and mine eyes do blind.

SONNET LXXXVIII.

IKE as the Culver, on the bared bough,
    Sits mourning for the absence of her mate;
    And, in her songs, sends many a wishful vow
    For his return that seems to linger late:
So I alone, now left disconsolate,
Mourn to myself the absence of my love;
And, wandering here and there all desolate,
Seek with my plaints to match that mournful dove.
Ne joy of aught that under heaven doth hove
Can comfort me, but her own joyous sight:
Whose sweet aspect both God and man can move,
In her unspotted pleasance to delight.
    Dark is my day, while her fair light I miss,
    And dead my life that wants such lively bliss.

Fidessa, more
chaste than
kind.

By B. GRIFFIN, Gent.

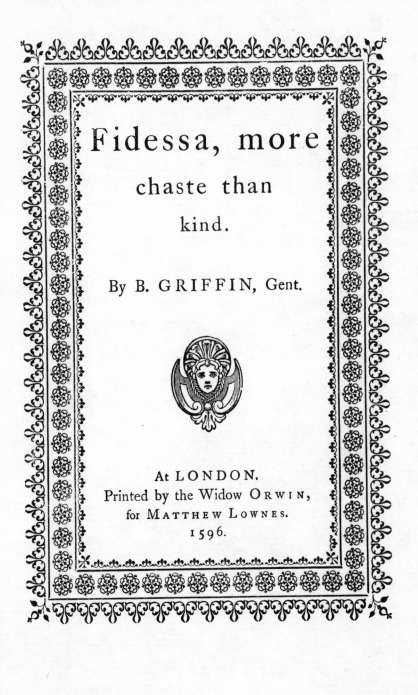

At LONDON.
Printed by the Widow ORWIN,
for MATTHEW LOWNES.
1596.

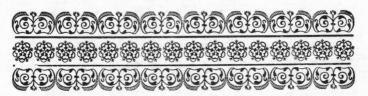

To the most kind and virtuous Gentleman, Master WILLIAM ESSEX of Lamebourne, in the County of Berk[shire], Esquire.

SIR,

IT MAY seem strange that I should be thus far bold to make choice of yourself, a Patron of so slender a work ; especially being so little known unto you as I am : but, howsoever, I protest what is done, proceeded from the unfeigned love I bear unto you, your own demerit, your friends' hope, and the good report of all men. All which are lively witnesses of your love to the Muses, your grace with Fortune, and your fame with the World ; quickened in your birth, increased in your travails, and living after death.

Deign, sweet Sir, to pardon the matter ! judge favourably of the manner ! and accept both ! So shall I ever rest yours,

In all dutiful affection,

Yours ever,

B. GRIFFIN.

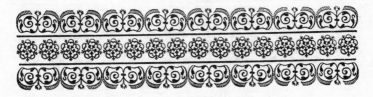

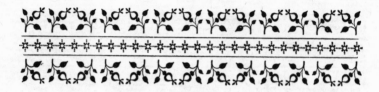

To the Gentlemen of the Inns of Court.

COURTEOUS GENTLEMEN.

*I*T MAY *please you, entertain with patience this poor pamphlet! unworthy I confess so worthy patronage. If I presume, I crave pardon! if offend, it is the first-fruit of any my writings! if dislike. I can be but sorry! Sweet Gentlemen, censure mildly, as protectors of a poor stranger! judge the best, as encouragers of a young beginner! So shall I make true report of your undeserved favours; and you shall be yourselves ever courteous!*

In this hope, if promise may go for current, I willingly make the same unto you, of a Pastoral, yet unfinished; that my purpose was to have added, for variety sake, to this little volume of Sonnets. The next Term you may expect it! In the meantime, I wholly rely on your gentle acceptance.

Yours ever,

B. GRIFFIN.

TO FIDESSA.

SONNET I.

Fertur Fortunam Fortuna favere ferenti.

FIDESSA fair! long live a happy maiden!
  Blest from thy cradle, by a worthy
   Mother,
  High-thoughted, like to her, with bounty
   laden,
  Like pleasing grace affording, one and
   other.
Sweet model of thy far renownèd Sire!
  Hold back a while thy ever-giving hand!
And though these free penned lines do nought require
  (For that they scorn at base Reward to stand),
Yet crave they most, for that they beg the least!
  Dumb is the message of my hidden grief,
And store of Speech by silence is increased;
  O let me die, or purchase some relief!
Bounteous FIDESSA cannot be so cruel
As for to make my heart, her Fancy's fuel!

SONNET II.

How can that piercing crystal-painted eye,
That gave the onset to my high aspiring,
Yielding each look of mine a sweet reply,
Adding new courage to my heart's desiring ?
How can it shut itself within her ark,
And keep herself and me both from the light ;
Making us walk in all misguiding dark,
Aye to remain, in confines of the night ?
How is it that so little room contains it,
(That guides the Orient, as the world, the Sun)
Which once obscured, most bitterly complains it,
Because it knows and rules whate'er is done.
The reason is, that they may dread her sight,
Who doth both give, and take away their light.

SONNET III.

Venus, and young Adonis sitting by her,
Under a myrtle shade, began to woo him ;
She told the youngling, how god Mars did try her,
And as he fell to her, so fell she to him.
" Even thus," quoth she, " the wanton god embraced me ! "
And then she clasped Adonis in her arms ;
" Even thus," quoth she, " the warlike god unlaced me ! "
As if the boy should use like loving charms.
But he, a wayward boy, refused the offer,
And ran away ! the beauteous Queen neglecting ;
Showing both folly to abuse her proffer,
And all his sex, of cowardice detecting.
O that I had my Mistress at that bay !
To kiss and clip me, till I ran away !

SONNET IV.

ID you sometimes three German brethren see;
 Rancour 'twixt two of them so raging rife,
That th'one could stick the other with his knife?
 Now if the third assaulted chance to be
By a fourth stranger; him set on the three!
 Them two 'twixt whom afore was deadly strife,
Made one to rob the stranger of his life.
 Then do you know our state as well as we!
Beauty and Chastity, with her were born,
 Both at one birth; and up with her did grow.
Beauty, still foe to Chastity was sworn;
 And Chastity sworn to be Beauty's foe:
And yet when I lay siege unto her heart,
Beauty and Chastity both take her part!

SONNET V.

RRAIGNED, poor captive at the Bar I stand;
 The Bar of Beauty, bar to all my joys,
And up I hold my ever trembling hand,
 Wishing, or life, or death to end annoys.
And when the Judge doth question of the guilt,
 And bids me speak: then, sorrow shuts up words!
Yea, though he say, "Speak boldly, what thou wilt!"
 Yet my confused affects no speech affords.
For why? Alas, my Passions have no bound!
 For fear of death that penetrates so near;
And still one grief another doth confound,
 Yet doth at length a way to speech appear.
Then, for I speak too late, the Judge doth give
His sentence, that "in prison, I shall live!"

SONNET VI.

UNHAPPY sentence ! Worst of worst of pains,
　　To be in darksome silence, out of ken,
Banished from all that bliss the world contains,
　　And thrust from out the companies of men.
Unhappy sentence ! Worse than worst of deaths,
　　Never to see FIDESSA's lovely face !
O better were I lose ten thousand breaths,
　　Than ever live in such unseen disgrace !
Unhappy sentence ! Worse than pains of hell,
　　To live in self-tormenting griefs alone ;
Having my heart, my prison and my cell,
　　And there consumed, without relief to moan !
If that the sentence so unhappy be,
Then what am I, that gave the same to me ?

SONNET VII.

OFT have mine Eyes, the Agents of mine Heart
　　(False traitor Eyes conspiring my decay !)
Pleaded for grace with dumb and silent art,
　　Streaming forth tears, my sorrows to allay.
Moaning the wrong, they do unto their Lord,
　　Forcing the cruel Fair, by means to yield ;
Making her, 'gainst her will, some grace t'afford ;
　　And striving sore, at length to win the field,
Thus work they means to feed my fainting hope,
　　And strengthened hope adds matter to each thought ;
Yet when they all come to their end and scope,
　　They do but wholly bring poor me, to nought.
She'll never yield ! although they ever cry ;
And therefore we must all together die !

SONNET VIII.

GRIEF-URGING Guest! great cause have I to plain me,
    Yet hope persuading hope expecteth grace,
And saith, " None but myself shall ever pain me!"
    But grief, my hopes exceedeth, in this case.
For still my fortune ever more doth cross me,
    By worse events than ever I expected ;
And, here and there, ten thousand ways doth toss me,
    With sad remembrance of my time neglected.
These breed such thoughts as set my heart on fire,
    And like fell hounds, pursue me to my death.
Traitors unto their sovereign Lord and Sire,
    Unkind exactors of their father's breath.
Whom, in their rage, they shall no sooner kill
Than they themselves, themselves unjustly spill !

SONNET IX.

MY SPOTLESS love, that never yet was tainted,
    My loyal heart, that never can be moved,
My growing hope, that never yet hath fainted,
    My constancy, that you full well have proved :
All these consented have, to plead for grace,
    These all lie crying at the door of Beauty !
This wails! this sends out tears ! this cries apace !
    All do reward expect of faith and duty !
Now either thou must prove th'unkindest one ;
    And as thou fairest art, must cruelest be !
Or else, with pity, yield unto their moan !
    Their moan that ever will importune thee.
Ah, thou must be unkind, and give denial ;
And I, poor I, must stand unto my trial !

SONNET X.

Lip not, sweet Love, the wings of my Desire,
　　Although it soar aloft, and mount too high:
But rather, bear with me, though I aspire,
　　For I have wings to bear me to the sky.
What though I mount, there is no sun but thee!
　　And sith no other sun, why should I fear?
Thou wilt not burn me, though thou terrify!
　　And though thy brightness do so great appear.
Dear! I seek not to batter down thy glory;
　　Nor do I envy that thy hope increaseth!
O never think, thy fame doth make me sorry!
　　For thou must live by fame, when beauty ceaseth.
Besides, since from one root we both did spring,
Why should not I, thy fame and beauty sing?

SONNET XI.

Winged with sad woes, why doth fair Zephyr blow
　　Upon my face (the map of discontent)?
Is it to have the weeds of sorrow grow
　　So long and thick, that they will ne'er be spent?
"No, fondling! No! It is to cool the fire
　　Which hot Desire within thy breast hath made.
Check him but once, and he will soon retire!"
　　O but he sorrows brought which cannot fade.
"The sorrows that he brought, he took from thee,
　　Which fair Fidessa span, and thou must wear!
Yet hath she nothing done of cruelty,
　　By (for her sake) to try what thou wilt bear!"
Come, sorrows! come! You are to me assigned!
I'll bear you all! It is Fidessa's mind!

SONNET XII.

IF my heavenly sighs must prove annoy
    (Which are the sweetest music to my heart),
Let it suffice, I count them as my joy!
    Sweet bitter joy, and pleasant painful smart!
For when my breast is clogged with thousand cares,
    That my poor loaded heart is like to break;
Then every sigh doth question " How it fares ? "
    Seeming to add their strength, which makes me weak.
Yet, for they friendly are, I entertain them;
    And they too well are pleasèd with their host.
But I, had not FIDESSA been, ere now, had slain them!
    It's for her cause they live! in her, they boast!
They promise help, but when they see her face;
They fainting, yield! and dare not sue for grace!

SONNET XIII.

COMPARE me to the child that plays with fire!
    Or to the fly that dieth in the flame!
Or to the foolish boy that did aspire
    To touch the Glory of high heaven's frame!
Compare me to LEANDER struggling in the waves,
    Not able to attain his safety's shore!
Or to the sick, that do expect their graves!
    Or to the captive crying evermore!
Compare me to the weeping wounded hart,
    Moaning with tears the period of his life!
Or to the boar that will not feel the smart,
    When he is stricken with the butcher's knife!
No man to these, can fitly me compare:
These live to die! I die to live in care!

SONNET XIV.

WHEN silent sleep had closèd up mine eyes,
   My watchful mind did then begin to muse;
   A thousand pleasing thoughts did then arise,
That sought by slights, their master to abuse.
I saw (O heavenly sight !) FIDESSA's face,
   And fair dame Nature blushing to behold it !
Now did She laugh ! now wink ! now smile apace !
   She took me by the hand, and fast did hold it !
Sweetly her sweet body did She lay down by me,
   " Alas, poor wretch," quoth She, " great is thy sorrow !
But thou shall comfort find, if thou wilt try me !
   I hope, sir boy ! you'll tell me news to-morrow !"
With that, away She went ! and I did wake withal :
When, ah ! my honey thoughts were turned to gall.

SONNET XV.

CARE-CHARMER Sleep ! Sweet ease in restless misery !
   The captive's liberty, and his freedom's song !
Balm of the bruised heart ! Man's chief felicity !
   Brother of quiet Death, when life is too too long !
A Comedy it is ! and now an History !
   What is not sleep unto the feeble mind ?
It easeth him that toils, and him that's sorry !
   It makes the deaf to hear ; to see, the blind !
Ungentle Sleep ! thou helpest all but me !
   For when I sleep, my soul is vexèd most.
It is FIDESSA that doth master thee !
   If She approach ; alas, thy power is lost !
But here She is ! See, how he runs amain !
I fear, at night, he will not come again.

SONNET XVI.

FOR I have lovèd long, I crave reward!
   Reward me not unkindly! Think on kindness!
Kindness becometh those of high regard;
   Regard with clemency a poor man's blindness!
Blindness provokes to pity, when it crieth;
   It crieth "Give!" Dear Lady, shew some pity!
Pity, or let him die, that daily dieth!
   Dieth he not oft, who often sings this ditty?
This ditty pleaseth me, although it choke me.
   Methinks, dame ECHO weepeth at my moaning,
Moaning the woes, that to complain provoke me.
   Provoke me now no more; but hear my groaning!
Groaning both day and night, doth tear my heart:
My heart doth know the cause, and triumphs in the smart.

SONNET XVII.

SWEET stroke! (so might I thrive as I must praise)
   But sweeter hand that gives so sweet a stroke!
The Lute itself is sweetest when she plays.
   But what hear I? A string, through fear, is broke!
The Lute doth shake as if it were afraid.
   O, sure, some goddess holds it in her hand!
A Heavenly Power that oft hath me dismayed,
   Yet such a power as doth in beauty stand!
Cease Lute! my ceaseless suit will ne'er be heard!
   (Ah, too hard-hearted She that will not hear it!)
If I but think on joy, my joy is marred!
   My grief is great, yet ever must I bear it!
But love twixt us, will prove a faithful page;
And she will love my sorrows to assuage!

SONNET XVIII.

, SHE must love my sorrows to assuage.
　　O God! what joy felt I when She did smile!
Whom killing grief before did cause to rage.
　　(Beauty is able Sorrow to beguile)
Out, traitor Absence! thou dost hinder me!
　　And mak'st my Mistress often to forget,
Causing me to rail upon her cruelty,
　　Whilst thou my suit injuriously dost let!
Again, her Presence doth astonish me,
　　And strikes me dumb, as if my Sense were gone.
Oh! is not this a strange perplexity?
　　In presence, dumb! she hears not absent moan!
Thus absent, presence; present, absence maketh:
That, hearing my poor suit, she it mistaketh!

SONNET XIX.

Y PAIN paints out my love in doleful Verse.
　　(The lively Glass wherein she may behold it!)
My Verse her wrong to me doth still rehearse,
　　But so, as it lamenteth to unfold it.
Myself with ceaseless tears my harms bewail,
　　And her obdurate heart not to be moved.
Though long-continued woes my senses fail,
　　And curse the day, the hour when first I loved.
She takes the Glass, wherein herself She sees,
　　In bloody colours cruelly depainted;
And her poor prisoner humbly on his knees,
　　Pleading for grace, with heart that never fainted:
She breaks the Glass! alas, I cannot choose!
But grieve that I should so, my labour lose.

SONNET XX.

REAT is the joy that no tongue can express !
　　Fair babe, new born, how much dost thou delight
　　　me !
　　But what, is mine so great ?　Yea, no whit less !
So great, that of all woes it doth acquite me.
It's fair FIDESSA that this comfort bringeth,
　　Who sorry for the wrongs, by her procured,
Delightful tunes of love, of true love singeth ;
　　Wherewith her too chaste thoughts were ne'er inured.
" She loves," she saith, " but with a love not blind."
　　Her love is counsel that I should not love ;
But upon virtues, fix a stayed mind.
　　But what !　This new-coined love, love doth reprove !
If this be love of which you make such store ;
Sweet ! love me less, that you may love me more !

SONNET XXI.

E THAT will CÆSAR be, or else not be,
　　(Who can aspire to CÆSAR's bleeding fame !)
Must be of high resolve ; but what is he
　　That thinks to gain a second CÆSAR's name ?
Whoe'er he be that climbs above his strength,
　　And climbeth high ; the greater is his fall !
For though he sit awhile, we see at length,
　　His slippery place no firmness hath at all !
Great is his bruise that falleth from on high.
　　This warneth me that I should not aspire ;
Examples should prevail !　I care not, I !
　　I perish must, or have what I desire !
This humour doth with mine full well agree.
I must FIDESSA's be, or else not be !

SONNET XXII.

IT WAS of love, ungentle gentle boy!
  That thou didst come and harbour in my breast;
Not of intent my body to destroy,
  And have my soul, with restless cares opprest.
But sith thy love doth turn unto my pain,
  Return to Greece, sweet lad! where thou wast born.
Leave me alone my griefs to entertain!
  If thou forsake me, I am less forlorn;
Although alone, yet shall I find more ease.
  Then see thou hie thee hence, or I will chase thee!
Men highly wrongèd, care not to displease!
  My fortune hangs on thee! Thou dost disgrace me!
Yet, at thy farewell, play a friendly part;
To make amends, fly to FIDESSA's heart!

SONNET XXIII.

FLY to her heart! Hover about her heart!
With dainty kisses, mollify her heart!
Pierce with thy arrows, her obdurate heart!
With sweet allurements ever move her heart!
At midday and at midnight, touch her heart!
Be lurking closely, nestle about her heart!
With power (thou art a god!) command her heart!
Kindle thy coals of love about her heart!
Yea, even into thyself, transform her heart!
Ah, she must love! Be sure thou have her heart!
And I must die, if thou have not her heart!
Thy bed (if thou rest well) must be her heart!
He hath the best part sure, that hath her heart,
What have I not? if I have but her heart!

SONNET XXIV.

STRIVING is past! Ah, I must sink and drown,
    And that in sight of long descrièd shore!
I cannot send for aid unto the town!
    All help is vain, and I must die therefore.
Then poor distressèd caitiff, be resolved
    To leave this earthly dwelling fraught with care!
Cease will, thy woes! Thy corpse in earth involved,
    Thou diest for her that will no help prepare.
O see, my case, herself doth now behold!
    The casement open is! She seems to speak!
But She is gone! O then I dare be bold
    And needs must say, " She caused my heart to break!"
I die before I drown, O heavy case!
It was because I saw my Mistress's face.

SONNET XXV.

COMPARE me to PYGMALION with his Image 'sotted!
    For (as was he) even so, am I deceived.
The shadow only is to me allotted,
    The substance hath of substance me bereaved.
Then poor and helpless, must I wander still
    In deep laments to pass succeeding days,
Welt'ring in woes, that poor and mighty kill.
    O who is mighty, that so soon decays!
The dread Almighty hath appointed so,
    The final period of all worldly things.
Then as in time they come, so must they go.
    (Death common is to beggars and to kings)
For whither do I run beside my text?
I run to death, for death must be the next!

FIDESSA. [B. Griffin.
1596.

SONNET XXVI.

THE silly bird that hastes unto the net,
 And flutters to and fro till she be taken,
Doth look some food or succour there to get,
 But loseth life : so much is she mistaken !
The foolish fly that fleeth to the flame
 With ceaseless hovering, and with restless flight,
Is burnèd straight to ashes in the same,
 And finds her death, where was her most delight.
The proud aspiring boy, that needs would pry
 Into the secrets of the highest seat,
Had some conceit to gain content thereby,
 Or else his folly, sure, was wondrous great.
These did through folly perish all and die :
And, though I know it ! even so do I !

SONNET XXVII.

POOR worm, poor silly worm, alas, poor beast !
 Fear makes thee hide thy head within the ground,
Because of creeping things thou art the least ;
 Yet every foot gives thee thy mortal wound.
But I, thy fellow worm, am in worse state ;
 For thou thy sun enjoyest, but I want mine !
I live in irksome night, O cruel fate !
 My sun will never rise, nor ever shine.
Thus blind of light, mine eyes misguide my feet,
 And baleful darkness makes me still afraid ;
Men mock me when I stumble in the street,
 And wonder how my young sight so decayed.
Yet do I joy in this, even when I fall,
That I shall see again, and then see all !

SONNET XXVIII.

WELL may my soul, immortal and divine,
    That is imprisoned in a lump of clay,
    Breathe out laments until this body pine.
        That from her takes her pleasures all away.
Pine then, thou loathèd prison of my life!
    Untoward subject of the least aggrievance!
O let me die! Mortality is rife!
    Death comes by wounds, by sickness, care, and chance.
O earth, the time will come when I'll resume thee,
    And in thy bosom make my resting-place;
Then do not unto hardest sentence doom me!
    Yield, yield betimes! I must, and will have grace!
" Richly shalt thou be entombed! since for thy grave,
    FIDESSA, fair FIDESSA! thou shalt have!"

SONNET XXIX.

EARTH! take this earth wherein my spirits languish!
    Spirits, leave this earth that doth in griefs retain!
    Griefs, chase this earth, that it may fade with
        anguish!
    Spirits, avoid these furies which do pain you!
O leave your loathsome prison! Freedom, gain you!
    Your essence is divine! Great is your power!
And yet you moan your wrongs and sore complain you,
    Hoping for joy, which fadeth every hour!
O Spirits, your prison loathe, and freedom gain you!
    The Destinies, in deep laments, have shut you,
Of mortal hate! because they do disdain you!
    And yet of joy that they in prison put you.
Earth, take this earth with thee to be enclosed!
Life is to me, and I to it, opposed!

SONNET XXX.

WEEP now no more, mine eyes; but be you drowned
   In your own tears, so many years distilled!
   And let her know, that at them long hath frowned,
   That you can weep no more, although She willed,
This hap, her cruelty hath her allotten,
  Who whilom was Commandress of each part;
That, now, her proper griefs must be forgotten,
  By those true outward signs of inward smart.
For how can he, that hath not one tear left him,
  Stream out those floods that're due unto her moaning;
When, both of eyes and tears She hath bereft him?
  O yet I'll signify my grief with groaning!
True sighs, true groans shall echo in the air
And say, " FIDESSA, though most cruel, is most fair!"

SONNET XXXI.

TONGUE, never cease to sing FIDESSA's praise!
   Heart, however she deserve, conceive the best!
   Eyes, stand amazed to see her beauty's rays!
   Lips, steal one kiss, and be for ever blest!
Hands, touch that hand wherein your life is closed!
  Breast, lock up fast in thee thy life's sole treasure!
Arms, still embrace, and never be disclosed!
  Feet, run to her, without, or pace, or measure!
Tongue, heart, eyes, lips, hands, breast, arms, feet,
  Consent to do true homage to your Queen!
Lovely, fair, gentle, wise, virtuous, sober, sweet!
  Whose like shall never be, hath never been!
O that I were all tongue, her praise to shew;
Then surely my poor heart were freed from woe!

SONNET XXXII.

SORE sick of late, Nature her due would have,
    Great was my pain where still my mind did rest;
No hope but heaven! no comfort but my grave,
    Which is of comforts both the last and least!
But on a sudden, th'Almighty sent
    Sweet ease to the distressed and comfortless,
And gave me longer time for to repent;
    With health and strength, the foes of feebleness.
Yet I my health no sooner 'gan recover,
    But my old thoughts, though full of cares, retained,
Made me, as erst, become a wretched lover
    Of her, that Love and lovers aye disdained.
Then was my pain, with ease of pain increased,
And I ne'er sick until my sickness ceased.

SONNET XXXIII.

HE that would fain FIDESSA's image see,
    My face, of force, may be his looking-glass!
There is she portrayed, and her cruelty!
    Which as a wonder, through the world must pass.
But were I dead, she would not be betrayed.
    It's I, that 'gainst my will, shall make it known!
Her cruelty by me, must be bewrayed:
    Or I must hide my head, and live alone.
I'll pluck my silver hairs from out my head,
    And wash away the wrinkles of my face!
Closely immured I'll live, as I were dead,
    Before She suffer but the least disgrace!
How can I hide that is already known?
I have been seen, and have no face but one!

SONNET XXXIV.

IE, Pleasure! fie!　Thou cloy'st me with delight;
　　Sweet thoughts, you kill me, if you lower stray!
　O many be the joys of one short night!
　　Tush, fancies never can Desire allay!
Happy, unhappy thoughts! I think, and have not.
　　Pleasure, O pleasing plain! Shews nought avail me!
Mine own conceit doth glad me, more I crave not!
　　Yet wanting substance, woe doth still assail me.
" Babies do children please! and shadows, fools! "
　　" Shews have deceived the wisest, many a time ! "
" Ever to want our wish, our courage cools! "
　　" The ladder broken, 'tis in vain to climb."
But I must wish, and crave, and seek, and climb;
It's hard, if I obtain not grace in time!

SONNET XXXV.

HAVE not spent the April of my time,
　　The Swelt of Youth in plotting in the air!
But do, at first adventure, seek to climb,
　　Whilst flowers of blooming years are green and
　　　　fair.
I am no leaving of all-withering Age.
　　I have not suffered many winter lours.
I feel no storm, unless my Love do rage.
　　And then, in grief I spend both days and hours.
This yet doth comfort that my flower lasted
　　Until it did approach my sun too near:
And then, alas, untimely was it blasted,
　　So soon as once thy beauty did appear!
But after all, my comfort rests in this,
That, for thy sake! my Youth decayed is.

SONNET XXXVI.

 LET my heart, my body, and my tongue
  Bleed forth the lively streams of faith unfeigned !
Worship my saint, the gods and saints among !
  Praise and extol her fair, that me hath pained !
O let the smoke of my suppressed Desire,
  Raked up in ashes of my burning breast,
Break out at length, and to the clouds aspire,
  Urging the heavens t'afford me rest !
But let my body naturally descend
  Into the bowels of our common mother !
And to the very centre let it wend,
  When it no lower can, her griefs to smother !
And yet when I so low do buried lie ;
Then shall my love ascend unto the sky !

SONNET XXXVII.

 AIR is my love that feeds among the lilies,
  The lilies growing in that pleasant garden
Where Cupid's Mount, that well beloved hill is,
  And where that little god, himself is Warden.
See where my Love sits in the beds of spices !
  Beset all round with camphor, myrrh, and roses.
And interlaced with curious devices
  Which, her from all the world apart incloses.
There, doth she tune her Lute for her delight !
  And with sweet music makes the ground to move ;
Whilst I, poor I, do sit in heavy plight,
  Wailing alone my unrespected love.
Not daring rush into so rare a place,
That gives to her, and she to it, a grace.

SONNET XXXVIII.

As never eye did see my Mistress's face,
  Was never ear did hear FIDESSA's tongue,
Was never mind that once did mind her grace,
  That ever thought the travail to be long!
" When her I see, no creature I behold."
  So plainly say, these Advocates of Love,
That now do fear, and now to speak are bold;
  Trembling apace, when they resolve to prove.
These strange effects do show a hidden power,
  A majesty, all base attempts reproving;
That glads or daunts as she doth laugh or lower;
  Surely some goddess harbours in their moving!
Who thus my Muse from base attempts hath raised,
Whom thus my Muse beyond compare hath praised.

SONNET XXXIX.

MY LADY's hair is threads of beaten gold.
  Her front, the purest, crystal eye hath seen.
Her eyes, the brightest stars the heavens hold.
  Her cheeks, red roses, such as seld have been.
Her pretty lips, of red vermillion die.
  Her hand, of ivory the purest white.
Her blush, AURORA or the morning sky.
  Her breast displays two silver fountains bright.
The spheres, her voice; her grace, the Graces three.
  Her body is the saint that I adore.
Her smiles and favours, sweet as honey be.
  Her feet, fair THETIS praiseth evermore.
But ah, the worst and last is yet behind :
For of a griffon she doth bear the mind!

SONNET XL.

INJURIOUS Fates! to rob me of my bliss,
    And dispossess my heart of all his hope:
    You ought, with just revenge, to punish miss,
    For unto you the hearts of men are ope.
Injurious Fates! that hardened have her heart,
    Yet make her face to send out pleasing smiles:
And both are done, but to increase my smart,
    And entertain my love with falsèd wiles.
Yet being, when She smiles, surprised with joy,
    I fain would languish in so sweet a pain!
Beseeching death, my body to destroy;
    Lest, on the sudden, She should frown again.
When men do wish for death, Fates have no force:
But they, when men would live, have no remorse.

SONNET XLI.

THE prison I am in is thy fair face!
    Wherein my liberty enchainèd lies;
    My thoughts, the bolts that hold me in the place;
    My food, the pleasing looks of thy fair eyes!
Deep is the prison where I lie enclosed,
    Strong are the bolts that in this cell contain me.
Sharp is the food necessity imposed,
    When hunger makes me feed on that which pains me.
Yet do I love, embrace, and follow fast,
    That holds, that keeps, that discontents me most:
And list not break, unlock, or seek to waste
    The place, the bolts, the food (though I be lost!),
Better in prison ever to remain;
Than, being out, to suffer greater pain.

SONNET XLII.

HEN never-speaking silence proves a wonder;
　　When ever-flying flame at home remaineth;
　When all-concealing night keeps darkness under;
　　When men-devouring wrong true glory gaineth ·
When soul-tormenting grief agrees with joy;
　　When LUCIFER foreruns the baleful night;
When VENUS doth forsake her little boy;
　　When her untoward boy obtaineth sight;
When SYSIPHUS doth cease to roll his stone;
　　When OTHES shaketh off his heavy chain;
When Beauty, Queen of Pleasure is alone;
　　When Love and Virtue, quiet peace disdain:
　　　When these shall be, and I not be;
　　　Then will FIDESSA pity me;

SONNET XLIII.

ELL me of love, Sweet LOVE, who is thy sire?
　　Or if thou mortal or immortal be?
　Some say " Thou art begotten by Desire!
　　Nourished with Hope! and fed with Fantasy!
Engendered by a heavenly Goddess's eye,
　　Lurking most sweetly in an angel's face."
Others that " Beauty, thee doth deify! "
　　(O sovereign Beauty, full of power and grace!)
But I must be absurd all this denying,
　　Because the fairest Fair alive ne'er knew thee.
Now, CUPID! comes thy godhead to the trying!
　　'Twas She alone (such is her power!) that slew me!
She shall be LOVE, and thou a foolish boy!
　　Whose virtue proves thy power is but a toy.

SONNET XLIV.

NO CHOICE of change can ever change my mind!
    Choiceless my choice, the choicest choice alive:
Wonder of women, were She not unkind:
    The pitiless of pity to deprive.
Yet She, the kindest creature of her kind,
    Accuseth me of self-ingratitude:
And well She may! Sith, by good proof I find
    Myself had died, had She not helpful stood.
For when my sickness had the upper hand,
    And death began to show his awful face;
She took great pains, my pains for to withstand;
    And eased my heart that was in heavy case.
But cruel now, she scorneth what it craveth:
Unkind in kindness, murdering while she saveth!

SONNET XLV.

MINE eye bewrays the secrets of my heart,
    My heart unfolds his grief before her face:
Her face (bewitching pleasure of my smart!)
    Deigns not one look of mercy and of grace.
My guilty eye of murder and of treason,
    (Friendly conspirator of my decay,
Dumb eloquence, the lover's strongest reason!)
    Doth weep itself for anger quite away;
And chooseth rather not to be, than be
    Disloyal, by too well discharging duty:
And being out, joys it no more can see
    The sugared charms of all deceiving Beauty,
But (for the other greedily doth eye it),
I pray you, tell me, What do I get by it?

SONNET XLVI.

O soon as peeping LUCIFER, AURORA's star,
  The sky with golden periwigs doth spangle;
So soon as PHŒBUS gives us light from far,
  So soon as fowler doth the bird entangle;
Soon as the watchful bird, Clock of the Morn!
  Gives intimation of the Day's appearing;
Soon as the jolly hunter winds his horn,
  His speech and voice with custom's echo clearing;
Soon as the hungry lion seeks his prey
  In solitary range of pathless mountains;
Soon as the passenger sets on his way,
  So soon as beasts resort unto the fountains;
So soon mine eyes their office are discharging;
And I, my griefs, with greater griefs enlarging!

SONNET XLVII.

SEE, I hear, I feel, I know, I rue
  My fate, my fame, my pain, my loss, my fall;
Mishap, reproach, disdain, a crown, her hue;
  Cruel, still flying, false, fair, funeral
To cross, to shame, bewitch, deceive, and kill
  My first proceedings in their flowing bloom.
My worthless pen fast chainèd to my will,
  My erring life through an uncertain doom,
My thoughts that yet in lowliness do mount,
  My heart the subject of her tyranny:
What now remains, but her severe account
  Of murder's crying guilt (foul butchery!)
She was unhappy in her cradle breath;
That given was, to be another's death.

SONNET XLVIII.

"MURDER! O murder!" I can cry no longer.
    "Murder! O murder!" Is there none to aid me?
Life feeble is in force, Death is much stronger.
    Then let me die that shame may not upbraid me,
Nothing is left me now, but shame or death!
    I fear She feareth not foul murder's guilt!
Nor do I fear to lose a servile breath.
    I know my blood was given to be spilt,
What is this life, but maze of countless strays?
    The enemy of true felicity!
Fitly compared to dreams! to flowers! to plays!
    O life! no life to me, but misery!
Of shame or death (if thou must one?),
Make choice of death! and both are gone.

SONNET XLIX.

MY CRUEL fortunes, clouded with a frown,
    Lurk in the bosom of eternal night;
My climbing thoughts are basely haulèd down!
    My best devices prove but after-sight.
Poor outcast of the world's exilèd room,
    I live in wilderness of deep lament:
No hope reserved me, but a hopeless tomb,
    When fruitless life and fruitful woes are spent.
Shall PHŒBUS hinder little stars to shine,
    Or lofty cedar, mushrooms leave to grow?
Sure, mighty men at little ones repine,
    The rich is to the poor a common foe.
FIDESSA, seeing how the world doth go,
Joineth with Fortune, in my overthrow.

SONNET L.

HEN I the hooks of pleasure first devoured,
 Which undigested, threaten now to choke me;
Fortune on me, her golden graces showered :
 O then Delight did to delight provoke me !
Delight, false instrument of my decay !
 Delight the nothing that doth all things move ;
Made me first wander from the perfect way,
 And fast entangled me in the snares of love.
Then my unhappy happiness, at first, began,
 Happy in that I loved the fairest Fair ;
Unhappily despised, a hapless man :
 Thus Joy did triumph ! Triumph did despair !
My conquest is, which shall the conquest gain ?
FIDESSA, author both of joy and pain !

SONNET LI.

ORK ! work apace, you blessed Sisters three !
 In restless twining of my fatal thread.
O let your nimble hands at once agree,
 To weave it out, and cut it off with speed !
Then shall my vexèd and tormented ghost
 Have quiet passage to the Elysian rest !
And sweetly over Death and Fortune boast,
 In everlasting triumphs with the blest !
But, ah, (too well I know !) you have conspired
 A lingering death for him that loatheth life ;
As if with woes he never could be tired.
 For this, you hide your all-dividing knife.
One comfort yet, the heavens have assigned me ;
That I must die, and leave my griefs behind me.

SONNET LII.

T is some comfort to the wrongèd man,
 The wronger, of injustice to upbraid.
Justly myself, herein I comfort can,
 And justly call her " An ungrateful maid ! "
Thus am I pleased to rid myself of crime,
 And stop the mouth of all-reporting fame ;
Counting my greatest cross, the loss of time,
 And all my private grief, her public shame.
Ah, (but to speak the truth) hence are my cares,
 And in this comfort, all discomfort resteth ;
My harms I cause (her scandal) unawares,
 Thus love procures the thing that love detesteth.
For he that views the glasses of my smart
Must needs report " She hath a flinty heart ! "

SONNET LIII.

Was a King of sweet Content at least ;
 But now from out my Kingdom banished !
I was chief guest at fair Dame Pleasure's feast ;
 But now I am for want of succour famished !
I was a saint, and heaven was my rest ;
 But now cast down into the lowest hell !
Vile caitiffs may not live among the blest !
 Nor blessed men, amongst cursed caitiffs dwell !
Thus am I made an exile, of a King.
 Thus choice of meats, to want of food is changed.
Thus heaven's loss doth hellish torments bring.
 Self crosses make me from myself estranged.
Yet am I still the same, but made another !
 Then not the same ! Alas, I am no other !

SONNET LIV.

IF GREAT APOLLO offered as a dower,
    His burning throne to Beauty's excellence;
If JOVE himself came in a golden shower,
    Down to the earth, to fetch fair Io thence;
If VENUS, in the curlèd locks was tied
    Of proud ADONIS, not of gentle kind;
If TELLUS, for a shepherd's favour died,
    (The favour cruel Love to her assigned);
If Heaven's-winged herald HERMES had
    His heart enchanted with a country maid;
If poor PYGMALION was for beauty mad:
    If gods and men have all for beauty strayed:
I am not then ashamed to be included
'Mongst those that love, and be with love deluded.

SONNET LV.

O, No, I dare not! O, I may not speak!
    Yes, yes, I dare! I can! I must! I will!
Then heart, pour forth thy plaints, and do not
      break!
    Let never Fancy, manly courage kill!
Intreat her mildly! (words have pleasing charms,
    Of force to move the most obdurate heart)
To take relenting pity of my harms.
    And with unfeigned tears to wail my smart!
Is She a stock, a block, a stone, a flint?
    Hath She, nor ears to hear, nor eyes to see?
If so, my cries, my prayers, my tears shall stint!
    Lord! how can lovers so bewitchèd be!
I took her to be Beauty's Queen alone;
But now, I see She is a senseless stone!

SONNET LVI.

 S Trust betrayed?   Doth Kindness grow unkind?
    Can Beauty, both at once, give life and kill?
    Shall Fortune alter the most constant mind?
    Will Reason yield unto rebelling will?
Doth Fancy purchase praise, and Virtue, shame?
    May shew of Goodness lurk in treachery?
Hath Truth unto herself procurèd blame?
    Must sacred Muses suffer misery?
Are women woe to men, traps for their falls?
    Differ their words, their deeds; their looks, their lives?
Have lovers ever been their tennis balls?
    Be husbands fearful of the chastest wives?
All men do these affirm; and so must I!
Unless Fidessa give to me the lie.

SONNET LVII.

Hree playfellows (such Three were never seen
    In Venus's Court!) upon a summer's day,
    Met altogether on a pleasant green,
    Intending at some pretty game to play.
They Dian, Cupid, and Fidessa were.
    Their wager, Beauty, bow, and Cruelty;
The conqueress the stakes away did bear,
    Whose fortune then was it to win all three?
Fidessa! which doth these, as weapons use,
    To make the greatest heart, her will obey:
And yet the most obedient to refuse
    As having power, poor lovers to betray.
With these, She wounds, She heals, gives life and death:
More power hath none, that lives by mortal breath!

SONNET LVIII.

BEAUTY! Siren! kept with CIRCE's rod!
　　The faintest good in seem, but foulest ill!
　　The sweetest plague ordained for man by GOD!
　　The pleasing subject of presumptuous will!
Th'alluring object of unstayed eyes!
　　Friended of all, but unto all a foe!
The dearest thing that any creature buys!
　　And vainest too (It serves but for a shoe)!
In seem, a heaven; and yet from bliss exiling!
　　Paying, for truest service, nought but pain!
Young men's undoing! Young and old beguiling!
　　Man's greatest loss, though thought his greatest gain!
True, that all this, with pain enough I prove;
And yet most true, I will FIDESSA love!

SONNET LIX.

DO I, UNTO a cruel tiger play;
　　That preys on me, as wolf upon the lambs?
(Who fear the danger, both of night and day,
　　And run for succour to their tender dams)
Yet will I pray (though She be ever cruel!)
　　On bended knee, and with submissive heart!
She is the fire, and I must be the fuel.
　　She must inflict, and I endure the smart.
She must, She shall be mistress of her will;
　　And I, poor I, obedient to the same:
As fit to suffer death, as She to kill;
　　As ready to be blamed, as She to blame.
And for I am the subject of her ire,
All men shall know thereby my love entire.

SONNET LX.

Let me sigh, weep, wail, and cry no more;
Or let me sigh, weep, wail, cry more and more!
Yea, let me sigh, weep, wail, cry evermore;
For She doth pity my complaints no more
Than cruel Pagan or the savage Moor:
But still doth add unto my torments more;
Which grievous are to me by so much more
As She inflicts them, and doth wish them more.
O let thy mercy, Merciless! be never more!
So shall sweet death to me be welcome, more
Than is to hungry beasts the grassy moor,
As She that to affliction, adds yet more,
Becomes more cruel by still adding more!
Weary am I to speak of this word " more ";
Yet never weary She, to plague me more!

SONNET LXI.

Idessa's worth in time begetteth praise,
    Time, praise; Praise, fame; Fame, wonderment
Wonder, fame, praise, time, her worth do raise
    To highest pitch of dread astonishment.
Yet Time in time, her hardened heart bewrayeth:
    And Praise itself, her cruelty dispraiseth.
So that through Praise, alas, her praise decayeth:
    And that which makes it fall, her honour raiseth.
Most strange! yet true. So wonder wonder still,
    And follow fast the wonder of these days!
For well I know (all wonder to fulfil)
    Her will at length unto my will obeys:
Meantime, let others praise her constancy!
    And me attend upon her clemency!

SONNET LXII.

Ost true that I must fair FIDESSA love.
Most true that I fair FIDESSA cannot love.
Most true that I do feel the pains of love.
Most true that I am captive unto love.
Most true that I deluded am with love.
Most true that I do find the sleights of love.
Most true that nothing can procure her love.
Most true that I must perish in my love.
Most true that She contemns the God of love.
Most true that he is snarèd with her love.
Most true that She would have me cease to love.
Most true that She herself alone is Love.
Most true that though She hated, I would love!
Most true that dearest life shall end with love.

B. GRIFFIN.

FINIS.

Talis apud tales, talis sub tempore tali :
Subque meo tali judice, talis ero.

DIELLA

Certain Sonnets, adjoined

to the amorous Poem of

Dom Diego and Gyneura

(∴)

By R. L., Gentleman.

Ben balla, á chi fortuna suona.

AT LONDON,

Printed for HENRY OLNEY, and are to be sold at
his shop in Fleet street, near the Middle Temple Gate.
1596.

*To the most worthily honoured and
virtuously beautified Lady, the Lady ANNE
GLEMNHAM, wife to the most
noble, magnanimous, and worthy Knight,
Sir HENRY GLEMNHAM, &c.*

MADAM,

 OUR many honourable virtues having tied me to
your eternal service; to shew some part of my
duty, I present your Ladyship with a few passionate Sonnets intermingled with the Loves of
Dom DIEGO and GYNEURA.

Deign, gentle Lady, to accept them, and therein shew the
greatness of your benignity, in receiving courteously a gift
of so small worth: which though it cannot any ways equal
either the number of your virtues, or the greatness of that
noble House, whence your Ladyship is descended; impute it
not, Madam, to my defect of Judgement, but of Fortune;
for were I furnished with the greatest riches that blind
goddess could bestow on a man of my state, both they and I
would fall prostrate at your feet, and ever rest at your Ladyship's devotion.

Yet, Madam, as it is, it is a Child of the Muses, and, therefore, worthy to be cherished; conceived in the brain of a
gallant Gentleman, and therefore to be favoured: sent into
the world by me, who have ever honoured your Ladyship,
and therefore crave of your Ladyship to be protected, to
whom I ever wish long life, lengthened with all honourable
happiness.

Your Ladyship's
in all duty,
HENRY OLNEY.

[SONNETS.]

SONNET I.

HEN first the feathered god did strike my
    heart
  with fatal and immedicable wound,
Leaving behind the head of his fell dart;
  my bloodless body fell unto the ground.
And, when with shame I reinforced my
    might,
  boldly to gaze on her so heavenly face,
Huge flames of fire She darted from her light,
  which since have scorched me in most piteous case.
To quench which heat, an ocean of tears
  have gushèd out from forth my red-swollen eyes.
But deep-fetched sighs, this raging flame uprears,
  and blow the sparks up to the purple skies:
Whereat, the gods, afraid that heaven should burn,
Intreated LOVE, that I, for e'er might mourn.

SONNET II.

SOON as the azure-coloured Gates of th'East·
　were set wide open by the watchful Morn,
I walked abroad, as having took no rest
　(for nights are tedious to a man forlorn);
And viewing well each pearl-bedewèd flower,
　then waxing dry by splendour of the sun :
All scarlet-hued I saw him 'gin to lower
　and blush, as though some heinous act were done.
At this amazed, I hied me home amain,
　thinking that I, his anger causèd had.
And at his set, abroad I walked again;
　when, lo, the moon looked wondrous pale and sad.
Anger, the one; and envy moved the other,
To see my Love more fair than LOVE's fair mother.

SONNET III.

SWIFT-FOOTED Time ! look back ! and here mark well
　those rare-shaped parts my pen shall now declare !
My Mistress' snow-white Skin doth much excel
　the pure soft wool Arcadian sheep do bear !
Her Hair exceeds gold forced in smallest wire,
　in smaller threads than those ARACHNE spun !
Her Eyes are crystal fountains, yet dart fire
　more glorious to behold than midday sun !
Her ivory Front, though soft as purest silk,
　looks like the table * of Olympic JOVE !　[* *portrait.*]
Her Cheeks are like ripe cherries laid in milk !
　her alabaster Neck, the throne of LOVE !
Her other parts so far excel the rest,
That wanting words, they cannot be expressed !

SONNET IV.

WHAT sugared terms, what all-persuading art,
    what sweet mellifluous words, what wounding
      looks,
    LOVE used for his admittance to my heart!
such eloquence was never read in books!
He promised Pleasure, Rest, and Endless Joy,
    Fruition of the fairest She alive.
His pleasure, pain; rest, trouble; joy, annoy;
    have I since found! which me, of bliss deprive.
The Trojan horse, thus have I now let in;
    wherein enclosed these armèd men were placed.
Bright Eyes, fair Cheeks, sweet Lips, and milk-white Skin,
    these foes, my life have overthrown and razed.
Fair outward shews prove inwardly the worst:
Love looketh fair, but lovers are accurst!

SONNET V.

THE little Archer viewing well my Love,
    stone-still amazed, admirèd such a sight;
    And swore he knew none such to dwell above:
    though many fair; none, so conspicuous bright!
With that enraged, flamigerous as he is,
    he now 'gan loathe his PSYCHE's lovely face;
And swore great oaths, "to rob me of my bliss,"
    saying that "earth for her, was too too base!"
But CYTHEREA checked her lordly son,
    commanding him to bring no giglet thither!
Fearing indeed, her amorous sports were done
    with hotspur MARS, if he should once but see her.
If then her beauty move the gods above;
Let all men judge, if I have cause to love!

SONNET VI.

MIRROR of Beauty! Nature's fairest Child!
    Empress of Love! my heart's high-prizèd jewel!
Learn of the Dove, to love and to be mild!
    be not to him that honours thee, so cruel!
But as the Asp, deaf, angry, nothing meek;
    thou will not listen to my doleful plaint!
Nor once wilt look on my discoloured cheek!
    which wanting blood, causeth me oft to faint.
Then, silent will I be! if that will please thee:
    yet so, as in my stead, each plain, each hill
Shall echo forth my grief! and thereby ease me;
    for I myself, of speaking have my fill.
If plains and hills be silent in my pain;
    My death shall speak! and tell what I sustain!

SONNET VII.

[Cf. BARNES' *Parthenophil*, vol. i. p. 200, and PERCY's *Coelia*, vol. ii. p. 146 *supra*.]

WHEN LOVE had first besieged my heart's strong wall,
    rampiered and countermured with Chastity,
And had with ordnance made his tops to fall
    stooping their glory to his surquedry:
I called a parley, and withal did crave
    some Composition, or some friendly Peace;
To this request, he, his consent soon gave,
    as seeming glad such cruel wars should cease.
I, nought mistrusting, opened all the gates,
    yea, lodged him in the palace of my heart:
When, he, in dead of night, he seeks his mates,
    And shews each traitor how to play his part;
With that, they fired my heart! and thence 'gan fly!
Their names, Sweet Smiles, Fair Face, and Piercing Eye.

SONNET VIII.

IKE to a falcon watching for a flight,
    duly attending his desirèd game;
Have I oft watched and marked to have a sight.
    of thy fair face, exceeding niggard Fame!
Thine eyes, those seminaries of my grief!
    have been more gladsome to my tirèd sprite,
Than naked savages receive relief
    by comfort-bearing warmth of PHŒBUS' light.
But when each part so glorious I had seen;
    I trembled more than Autumn's parchèd leaves!
Mine eyes were greedy whirlpools sucking in
    that heavenly Fair, which me of rest bereaves.
Then as thy Beauty thus hath conquered me,
Fair! let relenting Pity conquer thee!

SONNET IX.

LOT not thy beauty (Fairest, yet unkind!)
    with cruel usage of a yielding heart!
The stoutest Captain scorns such bloody mind:
    then mingle mercy, where thou causedst smart!
Let him not die, in his May-springing days!
    that living, vows to honour thee for ever.
Shine forth some pity from thy sun-like rays!
    that hard-frozed hate may so dissolve and sever!
O were thou not much harder than a flint,
    thou hadst ere this, been melted into love!
In firmest stone, small rain doth make a print:
    but seas of tears cannot thy hardness move!
Then, wretched I, must die before my time!
Blasted and spoilèd in my budding prime.

SONNET X.

HEN FLORA vaunts her in her proud array,
    clothing fair TELLUS in a spangled gown;
When BOREAS' fury is exiled away,
    and all the welkin cleared from angry frown:
At that same time, all Nature's children joy;
    trees leave, flowers bud, plants spring, and beasts increase.
Only my soul, surcharged with deep annoy,
    cannot rejoice, nor sighs nor tears can cease:
Only the grafts of sorrow seem to grow;
    set in my heart, no other spring I find.
Delights and pleasures are o'ergrown with woe,
    laments and sobs possess my weeping mind.
The frost of grief so nips Delight at root:
No sun but She can do it any boot.

SONNET XI.

HAT She can be so cruel as my Love,
    or bear a heart so pitiless as She?
    Whom love, looks, words, tears, prayers do not
        move;
        nor sighs, nor vows prevail to pity me.
She calls my love, "a SINON to her heart!"
    "my looks," she saith, "are like the crocodile's!"
"My words the Sirens sing, with guileful art!"
    tears, "CIRCE's floods!" sighs, vows, "deceitful guiles!"
But my poor heart hath no interpreter
    but love, looks, words, tears, prayers, sighs, or vows!
Then must it die! sith She, my comforter,
    whate'er I do, nor liketh, nor allows.
With TITIUS, thus the vulture Sorrow eats me!
With steel-twigged rods, thus tyrant CUPID beats me!

SONNET XII.

Hou (like the fair-faced, gold-encovered book,
 whose lines are stuffed with damnèd heresies)
Dost in thy face, bear a celestial look;
 when, in thy heart, live hell-born cruelties!
With poisonous toads, the clearest spring 's infected;
 and purest lawn 's nought worth, if full of stains ·
So is fair Beauty, when true love 's rejected;
 when coal-black hate within the heart remains.
Then love, my Dear! let that be Methridate
 to overcome the venom of disdain!
Be pitiful! tread down this killing hate!
 Convert to sugared pleasure, gall-ful pain!
O, sith Disdain is foe unto thy Fair,
Exile him thence! there, let him not repair!

SONNET XIII.

Know, within my mouth, for bashful fear
 and dread of your disdain, my words will die!
I know, I shall be stricken dumb, my Dear!
 with doubt of your unpitiful reply.
I know, when as I shall before you lie
 prostrate and humble, craving help of you;
Misty aspects will cloud your sun-bright eye,
 and scornful looks o'ershade your beauty's hue.
I know, when I shall plead my love so true,
 so stainless, constant, loyal, and upright;
My truthful pleadings will not cause you rue
 The ne'er-heard state of my distressèd plight.
I know, when I shall come with face bedight
 with streaming tears, fallen from my fountain eyes,

SONNET XIII.

[The same number is repeated, a kind of double Sonnet on the same thought, being attempted.]

BREATHING forth sighs of most heart-breaking might,
  my tears, my sighs, and me, you will despise!
I know, when with the power that in me lies,
  and all the prayers and vows that women move,
I shall in humblest mercy-moving wise,
  intreat, beseech, desire, and beg your love:
I know, sweet Maiden! all will not remove
  flint-hearted rigour from your rocky breast!
But all my means, my suit, and what I prove,
  prove bad, and I must live in all unrest.
Dying in life, and living still in death,
And yet nor die, nor draw a life-like breath.

SONNET XIV.

WHEN broad-faced rivers turn unto their fountains
  and hungry wolves devourèd are by sheep;
When marine dolphins play on snow-tipped moun-
    tains,
  and foul-formed bears do in the ocean keep:
Then shall I leave to love, and cease to burn
  in these hot flames, wherein I now delight!
But this I know, the rivers ne'er return,
  nor silly sheep with ravening wolves dare fight,
Nor dolphins leave the seas, nor bears, the woods;
  for Nature bids them all to keep their kind.
Then eyes, rain forth your over-swellèd floods,
  till, drownèd in such seas, may make you blind!
Then, Heart's Delight! sith I must love thee ever,
Love me again! and let thy love persèver!

SONNET XV.

NO SOONER leaves HYPERION, THETIS' bed,
    and mounts his coach to post from thence away;
Richly adorning fair LEUCOTHEA's head,
    giving to mountains, tincture from his ray:
But straight I rise, where I could find no rest,
    where visions and fantasies appear;
And when, with small ado, my body's dresst,
    abroad I walk, to think upon my Dear!
Where, under umbrage of some agèd tree,
    with lute in hand I sit and, sighing, say,
" Sweet groves, tell forth with echo, what you see!
    good trees, bear witness, who is my decay!
And thou, my soul, speak! speak what rest I have,
When each our joy's despair doth make me rave!"

SONNET XVI.

BUT thou, my dear sweet-sounding lute, be still!
    repose thy troubled strings upon this moss!
Thou hast full often eased me 'gainst my will:
    lie down in peace, thy spoil were my great loss!
I'll speak enough of her too cruel heart,
    enough to move the stony rocks to ruth!
And cause these trees weep tears to hear my smart,
    though cruel She will not once weigh my truth.
Her face is of the purest white and red,
    her eyes are crystal, and her hair is gold.
The World, for shape with garlands crown her head,
    and yet a tigress' heart dwells in this mould.
But I must love her, Tigress! too too much!
Forced; must I love! because I find none such.

SONNET XVII.

HE sun-scorched seaman, when he sees the seas,
    all in a fury, hoist him to the sky;
And throw him down again, as waves do please,
    (so chaséd clouds, from Æol's mastiffs fly!)
In such distress, provideth with great speed
    all means to save him from the tempest's rage:
He shews his wit, in such like time of need,
    the big swoll'n billows' fury to assuage.
But foolish I, althouth I see my death,
    and feel her proud disdain too feelingly
(Which me of all felicity bereaveth):
    yet seek no means t' escape this misery.
So am I charmed with heart-enchanting beauty,
That still to wail, I think it is my duty.

SONNET XVIII.

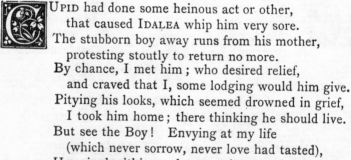UPID had done some heinous act or other,
    that caused IDALEA whip him very sore.
The stubborn boy away runs from his mother,
    protesting stoutly to return no more.
By chance, I met him; who desired relief,
    and craved that I, some lodging would him give.
Pitying his looks, which seemed drowned in grief,
    I took him home; there thinking he should live.
But see the Boy! Envying at my life
    (which never sorrow, never love had tasted),
He raised within my heart such uncouth strife;
    that, with the same, my body now is wasted,
By thankless LOVE, thus vilely am I used!
By using kindness, I am thus abused;

SONNET XIX.

WHEN Night returns back to his ugly mansion,
    and clear-faced Morning makes her bright uprise;
In sorrow's depth, I murmur out his cantion
    (salt tears distilling from my dewy eyes),
"O thou deceitful SOMNUS, god of dreams!
    cease to afflict my over-painèd sprite
With vain illusions, and idle themes!
    thy spells are false! thou canst not charm aright!
For when, in bed, I think t'embrace my Love
    (enchanted by thy magic so to think),
Vain are my thoughts! 'tis empty air, I prove!
    that still I wail, till watching make me wink:
And when I wink, I wish I ne'er might wake,
But sleeping, carried to the Stygian lake."

SONNET XX.

THE strongest pine, that Queen FERONIA hath,
    growing within her woody empiry,
Is soon thrown down by BOREAS' wintry wrath,
    if one root only his supporter be.
The tallest ship that cuts the angry wave,
    and plows the seas of SATURN's second sun,
If but one anchor for a journey have,
    when that is lost, 'gainst every rock doth run.
I am that pine, fair Love! that ship am I!
    and thou, that anchor art and root to me!
If then thou fail (O fail not!) I must die!
    and pine away in endless misery!
But words prevail not! nor can sighs devise
To move thy heart, if bent to tyrannize.

SONNET XXI.

S WINTER's rage, young plants unkindly spilleth;
    as hail, green corn; and lightnings, flowers perish;
So man's decay is Love! whose heart it killeth,
    if in his soul, he carefully it cherish.
O how alluringly he offers grace;
    and breathes new hope of life into our thought.
With cheerful, pleasant (yet deceitful) face
    he creeps and fawns, till, in his net w' are caught;
Then, when he sees us captives by him led,
    and sees us prostrate, humbly craving help,
So fierce a lion, Lybia never bred!
    nor adder's sting! nor any tigress' whelp!
O blest be they that never felt his force!
LOVE hath, nor pity, mercy, nor remorse!

SONNET XXII.

Look, as a bird, through sweetness of the call,
    doth clean forget the fowler's guileful trap;
Or one that gazing on the stars, doth fall
    in some deep pit, bewailing his mishap:
So wretched I, whilst, with Lynceus' eyes,
    I greedily beheld her angel's face,
Was straight entangled with such subtilties,
    as, ever since, I live in woful case.
Her cheeks were roses laid in crystal glass;
    her breasts, two apples of Hesperides;
Her voice, more sweet than famous THAMIRAS,
    reviving death with Doric melodies:
I, hearkening so to this attractive call,
Was caught, and ever since have lived in thrall.

SONNET XXIII.

MY LIFE's preserver! hope of my heart's bliss!
    when shall I know the doom of life or death ?
Hell's fearful torments easier are, than this
    soul's agony, wherein I now do breathe.
If thou wouldst look! this my tear-stainèd face,
    dreary and wan, far differing from what it was,
Would well reveal my most tormentful case,
    and shew thy Fair, my Grief as in a glass.
Look, as a deer late wounded very sore,
    among the herd, full heavily doth feed ;
So do I live! expecting evermore,
    when as my wounded heart should cease to bleed.
How patient then, would I endure the smart
Of pitchy-countenanced Death's dead-doing dart!

SONNET XXIV.

WHEN leaden-hearted sleep had shut mine eyes,
    and close o'erdrawn their windowlets of light ;
Whose wateriness the fire of grief so dries,
    that weep they could no longer, sleep they might!
Methought, I sank down to a pool of grief,
    and then, methought, such sinking much did please me :
But when I, down was plunged past all relief ;
    with flood-filled mouth, I called that some would ease me!
Whereat, methought, I saw my dearest Love,
    fearing my drowning, reach her hand to mine ;
Who pulled so hard to get me up above,
    that with the pull, sleep did forsake mine eyen.
But when awaked, I saw 'twas but a dream ;
I wished to have slept, and perished in that stream.

SONNET XXV.

ROUGH storms have calms, lopt boughs do grow again;
  the naked Winter is reclothed by Spring;
No year so dry but there doth fall some rain:
  Nature is kind, save me, to everything.
Only my griefs do never end nor cease!
  no ebb doth follow my still-flowing tears!
My sighs are storms, which never can appease
  their furious blasts, procured by endless cares!
Then Sighs and Sobs tell TANTALUS, "he's blest!"
  go fly to TITIUS, tell him "he hath pleasure!"
So tell IXION "though his wheel ne'er rest;
  his pains are sports, imposèd with some measure!"
Bid them be patient! bid them look on me,
And they shall see the Map of Misery.

SONNET XXVI.

THE love-hurt heart, which tyrant CUPID wounds,
  (proudly insulting o'er his conquered prey)
Doth bleed afresh where pleasure most abounds:
  for Mirth and Mourning always make a fray.
Look, as a bird sore bruisèd with a blow
  (lately dividing notes most sweetly singing),
To hear her fellows, how in tunes they flow,
  doth droop and pine, as though her knell were ringing.
The heavy-thoughted prisoner, full of doubt,
  dolefully sitting in a close-barred cage,
Is half contented; till he looketh out.
  he sees each free: then storms he in a rage!
The sight of Pleasure trebleth every pain;
As small brooks swell, and are enraged with rain.

SONNET XXVII.

THe heaven's herald may not make compare
    of working words, which so abound in thee.
Thy honey-dewed tongue exceeds his far,
    in sweet discourse and tuneful melody.
Th' amber-coloured tress which BERENICE
    for her true-loving PTHOLOMEUS, vowed
Within IDALEA's sacred Aphrodrice,
    is worthless, with thy locks to be allowed.
To thee, my thoughts are consecrate, dear Love!
    my words and phrases bound to please thine ears!
My looks are such, as any heart could move:
    I still solicit thee with sighs and tears!
O let not hate eclipse thy beauty's shine!
Then none would deem thee earthly, but divine.

SONNET XXVIII.

WEARY with serving, where I naught could get;
    I thought to cross great NEPTUNE's greatest seas,
To live in exile : but my drift was let
    by cruel Fortune, spiteful of such ease.
The ship I had to pass in, was my Mind;
    greedy Desire was topsail of the same,
My Tears were surges, Sighs did serve for wind,
    of all my ship, Despair was chiefest frame;
Sorrow was Master, Care, the cable rope;
    Grief was the mainmast, Love, the captain of it;
He that did rule the helm was foolish Hope,
    but Beauty was the rock that my ship split,
Which since hath made such shipwreck of my Joy,
That still I swim in th' ocean of Annoy.

SONNET XXIX.

CEASE, Eyes, to cherish with still flowing tears,
　　the almost withered roots of dying grief!
　Dry up your running brooks! and dam your meres!
　　and let my body die for moist relief!
But DEATH is deaf! for well he knows my pain,
　my slackless pain, hell's horror doth exceed.
There is no hell so black as her disdain!
　　whence cares, sighs, sorrows, and all griefs do breed.
Instead of sleep, when day incloistered is
　in dusty prison of infernal night,
With broad-waked eyes, I wail my miseries;
　and if I wink, I fear some ugly sight,
Such fearful dreams do haunt my troubled mind:
My Love 's the cause, 'cause She is so unkind.

SONNET XXX.

HE THAT can count the candles of the sky,
　　reckon the sands whereon Pactolus flows,
　Or number numberless small atomie[s],
　　what strange and hideous monsters Nilus shows,
What mis-shaped beasts vast Africa doth yield,
　　what rare-formed fishes live in the ocean,
What coloured flowers do grow in Tempe's field,
　　how many hours are since the world began:
Let him, none else, give judgement of my grief!
　　let him declare the beauties of my Love!
And he will say my pains pass all relief:
　　and he will judge her for a Saint above!
But, as those things, there's no man can unfold
So, nor her Fair, nor my Grief may be told!

SONNET XXXI.

FAIR ivory Brow, the board LOVE banquets on !
    sweet Lips of coral hue, but silken softness !
Fair Suns that shine, when PHŒBUS' eyes are gone!
    sweet Breath that breathes incomparable sweet-
        ness !
Fair Cheeks of purest roses red and white !
    sweet Tongue containing sweeter thing than sweet !
O that my Muse could mount a lofty flight,
    and were not all so forceless, and unmeet
To blaze the beauty of thy several shine,
    And tell the sweetness of thy sundry taste !
Able of none but of the Muses nine,
    to be arightly honourèd and graced.
The first so fair, so bright, so purely precious !
The last so sweet, so balmy, so delicious !

SONNET XXXII.

THE last so sweet, so balmy, so delicious !
    lips, breath, and tongue, which I delight to
        drink on :
    The first so fair, so bright, so purely precious !
    brow, eyes, and cheeks, which still I joy to
        think on ;
But much more joy to gaze, and aye to look on.
    those lily rounds which ceaseless hold their moving,
From whence my prisoned eyes would ne'er be gone ;
    which to such beauties are exceeding loving.
O that I might but press their dainty swelling !
    and thence depart, to which must now be hidden,
And which my crimson verse abstains from telling ;
    because by chaste ears, I am so forbidden.
There, in the crystal-pavèd Vale of Pleasure,
Lies lockèd up, a world of richest treasure.

SONNET XXXIII.

HINKING to close my over-watchèd eyes,
    and stop the sluice of their uncessant flowing;
I laid me down; when each one 'gan to rise:
    new risen Sol his flame-like countenance shewing.
But Grief, though drowsy ever, yet never sleeps;
    but still admits fresh intercourse of thought:
Duly the passage of each hour he keeps,
    nor would he suffer me with sleep be caught.
Some broken slumbers, MORPHEUS had lent
    (who greatly pitièd my want of rest);
Whereat my heart, a thousand thanks him sent:
    and vowed, to serve him he was ready prest.
Let restless nights, days, hours do their spite;
I'll love her still! and Love for me shall fight!

SONNET XXXIV.

HY should a Maiden's heart be of that proof
    as to resist the sharp-pointed dart of Love?
My Mistress' eye kills strongest man aloof;
    methinks, he's weak, that cannot quail a Dove!
A lovely Dove so fair and so divine,
    able to make what cynic soe'er liveth,
Upon his knees, to beg of their bright eyen,
    one smiling look, which life from death reviveth.
The frozen heart of cold ZENOCRATES
    had been dissolvèd into hot Desire,
Had PHRYNE cast such sunbeams from her eyes
    (such eyes are cause that my heart flames in fire!):
And yet with patience I must take my woe;
In that my dearest Love will have it so.

SONNET XXXV

ENd this enchantment, Love! of my desires!
   let me no longer languish for thy love!
Joy not, to see me thus consume in fires!
   but let my cruel pains, thy hard heart move!
And now, at last, with pitiful regard,
   eye me, thy lover! 'lorn for lack of thee!
Which, dying, lives in hope of sweet reward,
   which hate hath hitherto withheld from me.
Constant have I been, still in Fancy fast,
   ordained by heavens to doat upon my Fair,
Nor will I e'er, so long as life shall last,
   say any " 's fairer! breathing vital air."
But when the ocean sands shall lie unwet;
That shall my soul, to love thee, Dear! forget!

SONNET XXXVI.

LOng did I wish, before I could attain
   the looked-for sight, I so desired to see;
Too soon, at last I saw what bred my bane,
   and ever since hath sore tormented me.
I saw Herself, whom had I never seen,
   my wealth of bliss had not been turned to bale.
Greedy regard of Her, my heart's sole queen,
   hath changed my summer's sun to winter's hail.
How oft have I, since that first fatal hour,
   beheld her all-fair shape with begging eye,
Till She, unkind, hath killed me with a lower,
   and bade my humble-suing looks look by.
O pity me, fair Love! and highest fame
Shall blazèd be, in honour of thy name.

[R. L [inche?]
1596.

SONNET XXXVII.

DID I not love her as a lover ought,
    with purest zeal and faithfulness of heart;
Then She had cause to set my love at naught,
    and I had well deserved to feel this smart!
But holding her so dearly as I do,
    as a rare jewel of most high esteem;
She most unkindly wounds and kills me, so,
    my ne'er-stained troth most causeless to misdeem!
Never did one account of woman more
    than I of her! nor ever woman yet
Respected less, or held in lesser store
    her lover's vows, than She by mine doth set!
What resteth then? but I despair and die!
That so my death may glut her ruthless eye.

SONNET XXXVIII.

[This is a Preface to the Poem of *Diego and Gyneura*, which was originally included
in the same volume as the *Diella* Sonnets.]

HEARKEN awhile, DIELLA! to a story
    that tells of Beauty, Love, and great Disdain!
The last, caused by suspect; but She was sorry
    that took that cause, true love so much to pain.
For when She knew his faith to be unfeigned,
    spotless, sincere, most true and pure unto her;
She joyed as if a kingdom She had gained;
    and loved him now, as when he first did woo her.
I ne'er incurred suspicion of my truth;
    fairest DIELLA! why wilt thou be cruel?
Impose some end to undeservèd ruth!
    and learn by others, how to quench hate's fuel!
Read all, my Dear! but chiefly mark the end!
And be to me, as She to Him, a friend!

CHLORIS,

or

The Complaint of the passionate despised Shepherd.

By WILLIAM SMITH.

Imprinted at London, by EDMUND BOLLIFANT. 1596.

To the most excellent and learned
Shepherd COLIN CLOUT
[i.e. EDMUND SPENSER].

OLIN, my dear and most entire beloved,
    My Muse audacious stoops her pitch to thee!
Desiring that thy patience be not moved
    By these rude lines, written here you see.
Fain would my Muse, whom cruel Love hath wronged,
Shroud her love-labours under thy protection!
And I myself, with ardent zeal, have longed
That thou mightst know, to thee my true affection.
    Therefore, good COLIN, graciously accept
A few sad Sonnets which my Muse hath framed:
Though they but newly from the shell are crept,
Suffer them not by envy to be blamed!
    But, underneath the shadow of thy wings,
    Give warmth to these young-hatchèd orphan things!

    Give warmth to these young-hatchèd orphan things!
Which, chill with cold, to thee for succour creep.
They of my study are the budding springs:
Longer I cannot them in silence keep.
    They will be gadding! sore against my mind.
But, courteous Shepherd, if they run astray,
Conduct them, that they may the pathway find:
And teach them how the Mean observe they may!
    Thou shalt them ken by their discording notes!
Their weeds are plain, such as poor shepherds wear;
Unshapen, torn, and ragged are their coats:
Yet forth they wandering are, devoid of fear.
    They which have tasted of the Muses' spring,
    I hope, will smile upon the tunes they sing.
                 W. SMITH.

F I N I S.

To all Shepherds in general.

Ou whom the World admires for rarest style,
  You which have sung the Sonnets of True
    Love,
  Upon my maiden verse with favour smile !
Whose weak-penned Muse, to fly too soon doth prove :
Before her feathers have their full perfection,
She soars aloft, pricked on by blind affection.

  You whose deep wits, ingine, and industry,
The everlasting palm of praise have won !
You paragons of learned Poesy
Favour these mists ! which fall before you sun :
Intentions leading to a more effect,
If you them grace but with your mild aspect.

  And Thou, the Genius of my ill tuned note !
Whose beauty urgèd hath my rustic vein,
Through mighty oceans of despair to float ;
That I in rhyme thy cruelty complain :
Vouchsafe to read these lines both harsh and bad !
Nuntiates of Woe, with sorrow being clad.

                              W. Smith.

CHLORIS.

SONNET I.

COURTEOUS CALLIOPE, vouchsafe to lend
Thy helping hand to my untunèd Song!
And grace these Lines, which I to write
 pretend,
Compelled by love which doth poor CORIN
 wrong.
 And those, thy sacred Sisters, I beseech,
Which on Parnassus' Mount do ever dwell,
To shield my country Muse and rural speech
By their divine authority and spell.
 Lastly to thee, O PAN, the shepherds' King ;
And you swift footed Dryades, I call !
Attend to hear a swain in verse to sing
Sonnets of her that keeps his heart in thrall !
 O CHLORIS, weigh the task I undertake !
 Thy beauty, subject of my Song I make.

SONNET II.

THY beauty, subject of my Song I make ;
O fairest Fair ! on whom depends my life :
Refuse not then the task I undertake
To please thy rage, and to appease my strife !
 But with one smile remunerate my toil ;
None other guerdon I, of thee desire.
Give not my lowly Muse new-hatched the foil,
But warmth ; that she may at the length aspire
 Unto the temples of thy star-bright Eyes ;
Upon whose round orbs perfect Beauty sits :
From whence such glorious crystal Beams arise
As best my CHLORIS' seemly Face befits.
 Which Eyes, which Beauty, which bright crystal Beam,
 Which Face of thine, hath made my love extreme.

SONNET III.

EED, silly sheep! although your keeper pineth;
Yet, like to TANTALUS, doth see his food.
Skip you and leap! now bright APOLLO shineth
Whilst I bewail my sorrows in yon wood:
Where woeful PHILOMELA doth record
(And sings with notes of sad and dire lament),
The tragedy wrought by her sister's Lord.
I'll bear a part in her black discontent!
    That pipe, which erst was wont to make you glee,
Upon these downs whereon you careless graze,
Shall to her mournful music tunèd be!
Let not my plaints, poor lambkins, you amaze!
    There, underneath that dark and dusky bower,
    Whole showers of Tears to CHLORIS I will pour!

SONNET IV.

HOLE showers of Tears to CHLORIS I will pour
As true oblations of my sincere love.
If that will not suffice, most fairest Flower!
Then shall my Sighs, thee to pity move.
    If neither Tears nor Sighs can ought prevail;
My streaming Blood thine anger shall appease!
This hand of mine by vigour shall assail
To tear my heart asunder, thee to please!
    Celestial powers, on you I invocate!
You know the chaste affections of my mind!
I never did my faith yet violate!
Why should my CHLORIS then be so unkind?
    That neither Tears, nor Sighs, nor streaming Blood
    Can unto mercy move her cruel mood.

SONNET V.

YOu Fauns and Silvans, when my CHLORIS brings
Her flocks to water in your pleasant plains,
Solicit her to pity CORIN's stings!
The smart whereof, for her, he still sustains.
For she is ruthless of my woeful song.
My oaten reed she not delights to hear.
O CHLORIS! CHLORIS! CORIN thou dost wrong;
Who loves thee better than his own heart dear.
The flames of Etna are not half so hot
As is the fire which thy disdain hath bred.
Ah, cruel Fates! why do you then besot
Poor CORIN's soul with love? when love is fled!
Either cause cruel CHLORIS to relent,
Or let me die upon the wound she sent!

SONNET VI.

YOu lofty Pines, co-partners of my woe,
When CHLORIS sitteth underneath your shade;
To her those sighs and tears, I pray you show,
Whilst you attending, I for her have made.
Whilst you attending droppèd have sweet balm,
In token that you pity my distress:
ZEPHIRUS hath your stately boughs made calm;
Whilst I, to you my sorrows did express.
The neighbour mountains bendèd have their tops,
When they have heard my rueful melody;
And Elves, in rings about me leap and hop,
To frame my passions to their jollity.
Resounding echoes, from their obscure caves
Reiterate what most my fancy craves.

SONNET VII.

HAT need I mourn? seeing PAN, our sacred King,
Was, of that Nymph, fair SYRINX coy, disdained.
The World's great Light, which comforteth each
    thing,
All comfortless for DAPHNE's sake remained.
  If gods can find no help to heal the sore
Made by LOVE's shafts, which pointed are with fire;
Unhappy CORIN, then thy chance deplore!
Since they despair by wanting their desire.
  I am not PAN, though I a shepherd be;
Yet is my Love as fair as SYRINX was.
My Song cannot with PHŒBUS's tunes agree;
Yet CHLORIS doth his DAPHNE far surpass.
    How much more fair, by so much more unkind
    Than SYRINX coy, or DAPHNE, I her find.

SONNET VIII.

O sooner had fair PHŒBUS trimmed his car,
Being newly arisen from AURORA's bed;
But I, in whom Despair and Hope did war,
My unpenned flock unto the mountains led.
  Tripping upon the snow-soft downs I spied
Three Nymphs, more fairer than those Beauties Three
Which did appear to PARIS on Mount Ide.
Coming more near, my goddess I there see.
  For She, the field Nymphs oftentimes doth haunt,
To hunt with them the fierce and savage boar:
And having sported, Virelays they chant;
Whilst I, unhappy, helpless cares deplore.
    There did I call to her, ah, too unkind!
    But tiger-like, of me she had no mind.

SONNET IX.

NTO the fountain, where fair DIANA chaste
The proud ACTEON turnèd to a hart,
I drave my flock that water sweet to taste;
'Cause from the welkin, PHŒBUS 'gan depart.
There did I see the Nymph whom I admire,
Remembering her locks; of which the yellow hue
Made blush the beauties of her curlèd wire,
Which JOVE himself with wonder well might view.
Then red with ire, her tresses she berent;
And weeping hid the beauty of her face:
Whilst I, amazèd at her discontent,
With tears and sighs do humbly sue for grace.
But she, regarding neither tears nor moan,
Flies from the fountain, leaving me alone.

SONNET X.

M I a GORGON? that she doth me fly!
Or was I hatchèd in the river Nile?
Or doth my CHLORIS stand in doubt that I,
With Siren songs, do seek her to beguile?
If any one of these she can object
'Gainst me, which chaste affectèd love protest;
Then might my fortunes by her frowns be checked:
And blameless She from scandal free might rest.
But seeing I am no hideous monster born;
But have that shape which other men do bear:
Which form great JUPITER did never scorn
Amongst his subjects here on earth to wear.
Why should she then that soul with sorrow fill
Which vowèd hath to love and serve her still?

SONNET XI.

ELL me, my dear, what moves thy ruthless mind
To be so cruel, seeing thou art so fair?
Did Nature frame thy beauty so unkind;
Or dost thou scorn to pity my despair?
O no, it was not Nature's ornament,
But wingèd LOVE's impartial cruel wound,
Which in my heart is ever permanent,
Until my CHLORIS makes me whole and sound.
O glorious Love-God, think on my heart's grief!
Let not thy vassal pine through deep disdain!
By wounding CHLORIS, I shall find relief;
If thou impart to her some of my pain.
She doth thy temples and thy shrines abject!
They with AMINTA's flowers by me are decked.

SONNET XII.

EASE eyes to weep, sith none bemoans your
weeping!
Leave off, good Muse, to sound the cruel name
Of my love's Queen! which hath my heart in
keeping;
Yet of my love doth make a jesting game.
Long hath my sufferance laboured to enforce
One pearl of pity from her pretty eyes;
Whilst I, with restless oceans of remorse,
Bedew the banks where my fair CHLORIS lies,
Where my fair CHLORIS bathes her tender skin;
And doth triumph to see such rivers fall
From those moist springs, which never dry have been
Since she their honour hath detained in thrall.
And still she scorns one favouring smile to show
Unto those waves proceeding from my woe.

A Dream.

SONNET XIII.

HAT time fair TITAN in the zenith sat
And equally the fixèd poles did heat ;
When to my flock my daily woes I chat,
And underneath a broad beech took my seat :
The dreaming god, which MORPHEUS Poets call,
Augmenting fuel to my Etna's fire,
With sleep possessing my weak senses all,
In apparitions makes my hopes aspire.
  Methought I saw the Nymph I would embrace,
With arms abroad, coming to me for help :
A lust-led Satyr having her in chase ;
Which after her, about the fields, did yelp.
I seeing my Love in perplexed plight,
A sturdy bat from off an oak I reft ;
And with the ravisher continued fight
Till breathless I upon the earth him left.
Then when my coy Nymph saw her breathless foe,
With kisses kind she gratifies my pain ;
Protesting never rigour more to show.
Happy was I this good hap to obtain.
  But drowsy slumbers, flying to their cell,
My sudden joy convertèd was to bale.
My wontèd sorrows still with me.do dwell.
I lookèd round about on hill and dale :
But I could neither my fair CHLORIS view ;
Not yet the Satyr, which erst while I slew.

SONNET XIV.

OURNFUL AMYNTAS, thou didst pine with care,
    Because the Fates, by their untimely doom,
    Of life bereft thy loving PHILLIS fair;
    When thy love's Spring did first begin to bloom.
My care doth countervail that care of thine;
And yet my CHLORIS draws her angry breath:
My hopes, still hoping, hopeless now repine;
For living, She doth add to me but death.
    Thy PHILLIS dying, lovèd thee full dear.
My CHLORIS living, hates poor CORIN's love.
Thus doth my woe as great as thine appear;
Though sundry accents both our sorrows move.
    Thy swan-like Song did shew thy dying anguish:
    These weeping Truce-men shew I living languish.

SONNET XV.

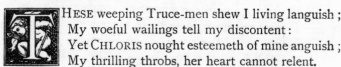

HESE weeping Truce-men shew I living languish;
    My woeful wailings tell my discontent:
    Yet CHLORIS nought esteemeth of mine anguish;
    My thrilling throbs, her heart cannot relent.
My kids to hear the rhymes and roundelays,
Which I, on wasteful hills, was wont to sing,
Did more delight than lark in summer days:
Whole echo made the neighbour groves to ring.
    But now my flock, all drooping, bleats and cries;
Because my Pipe, the author of their sport,
All rent, and torn, and unrespected, lies:
Their lamentations do my cares consort.
    They cease to feed, and listen to the plaint;
    Which I pour forth unto a cruel Saint.

SONNET XVI.

HICH I pour forth unto a cruel Saint,
Who merciless my prayers doth attend :
Who tiger-like doth pity my complaint ;
And never unto my woes will lend.
But still false hope despairing life deludes ;
And tells my fancy I shall grace obtain.
But CHLORIS fair, my orisons concludes
With fearful frowns, presagers of my pain.
Thus do I spend the weary wandering day,
Oppressèd with a chaos of heart's grief :
Thus I consume the obscure night away,
Neglecting sleep which brings all cares relief.
Thus I pass my lingering life in woe :
But when my bliss will come, I do not know !

SONNET XVII.

HE perils which LEANDER took in hand,
Fair HERO's love and favour to obtain ;
When, void of fear, securely leaving land,
Through Hellespont he swam to Cestos main :
His dangers should not counterpoise my toil.
If my dear Love would once but pity show,
To quench these flames which in my breast do broil,
Or dry these springs which from mine eyes do flow ;
Not only Hellespont, but ocean seas,
For her sweet sake, to ford I would attempt !
So that my travails would her ire appease ;
My soul, from thrall and languish to exempt.
O what is't not, poor I, would undertake ;
If labour could my peace with CHLORIS make ?

SONNET XVIII.

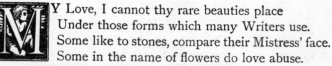

Y Love, I cannot thy rare beauties place
Under those forms which many Writers use.
Some like to stones, compare their Mistress' face.
Some in the name of flowers do love abuse.
  Some make their love a goldsmith's shop to be,
Where orient pearls and precious stones abound.
In my conceit these far do disagree
The prefect praise of beauty forth to sound.
  O CHLORIS, thou dost imitate thyself!
Self's imitating passeth precious stones
Or all the Eastern Indian golden pelf,
Thy red and white, with purest fair atones,
    Matchless for beauty Nature hath thee framed:
    Only "unkind" and "cruel" thou art named.

SONNET XIX.

HE Hound, by eating grass, doth find relief:
For, being sick, it is his choicest meat.
The wounded Hart doth ease his pain and grief;
If he, the herb *Dictamion* may eat.
  The loathsome Snake renews his sight again,
When he casts off his withered coat and hue.
The sky-bred Eagle fresh age doth obtain
When he, his beak decayèd doth renew.
  I worse than these, whose sore no salve can cure;
Whose grief, no herb, nor plant, nor tree can ease:
Remediless, I still must pain endure
Till I, my CHLORIS's furious mood can please.
    She, like the scorpion, gave to me a wound;
    And, like the scorpion, she must make me sound.

SONNET XX.

E wasteful woods, bear witness of my woe!
Wherein my plaints did oftentimes abound.
Ye, careless birds, my sorrows well do know!
They, in your songs, were wont to make a sound.
Thou, pleasant spring, canst record likewise bear.
Of my designs and sad disparagement!
When thy transparent billows mingled were
With those downfalls which from mine eyes were sent.
The echo of my still-lamenting cries,
From hollow vaults, in treble voice resoundeth;
And then into the empty air it flies,
And back again from whence it came reboundeth.
That Nymph, unto my clamours doth reply,
"Being likewise scorned in love, as well as I."

SONNET XXI.

"EING likewise scorned in love as well as I"
By that self-loving Boy; which did disdain
To hear her, after him for love to cry:
For which in dens obscure she doth remain.
Yet doth she answer to each speech and word
And renders back the last of what we speak.
But 'specially, if she might have her choice,
She of "Unkindness" would her talk forth break.
She loves to hear of Love's most sacred name;
Although, poor Nymph, in love she was despised:
And ever since she hides her head for shame,
That her true meaning was so lightly prized.
She, pitying me, part of my woes doth hear;
As you, good Shepherds, list'ning now shall hear.

SONNET XXII.

[For similar 'Echo' poems, see vol. i. pp. 220-1, 273-6, 301, and vol. ii. p. 148 *supra*].

O FAIREST Fair, to thee I make my plaint, my plaint,
To thee from whom my cause of grief
    doth spring :   doth spring.
Attentive be unto the groans, sweet Saint ! sweet Saint !
Which unto thee in doleful tunes I sing.   I sing.
    My mournful Muse doth always speak
      of thee.   of thee.
My love is pure, O do not it disdain !   disdain !
With bitter sorrow still oppress not me ; not me ;
But mildly look upon me which complain. which complain.
    Kill not my true-affecting thoughts; but
      give   but give
Such precious balm of comfort to my
    heart,   my heart,
That casting off despair, in hope to live, hope to live,
.I may find help at length to ease my
    smart.   to ease my smart.
    So shall you add such courage to my love, my love,
    That fortune false, my faith shall not
      remove.   shall not remove.

SONNET XXIII.

HE Phœnix fair which rich Arabia breeds,
When wasting time expires her tragedy ;
No more on PHŒBUS' radiant rayes she feeds :
But heapeth up great store of spicery ;
    And on a lofty tow'ring cedar tree,
With heavenly substance, she herself consumes.
From whence she young again appears to be,
Out of the cinders of her peerless plumes.
    So I, which long have fri̇ed in love's flame,
The fire, not made of spice, but sighs and tears,
Revive again, in hope Disdain to shame,
And put to flight the author of my fears.
    Her eyes revive decaying life in me ;
    Though they augmentors of my thraldom be.

SONNET XXIV.

HOUGH they augmentors of my thraldom be:
For her I live, and her I love and none else.
O then, fair eyes, look mildly upon me!
Who poor, despised, forlorn, must live alone else:
And, like AMYNTAS, haunt the desert cells
(And moneyless there breathe out thy cruelty)
Where none but Care and Melancholy dwell.
I, for revenge, to NEMESIS will cry!
If that will not prevail; my wandering ghost,
Which breathless here this love-scorched trunk shall leave,
Shall unto thee, with tragic tidings post!
How thy disdain did life from soul bereave.
    Then, all too late, my death thou wilt repent!
    When murder's guilt, thy conscience shall torment.

SONNET XXV.

HO doth not know that LOVE is triumphant,
Sitting upon the throne of majesty?
The gods themselves, his cruel darts do daunt:
And he, blind boy, smiles at their misery!
LOVE made great JOVE ofttimes transform his shape.
LOVE made the fierce ALCIDES stoop at last.
ACHILLES, stout and bold, could not escape
The direful doom which LOVE upon him cast.
    LOVE made LEANDER pass the dreadful flood,
Which Cestos from Abydos doth divide.
LOVE made a chaos where proud Ilion stood.
Through LOVE the Carthaginian DIDO died.
    Thus may we see how LOVE doth rule and reign;
    Bringing those under, which his power disdain.

SONNET XXVI.

HOUGH you be fair and beautiful withal;
And I am black, for which you me despise:
Know that your beauty subject is to fall!
Though you esteem it at so high a price.
And time may come when that whereof you boast,
Which is your youth's chief wealth and ornament,
Shall withered be by winter's raging frost;
When beauty's pride and flowering years are spent.
Then wilt thou mourn! when none shall thee respect.
Then wilt thou think how thou hast scorned my tears!
Then, pitiless, each one will thee neglect;
When hoary grey shall dye thy yellow hairs.
Then wilt thou think upon poor CORIN's case!
Who loved thee dear, yet lived in thy disgrace.

SONNET XXVII.

LOVE, leave off with sorrows to torment me!
Let my heart's grief and pining pain content thee!
The breach is made; I give thee leave to enter!
Thee to resist, great god, I dare not venture!
Restless desire doth aggravate my anguish;
Careful conceits do fill my soul with languish:
Be not too cruel, in thy conquest gained!
Thy deadly shafts have victory obtained!
Batter no more my Fort with fierce affection;
But shield me, captive, under thy protection!
[Two lines wanting.]
I yield to thee, O LOVE, thou art the stronger!
Raise then thy siege, and trouble me no longer!

SONNET XXVIII.

WHAT cruel star, or fate, had dominion
When I was born? that thus my love is crossed.
Or from what planet had I derivation?
That thus my life in seas of woe is crossed.

Doth any live that ever hath such hap,
That all their actions are of none effect?
Whom Fortune never dandled in her lap;
But, as an abject, still doth me reject.

Ah, fickle Dame! and yet thou constant art
My daily grief and anguish to increase!
And to augment the troubles of my heart;
Thou, of these bonds will never me release!

So that thy darlings, me to be may know,
The true Idea of all Worldly Woe.

SONNET XXIX.

SOME in their hearts, their Mistress's colours bear;
Some hath her gloves; some other hath her
garters;
Some in a bracelet wear her golden hair;
And some with kisses seal their loving charters:

But I, which never favour reapèd yet,
Nor had one pleasant look from her fair brow;
Content myself in silent shade to sit,
In hope at length my cares to overplow.

Meanwhile mine eyes shall feed on her fair face!
My sighs shall tell to her my sad designs!
My painful pen shall ever sue for grace!
To help my heart, which languishing now pines.

And I will triumph still amidst my woe,
Till mercy shall my sorrows overflow.

SONNET XXX.

HE raging sea, within his limits lies ;
And with an ebb, his flowing doth discharge :
The rivers, when beyond their bounds they rise
Themselves do empty in the ocean large :
But my love's sea, which never limit keepeth ;
Which never ebbs, but always ever floweth,
In liquid salt unto my CHLORIS weepeth ;
Yet frustrate are the tears which he bestoweth.
This sea, which first was but a little spring,
Is now so great, and far beyond all reason,
That it a deluge to my thoughts doth bring ;
Which overwhelmèd hath my joying season.
So hard and dry is my Saint's cruel mind ;
These waves no way in her to sink can find.

SONNET XXXI.

HESE waves no way in her to sink can find ;
To penetrate the pith of contemplation.
These tears cannot dissolve her hardened mind,
Nor move her heart on me to take compassion.
O then, poor CORIN, scorned and quite despised,
Loathe now to live ! since life procures my woe.
Enough thou hast thy heart anatomised,
For her sweet sake which will no pretty show.
But as cold winter's storms and nipping frosts
Can never change sweet AMARANTHUS' hue ;
So, though my love and life by her are crossed,
My heart shall still be constant firm and true !
Although ERINNYES hinder HYMEN's rites,
My fixèd faith against oblivion fights.

SONNET XXXII.

Y fixèd faith against oblivion fights;
 And I cannot forget her, pretty Elf!
 Although she cruel be unto my plights;
 Yet let me rather clean forget myself,
Than her sweet name out of my mind should go:
Which is th' elixir of my pining soul;
From whence the essence of my life doth flow.
Whose beauty rare, my senses all control;
 Themselves most happy evermore accounting
That such a Nymph is Queen of their affection:
With ravished rage, they to the skies are mounting;
Esteeming not their thraldom nor subjection.
 But still do joy amidst their misery;
 With patience bearing LOVE's captivity.

SONNET XXXIII.

ITH patience bearing LOVE's captivity,
 Themselves unguilty of his wrath alleging;
 These homely Lines, abjects of Poesy,
 For liberty and for their ransom pledging:
 And being free, they solemnly do vow
Under his banner ever arms to bear
Against those rebels, which do disallow
That Love, of Bliss should be the sovereign Heir.
 And CHLORIS, if these weeping Truce-men may
One spark of pity from thine eyes obtain,
In recompense of their sad heavy Lay;
Poor CORIN shall thy faithful friend remain.
 And what I say, I ever will approve,
 "No joy may be comparèd to thy love!"

SONNET XXXIV.

HE bird of Thrace, which doth bewail her rape
And murdered ITIS eaten by his Sire,
When she her woes in doleful tunes doth shape;
She sets her breast against a thorny briar.
Because care-charmer Sleep should not disturb
The tragic tale which to the night she tells;
She doth her rest and quietness thus curb,
Amongst the groves where secret silence dwells.
Even so I wake; and waking, wail all night.
CHLORIS' unkindness, slumbers doth expel.
I need not thorns, sweet sleep to put to flight.
Her cruelty, my golden rest doth quell:
That day and night to me are only one;
Consumed in woe, in tears, in sighs, and moan.

SONNET XXXV.

IKE to the shipman, in his brittle boat,
Tossed aloft by the unconstant wind;
By dangerous rocks and whirling gulfs doth float,
Hoping, at length, the wishèd Port to find:
So doth my love in stormy billows sail,
And passing the gaping SCYLLA's waves,
In hope at length with CHLORIS to prevail;
And win that prize which most my fancy craves.
Which unto me of value will be more
Than was that rich and wealthy Golden Fleece;
Which JASON stout, from Colchos island bore,
With wind in sails, unto the shore of Greece,
More rich, more rare, more worth her love I prize;
Than all the wealth which under heaven lies.

SONNET XXXVI.

WHAT a wound, and what a deadly stroke,
  Doth CUPID give to us, perplexed lovers!
  Which cleaves, more fast than ivy doth to oak,
  Unto our hearts where he his might discovers.
Though warlike MARS were armèd at all points
With that tried coat which fiery VULCAN made;
LOVE's shafts did penetrate his steelèd joints,
And in his breast in streaming gore did wade.
  So pitiless is this fell conqueror,
That in his Mother's paps his arrows stuck!
Such is his rage! that he doth not defer
To wound those orbs, from whence he life did suck.
  Then sith no mercy he shews to his mother;
  We meekly must his force and rigour smother.

SONNET XXXVII.

ACH beast in field doth wish the morning light.
  The birds to HESPER pleasant Lays do sing.
  The wanton kids, well fed, rejoice in night;
  Being likewise glad when day begins to spring.
  But night, nor day, are welcome unto me:
Both can bear witness of my lamentation.
All day, sad sighing CORIN you shall see;
All night he spends in tears and exclamation.
  Thus still I live, although I take no rest;
But living look as one that is a dying:
Thus my sad soul, with care and grief opprest,
Seems as a ghost to Styx and Lethe flying.
  Thus hath fond love bereft my youthful years
  Of all good hap, before old age appears.

SONNET XXXVIII.

HAT day wherein mine eyes cannot her see,
    Which is the essence of their crystal sight;
    Both blind, obscure, and dim that day they be,
    And are debarrèd of fair heaven's light.
That day wherein mine ears do want to hear her;
Hearing, that day, is from me quite bereft.
That day wherein to touch I come not near her;
That day no sense of touching I have left.
    That day wherein I lack the fragrant smell,
Which from her pleasant amber breath proceedeth;
Smelling, that day, disdains with me to dwell.
Only weak hope, my pining carcase feedeth.
    But burst, poor heart! Thou hast no better hope,
    Since all thy senses have no further scope.

SONNET XXXIX.

HE stately lion and the furious bear,
    The skill of man doth alter from their kind;
    For where before they wild and savage were,
    By Art, both tame and meek you shall them find.
The elephant, although a mighty beast,
A man may rule according to his skill.
The lusty horse obeyeth our behest,
For with the curb, you may him guide at will.
    Although the flint most hard contains the fire,
By force we do his virtue soon obtain:
For with a steel you shall have your desire.
Thus man may all things by industry gain.
    Only a woman, if she list not love;
    No art, nor force, can unto pity move

SONNET XL.

O art nor force can unto pity move
    Her stony heart, that makes my heart to pant :
    No pleading passions of my extreme love
    Can mollify her mind of adamant.
  Ah, cruel sex, and foe to all mankind !
Either you love, or else you hate, too much !
A glist'ring show of gold in you we find ;
And yet you prove but copper in the touch.
  But why ? O why, do I so far digress ?
Nature you made of pure and fairest mould,
The pomp and glory of Man to depress ;
And as your slaves in thraldom them to hold :
    Which by experience now too well I prove,
    There is no pain unto the pains of love.

SONNET XLI.

AIR Shepherdess, when as these rustic lines
    Come to thy sight, weigh but with what affection
    Thy servile doth depaint his sad designs ;
    Which to redress, of thee he makes election.
  If so you scorn, you kill ; if you seem coy,
You wound poor CORIN to the very heart ;
If that you smile, you shall increase his joy ;
If these you like, you banish do all smart :
  And this I do protest, most fairest Fair,
My Muse shall never cease that hill to climb,
To which the learned Muses do repair !
And all to deify thy name in rhyme.
    And never none shall write with truer mind
    As by all proof and trial you shall find.

SONNET XLII.

IE, die my Hopes! for you do but augment
The burning accents of my deep despair ;
Disdain and scorn, your downfall do consent :
Tell to the World, She is unkind, yet fair.
O Eyes, close up those ever-running fountains !
For pitiless are all the tears you shed ;
Wherewith you watered have both dales and mountains.
I see, I see remorse from her is fled.

Pack hence, ye Sighs, into the empty air !
Into the air that none your sound may hear.
Sith cruel CHLORIS hath of you no care
(Although she once esteemèd you full dear) ;
Let sable night all your disgraces cover !
Yet truer sighs were never sighed by lover.

SONNET XLIII.

HOU glorious Sun (from whence my lesser light
The substance of his crystal shine doth borrow)
Let these my moans find favour in thy sight,
And with remorse extinguish now my sorrow !
Renew those lamps which thy disdain hath quenched,
As PHŒBUS doth his sister PHŒBE's shine :
Consider how thy CORIN, being drenched
In seas of woe, to thee his plaints incline !

And at thy feet, with tears, doth sue for grace ;
Which art the goddess of his chaste desire.
Let not thy frowns, these labours poor deface !
Although aloft they at the first aspire.
And time shall come, as yet unknown to men,
When I more large thy praises forth shall pen.

SONNET XLIV.

HEN I more large thy praises forth shall show,
 That all the World thy beauty shall admire ;
 Desiring that most sacred Nymph to know,
 Which hath the Shepherd's fancy set on fire.
  Till then, my dear, let these thine eyes content
Till then, fair Love, think if I merit favour !
Till then, O let thy merciful assent
Relish my hopes with some comforting savour !
  So shall you add such courage to my Muse,
That she shall climb the steep Parnassus' Hill :
That learned Poets shall my deeds peruse,
When I from thence obtainèd have more skill.
  And what I sing shall always be of thee,
  As long as life, or breath, remains in me.

SONNET XLV.

HEN she was born, whom I entirely love,
 Th' immortal gods, her birth-rites forth to grace,
 Descending from their glorious seat above ;
 They did on her, these several virtues place :
  First SATURN gave to her Sobriety ;
JOVE then enduèd her with Comeliness ;
And SOL with Wisdom did her beautify ;
MERCURY with Wit and Knowledge did her bless ;
  VENUS with Beauty did all parts bedeck ;
LUNA therewith did Modesty combine ;
DIANA chaste, all loose desires did check ;
And like a lamp in clearness she doth shine.
  But MARS, according to his stubborn kind,
  No virtue gave ; but a disdainful mind.

SONNET XLVI.

HEN CHLORIS first, with her heart-robbing eye,
    Enchanted had my silly senses all ;
    I little did respect LOVE's cruelty :
    I never thought his snares should me enthrall.
        But since her tresses have entangled me,
My pining flock did never hear me sing
Those jolly notes, which erst did make them glee ;
Nor do my kids about me leap and spring
    As they were wont : but when they hear my cry ;
They likewise cry, and fill the air with bleating.
Then do my sheep upon the cold earth lie,
And feed no more.   My griefs they are repeating.
    O CHLORIS, if thou then sawest them and me,
    I am sure thou would'st both pity them and me !

SONNET XLVII.

UT of thy heart too cruel I thee tell,
    Which hath tormented my young budding age ;
    And doth, (unless your mildness, passions quell)
    My utter ruin near at hand presage.
        Instead of blood, which wont was to display
His ruddy red upon my hairless face ;
By over-grieving, that is fled away :
Pale dying colour there hath taken place.
    Those curlèd locks, which thou wast wont to twist,
Unkempt, unshorn, and out of order been ;
Since my disgrace, I had of them no list,
Since when, these eyes no joyful day have seen :
    Nor never shall, till you renew again
    The mutual love which did possess us twain.

SONNET XLVIII.

YOU that embrace enchanting Poesy,
    Be gracious to perplexèd CORIN's lines !
You that do feel Love's proud authority,
    Help me to sing my sighs and sad designs !
      CHLORIS, requite not faithful love with scorn !
But, as thou oughtest, have commiseration.
I have enough anatomized and torn
My heart, thereof to make a pure oblation.
    Likewise consider how thy CORIN prizeth
Thy parts above each absolute perfection !
How he, of every precious thing deviseth,
To make thee Sovereign !   Grant me then affection !
    Else thus I prize thee, CHLORIS is alone
    More hard than gold, or pearl, or precious stone.

SONNET XLIX.

COLIN, I know that, in thy lofty wit,
    Thou wilt but laugh at these my youthful lines ;
Content I am, they should in silence sit,
    Obscured from light to sing their sad designs.
      But that it pleasèd thy grave Shepherdhood,
The Patron of my maiden verse to be ;
When I in doubt of raging envy stood :
And now I weigh not who shall *CHLORIS* see !
    For fruit before it comes to full perfection
But blossoms is, as every man doth know :
So these, being blooms, and under thy protection,
In time I hope to ripeness more will grow.
    And so I leave thee to thy worthy Muse ;
    Desiring thee, all faults here to excuse

F I N I S.

LAURA.

The Toys of a Traveller:

or

The Feast of Fancy.

DIVIDED INTO THREE PARTS.

BY

R[OBERT] T[OFTE],

Gentleman.

Poca favilla gran fiamma seconda.

LONDON,

Printed by VALENTINE SIMMES.
1597.

To the no less virtuous than fair, the
Honourable Lady LUCY, sister to
the thrice renowned and noble
Lord, HENRY [PERCY] Earl
of NORTHUMBERLAND.

OOD Madam, I make bold to present unto you a
few Toys of mine own travail: [the] most part
conceived in Italy, and some of them brought
forth in England. By which my imperfections,
you may see, as in a lively mirror, your own
perfections; and by the follies of my rechlesse [*heedless*]
youth, behold plainly the virtues of your flowering age:
hoping your Ladyship will keep them as privately, as I
send them unto you most willingly.

Neither doubt I at all but that your excellent spirit will
judge graciously of this my bare, yet bounden, conceit; and
to accept the same, as a mean[s], at idle times, to drive
away that self-pleasing, yet ill-easing, humour of never-glad
melancholy, which spiteful Fortune, seeking (though in vain)
most injuriously to insult over you, laboureth by all means
possible to inflict upon you: the virtuous behaviour of yourself being such as, even in the midst of all your crosses, you
cross her designs with an invincible heart, and with your
honourable carriage carry her, with all her devices, as a slave
to follow you, in all your generous and thrice-noble actions;
maugre the intricate labyrinth of so many and infinite
troubles allotted, most unworthily, unto you, by the irre-
vocable doom of your too partial and flinty Destiny. All

which notwithstanding, you bear and over-bear, with a
most resolute staiedness; and a resolved courage of a right
P E R C Y, and of a mind *A per se.*

But additions breed suspicions; and fair words, for the
most part are counted the blazons of flattery: therefore I
will leave to the temperate judgment of the wise, and to
the uncorrupt censure of the worthier sort, your heroical
and undaunted mind; and the integrity and never-stained
proceedings of your spotless self.

Only this, with submission, will I say, that if the richness
of the ground is known by the corn; the daintiness of the
water, by the sweetness of the fish; and the goodness of the
tree, by the rareness of the fruit: then may every man give
a guess of the internal habit and excellent qualities of your
inward mind, by the outward behaviour and apparent semblance of your exceeding chaste, and more than admirable,
demeanour in every respect.

And thus, hoping your Honour will as debonairly accept
of these Trifles, as I dutifully bequeath them unto you;
and with the sun-shining favour of your gracious aspect
deign to read these few lines: craving both privilege, and
pardon, for all such faults and defects as shall happen to
be discovered in the same,

I humbly devote myself unto

Your Ladyship's thrice-virtuous and immaculate
disposition and command whatsoever,

Who am bound, as a vasssal,

To do homage unto the same for ever,

R. T.

To the Gentle, and Gentlemen, Readers
whatsoever.

ENTLEMEN. As the Fencer first maketh a flourish with his weapon before he cometh to strokes, in playing [for] his prize: so I thought good, *pro formâ* only, to use these few lines unto you, before you come to the pith of the matter.

What the Gentleman was, that wrote these verses, I know not; and what She is, for whom they are devised, I cannot guess: but thus much I can say, That as they came into the hands of a friend of mine [? *the* R. B. *of page* 424] by mere fortune; so happened I upon them by as great a chance.

Only in this I must confess we are both to blame, that whereas he having promised to keep private the original; and I, the copy, secret: we have both consented to send it abroad, as common; presuming chiefly upon your accustomed courtesies. Assuring ourselves, if we may have your protections, we shall think ourselves as safe as ULYSSES did, when he was shadowed under the shield of PALLAS against furious AJAX; so we, by your countenances, shall be sufficiently furnished to encounter against any foul-mouthed JACKS whatsoever.

To censure of this Work is for better wits than

mine own: and it is for Poets, not Printers [*This therefore was written by* VALENTINE SIMMES, *the Printer of this Book. See also page* 424] to give judgement of this matter. Yet, if I may be bold to report what I have heard other Gentlemen affirm, Many have written worse; Some, better; Few, so well. The Work, being so full of Choice and Change as, it is thought, it will rather delight every way than dislike any way.

Thus, courteous Gentlemen, building upon my wonted foundation of your friendly acceptance, I rest your debtors; and will study, in what I can, daily to make you amends.

Yours always

[VALENTINE SIMMES.]

Alla bellissima sua Signora.

E. C.

[The Lady's name was E. CARIL.: see Book II., Poem XXXIII., at page 397.]

HROUGH thee, not of thee, Lady fair I write;
Through power of Beauty, not of Virtues, thine:
With zealous will, though slender be my might,
I, weakling, seek an eagle's nest to climb.
 Then guide my feet! and if to slip I chance,
 Uphold me by the favour of thy glance!

Accept in gree these verses rudely penned;
A sign of duty which to thee I owe:
And deign with sweet regard them to defend;
Which as condemnèd else are like to go.
 In thee, it rests the stamp on them to set:
 If current, Pass! Suppressed! if counterfeit.

And though the note, thy praises only fit,
Of sweetest bird, the dulcet nightingale:
[R and T stand here, and elsewhere, for the initials of the Author.] Disdain not little Robin RedbreasT yet!
 [A line wanting.]
 What he doth want in learning or in skill;
 He doth supply with zeal of his good will

For only Thee, they were devised alone :
And unto Thee, they dedicated are.
Who knows?   Perhaps this kindness, by thee shown,
Shall make this glimpse shine like a glittering star.
> Such is thy virtue in the World his sight ;
> Thy crow though black, may go for swan most white.

Then doubt me not, though parted we remain :
In England thou ; and I in Italy.
As I did part, I will return again,
Loyal to thee ; or else with shame I'll die !
> True Lovers, when they travel countries strange,
> The air, and not their constant minds, do change.

Cœlum, non animum, mutant, qui trans mare currunt.

*Affettionatissimo servid, della
divina Bellezza sua.*

R. T.

LAURA.

THE FIRST PART.

I.

ORTUNE, cross-friend to ever-conquering
  Love,
Our bodies, Lady, hath divided far;
But yet our constant minds she cannot move,
Which over-strong for her devices are.
  Woe's me! in England thou dost bide,
    and I,
    Scarce shadow of my self, in Italy.
But let her do her worst, and what is frail
And mortal seek to separate and undo;
Yet what immortal is, she never shall!
A string too high for her to reach unto.
  In spite of envious seeds, by malice sown,
  My heart shall aye be thine; and mine, thine own!

Padoa.

II.

HOUGH I do part, my heart yet doth not part;
  My poor afflicted body parts in twain,
  And doth in pieces two divide my heart:
  One piece my fainting spirit doth sustain,
The other part I leave with thee behind,
(The better part, and of my heart most dear);
Then to that part, so parted, be thou kind!
And to the same impart thy loving cheer!
  That I, returning, may again unite
  This parted heart; and find for grief, delight.

London.

III.

IKE to the blacksome Night, I may compare
 My Mistress' gown, when darkness 'plays his
  prize :
 But her sweet face, like to the sun most fair ;
  When he in glory 'ginneth to arise.
Yet this no whit the other doth disgrace ;
 But rather doubleth Beauty in the place.
Contraries like to these set opposite,
So dainty and so pleasing in their show
To lookers on, do breed no small delight ;
And pleasure great thereby to them doth grow.
 O wonder strange ! O solace sweet ! to see
 In one self subject, Night and Day to be.

IV.

N the Egean dangerous Sea of Love,
 In midst of faithless waves and wicked wind ;
 Where, to my cost, most bitter brunts I prove :
 A new ARION, there, myself I find.
And though, as he, I play on harp and sing ;
Yet cannot cunning mine so high aspire
As for to make the skipping fish me bring
Unto that wishèd shore I so desire.
 Only my LAURA, peerless for to see,
 May, in this troubled flood, my dolphin be !

V.

REAT was the strife between the sun on high
    And my fair Sun, when first she 'gan to 'pear,
    Who should exceed in brightest majesty;
    And show in sight of spacious world most clear.
The sun did shine; but she did lighten bright,
And so his burning beams extinguished quite.
Nay more, my Sun on sudden to the sun
Sent light; and yet no light at all did want:
Where else the other had been quite undone
For lack of brightness; which with him was scant.
    The beauty then the sun doth use to show,
    My Sun doth give; and from her, it doth grow.

VI.

URNED to a stone was he that did bewray,
    Unwitting, to the crafty thief himself
    The theft; not thinking he had stolen the prey,
    In hope to gain a little paltry pelf.
So I, who unawares to cruel Thee,
The robber of my heart, confessed the theft;
A senseless stone like BATTUS am to see:
Only in this unlike that shape bereft,
    That where to worthless stone he turnèd was;
    I for a Touchstone true of Love do pass

VII.

Own from the neck unto that dainty Breast,
　(Which Nature made a Mirror of Delight;
　And where a World of Beauties sweet do rest)
　Doth hang a costly Chain of Pearl most bright;
　　And of proportion are so just and round,
　　That such in India rich cannot be found.
Besides, their orient brightness is alike;
So that mine eyes are dazzled with the same,
And, not much used to see so fair a sight
(A sight which doth the sun in glory stain),
　　Cannot discern, though them they both do see,
　　If Breast be Pearl, or Pearl in Bosom be.

VIII.

To give that life, which had not breath before;
　PROMETHEUS, from above, stole heavenly fire:
　For which his boldness he was plaguèd sore,
　　A just reward for such a high aspire.
So whilst I steal from thee, my heaven above,
The heat which doth revive my dying sprite:
For rashness, mine eternal grief I prove.
Yet, though our fault 's all one—the plague 's not like:
　　He feels of vulture one, alone, the smart;
　　But I have thousands, which still gnaw my heart.

IX.

OVE, being blind, hath wrought me damage sore;
Thou, blind in this my loving, evil wast;
Nor would I see the snare, being blind far more,
Wherein myself, I did entangle fast.
    Yet hath this blindness harm done unto none
    But unto Beauty's buzzard, me alone.
When blinded Boy did catch my harmless heart;
Thou didst not see the net so intricate
Which bound me (being blind, blind as Thou art!)
To be a thrall in this most wretched state.
    So that, alone to work my misery,
    LOVE blind is; blind wert Thou; and blinder, I,

X.

F, LAURA, thou dost turn 'gainst me in hate;
Then me, such busses sweet why dost thou give?
Why check'st thou not the Cheeks which give the
    mate?
    The vital cause whereby I breathe and live?
Perhaps it is, because through too much joy,
As in sweet swound [*swoon*], I might away depart:
If so thou do, and think me so to 'noy;
Kiss hardly! and with kissing, breed my smart!
    Content am I to lose this life of mine;
    Whilst I do kiss that lovely lip of thine.

XI.

PON triumphant chariot, 'passing rare,
(In which my Sun doth sit like Majesty :
And makes the day shew unto us more fair ;
Whose cheerfulness delights each mortal eye.)
   I, rash, like to another PHAETON,
     With hare-brain haste, too hasty lept thereon.
But for my boldness dearly did I pay ;
And had like plague, as he, for being o'er-brave :
Yet though in equal fortune both did stay
(For life he lost ; and death She to me gave) ;
   The punisher of both was not the same,
    For he, by JOVE ; and I, by LOVE ; was slain.

XII.

HE beauty, that in Paradise doth grow,
   Lively appears in my sweet goddess's Face ;
From whence, as from a crystal river, flow
Favour divine and comeliness of grace.
But in her dainty, yet too cruel, Breast,
More cruelty and hardness doth abound ;
Than doth in painful Purgatory rest.
So that, at once, She's fair, and cruel, found :
   When in her Face and Breast, ah, grief to tell !
   Bright Heaven she shows ; and crafty, hides dark Hell.

XIII.

HILST angry JUNO, from the scowling skies,
  Thick swinging showers did downward send
    amain;
  My Lady, mounting up in stately wise,
    From heaven more fast did fiery lightning rain.
      So that the people, passing, had less harm
      By water wet, than by the fire o'erwarm.
The water only wet their outward skin;
A matter small, in which was danger none:
But this her fire did burn their hearts within;
And forced them, as they went, to sigh and groan.
  So that their grief was greater, sans all doubt,
  To have within fire, than water, without.

XIV.

HE swift Meander, turning, winds so fast,
  And with his stream in circle-wise so runs;
  That, wanton-like, from whence he springs, at last,
  Back to his fountain-head again he comes.
In me, a river huge of tears, from heart
To watery eyes ascend; from whence they flow,
And running down, do from mine eyes depart,
Descending to my heart again below.
  So that, through virtue of most mighty Love,
  In heart, a new Meander I do prove.

XV.

HOU stranger, who with wand'ring steps dost wend,
Thy gazing eyes turn quickly unto me!
And to my speech, with list'ning ear attend!
In whom four Elements united be.
Mark well; and, as a wonder, tell the same
Of CUPID's force! poor Lovers' TAMBURLAINE!
First this my body's Earth, and earth most cold.
The Fire within my heart, in covert lies.
The Air's my sighs. Mine eyes do Waters hold.
Thus for my Saint, he doth me martyrize.
Earth is my body; (Strange seems not this same?)
The Air, my sighs; eyes, Water; heart, the Flame.

XVI.

F lovely Lass, for Fairing thine, of me
Gold, in this Fair, thou meanest for to have;
Then give me of thy hairs! which golden be.
Give unto me! since thou of me dost crave.
Nor by this bargain, shalt thou loss sustain;
Or ought hereby shalt hindered be, sweet Wench!
Since I, to courteous thee, do give again,
As thankful, gold; for gold in recompence.
Thy treasure, so shall mine be; mine, as thine:
Nor shall th' exchange be worse than gold most fine.

XVII.

OCKED in a cradle, like as infants be,
　　When I was young, a little wanton child,
　　Two dainty dugs did nourish life in me ;
　　Whilst oft on them, with teat in mouth, I smiled.
　Ah, happy I ! thrice happy, might I say ;
　Whilst in that harmless state I then did stay.
But now that I am come to man's estate ;
Such dugs as nursed me in delight and joy
Do seek my death, by poisonous sugared bait ;
Whose sight, without possession, breeds me 'noy.
　So what, in childhood, causèd me to live ;
　Now, in my youth, doth death unto me give.

XVIII.

F Sea, no other thing doth shew to be
　　Than most unstable waters moving oft :
　　With pardon, Lady, you this seem to me ;
　　So most unstable is your changing thought.
I, likewise, hold a River, that o'erwhelms
With wat'ry salt, within these eyes of mine.
Then let us make a mixture 'mongst ourselves
Of this unsteadfastness and wat'ry brine !
　Let 's fashion, both of us, a novel Sea !
　So heaven, the Haven ; and Love, the Bay shall be.

XIX.

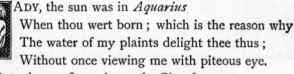

ADY, the sun was in *Aquarius*
  When thou wert born ; which is the reason why
  The water of my plaints delight thee thus ;
  Without once viewing me with piteous eye.
  But when as I was born, the Sign I guess
  In *Cancer* was ; a show of my distress.
This is the cause, within my boiling breast
Doth burn a hot and unextinguished fire :
But contrary these Signs in us do rest ;
Nor do they well accord to my desire.
  Far better had it been, *Aquarius's* Sign
  Had happed to me; and *Cancer's* had been thine !

XX.

HAT time, with brow, the Loveliest 'gins to scowl;
  Shewing disdain and fury in her face :
  Methinks I see the clouds wax dark and foul;
  And gloomy night begins to run his race.
But, then again, when She to show begins
Her smiling cheer, adorned with favour rare :
Straightways the sun, in chariot bright forth springs ;
Clear are the skies ; the gladsome day, most fair.
  Thus, in one face, I see, against my will,
  The rising of the sun ; and falling, still.

XXI.

R ANKLE the wound did in my head apace;
When fairest She, to play the Surgeon came:
And whilst her snow-white hand did me the grace
To lay the plaster on, which healed the same,
A wonder strange! No sooner did she touch
The hurt; but it appeared to be none such.
Yet, woe is me, no sooner by that hand
Was healed in head my outward fest'ring wound;
But that instead of that, as countermand,
One mortal scar at inward heart I found.
Thus, LOVE! thou seest is changèd my estate
She checks with Death, that 'fore gave Life for mate.

Venice.

XXII.

I F in the midst of kindling burning fire,
That worthy Roman burnt his valiant hand;
I like another MUTIUS in desire,
Have scorched my fist likewise, through LOVE's
command,
In freshest moisture; where my Lady sweet,
Her lily hands, for coolness, divèd oft.
But though desire between us was alike;
Yet was the matter diverse which we sought.
He chose to burn his hand, with courage bold,
In flaming fire; and I, in water cold.

XXIII.

THE Gentiles used, in sign of sacrifice,
    The blood of men to offer ; to appease
    The warlike goddess's wrath, in humble wise ;
    And through the same, her angry mind did please :
But Thou, more wicked Warrior far than she,
In reason may'st more cruel termèd be.
On Beauty's altar, to thee dedicate ;
Thousands of Lovers, mustering on a row,
Offer their blood and hearts ! yet mitigate
Thy hardened mind cannot : which flint doth show.
    Then is she cruel less than Thou art now :
    Since blood her pleased ; and Thee hearts cannot bow

XXIV.

FOR to behold my Sun, I from the sun
    Did seek my face to shadow with my hand,
    To shield me from the heat, that 'gan to come
    In place, where gazing on her I did stand.
But I no sooner from that sun was free,
But that, in that self instant and that time,
I, of mine own Sun, found myself to be
Burnt with the heat ; a most unlucky sign.
    So whilst a shade from sun did me defend,
    A Sun more hot did hurt me in the end.

XXV.

HITE was the orient pearl which, on a day,
 That hand me gave: which scorns the proud compare
Of purest white; and bears the palm away
As of all pearly Fairs, the orient'st fair.
  And whilst She offered unto me the same,
  I knew not which the Pearl was, of the twain.
So white the hand was of my peerless Pearl
As it did dazzle with delight mine eyes,
And pearl seemèd to me, giving me the pearl;
Which made me, sighing, say in whisp'ring wise,
 "Ah, why once may I not so happy be,
 This Pearl to have; which th' other gives to me?"

XXVI.

HEN you appear, appears the Break of Day;
 And shews to be most fair and passing bright:
But if you keep yourself unseen away,
 The Day shows not; but keepeth out of sight.
Then if again you 'gin yourself to show;
Behold the Day to shew itself afresh
With sky most clear. So both of you do grow
In beauty like: in heat nor are you less.
 Thus if your beams you ope, or hidden been:
 The Break of Day appears; else ne'er is seen.

XXVII.

USTLY of thee, Love partial, I complain
That, at one instant and with one self stroke,
Thou dartèd hast into my heart, with pain,
Cold chilly frost; and fiery flaming smoke.
  Ay me! within me, both I secret hold:
  And whilst th' one burns me, th' other makes
    me cold.
Then, Cruel, since thou wilt, two contraries,
Against my soul, within my heart shall rest:
Ah, yet make peace 'twixt them, in loving wise!
Or else, sweet Love, do promise this at least!
  Flame to my frost, and water to my fire;
  Life to my heart, to comfort my desire.

XXVIII.

IANA shineth in the heavens clear;
Because from purest Sun she takes her light:
And Fair, she shews that of DIANA here
On Earth, doth borrow beauty passing bright.
The virtue then that is infused in her,
She from DIANA hath; or else from none:
For other thews do all in her concur;
And unto her beholding are alone.
  O wonder strange of Nature to reveal!
  She, DIAN' gives; yet doth from DIAN' steal.

Sienna.

XXIX.

A S burnished gold, such are my Sovereign's Hairs;
    A brace of stars divine, her blackish Eyes;
    Like to the fairest black the raven bears;
    Or fairer, if you fairer can devise.
So likewise fair 's the beauty of her Breasts;
  Where Pleasure lurks, where joy still dallying rests.
This VENUS' Bower, you rightly may compare
To whitest snow that e'er from heaven fell;
Or to the mines of alabaster fair.
Woe 's me! 'Tis sweet to sleep in CUPID's cell!
  Whilst he, the heart makes surfeit with delight;
  Through golden Hair, black Eyes, and Breast most white.

XXX.

U NTO thy favour (which when Nature formed,
    She went beyond herself with cunning hand),
    I may compare what is, in world, adorned
    With beauty most; and with most grace doth
        stand.
But every mortal whiteness, ne'er so white,
The ivory white of thy white hand exceeds:
So that my soul, which doth fair whiteness like,
Rests on fair whiteness, and on whiteness feeds.
  For this is thought, and hopèd of from thee:
  White as thy hands. so white thy faith shall be.

XXXI.

 ADY, thou seemest like FORTUNE unto me;
    When I most wistly mark, how thou dost go
    With golden tresses loose (a joy to see!);
    Which gentle wind about thy ears doth blow.
And as thou her resemblest in this sort;
  So dost thou in attire, and all thy port.
Only thou wantest for thy swift right hand
The rolling Wheel: and shadowing Veil to hide
Those eyes; which, like Controllers, do command.
But if thou long'st of these to be supplied,
    Take me, thy prisoner, for to play this part!
    For my desire 's the Wheel, the Veil 's my heart.

XXXII.

 HOU, merry, laugh'st, and pleasantly dost smile:
    I woeful weep, and mestful sorrow still;
    Lest this thy mirth increasing, me beguile,
    And weave a web for me of greater ill.
Too well perceive I this thy deep disdain,
By this thy feignèd looks and cloakèd glee.
Thou of disaster mine art glad and fain;
And fain my death, as basilisk, would'st see;
    Since that of war and 'bate this laughter is,
    And not of gentle peace and calmy bliss.

XXXIII.

INCE thou hast changed thy gown and thine attire ;
Ah, change thy thoughts ! not always cruel be !
And with new clothes, put on a new desire !
That new, in every point, I may thee see :
And if thou heretofore unkind hast been ;
Be courteous now, and gentle be thou seen !
Thy glory great, thy praise more shalt thou find ;
If, of unconstant, constant thou become !
And of a foe, a faithful friend and kind !
Then change henceforth thy thoughts ! else I, undone.
Give me that colour which so likes mine eyen !
If death, then black : if life, then carnatine [*rosy red*].

XXXIV.

HANGED is my nature in me ; where before
I like was to a chilly freezing ice ;
I now a flame am, burning inward sore :
And such a flame that burneth in such wise
That if LOVE and my Mistress take no care
For this my hurt, my soul must quickly die.
Yet one doth see (for both not blinded are !)
The fire so hot doth burn, wherein I fry,
That fierce PERILLUS's boiling Bull of brass
May unto this for icy substance pass.

XXXV.

AR better had it been, I had been dead,
　　And laid full low in latest home, my grave；
　　Than with that drink myself for to have fed,
　　Which LAURA mine in crystal glass me gave.
The liquor pleased me, I must needs confess：
Yet to my heart, 'twas poison ne'ertheless.
So that I had contrary quite effect
To my desire；which I so much did wish.
Love was in fault, who Reason doth reject.
And see my cruel luck, what happed in this！
　　The wine was sweet；yet did his nature turn：
　　It cooled my mouth, but heart within did burn.

XXXVI.

WEET sang thy bird, in ebon cage shut fast,
　　And did delight thy dainty ears so much
　　As thou vouchsafedst to give him meat at last；
　　And gently did his feathers stroke and touch.
So, Lady, I likewise, in th' ebony
Of thy bright eyes am prisoner, and do sing
Thy Beauty's praise；and yet not fed am I
By thee：yet live through thee；a wondrous thing！
　　Love to my heart thy beauty doth supply
　　For food；which else, through famine starved, would die.

XXXVII.

F white 's the Moon, thou LAURA seem'st as white;
And white 's the gown which you on body wear.
And if her whitely horns, in calmy night,
She, smoothly gliding, shows to us most clear:
You, in the daytime, more and brighter far
Your beauty show; like bright AURORA's star.
Like brightness both of you abroad do cast;
Though not effect alike *per accidens:*
You shine, she shines, your powers eternal last;
But yet between you is great difference.
Her brightness freezeth, causing deadly cold:
Yours doth inflame, and lovely fire doth hold.

XXXVIII.

VEN as the lamp goeth out, that oil doth want,
Or as the sun doth fall in th' Occident;
So did my heart within me 'gin to pant;
My vital spirits away by little went:
When, taking on me pity, graciously
My Mistress's hem of garment, trailing down,
Touched me; and me revivèd suddenly.
Then if such virtue be within her gown;
Imagine what doth stay her corpse within!
Which who seeth, through sweetness needs must sin.

XXXIX.

EATED on marble was my Lady blithe,
  Holding in hand a crystal looking-glass;
  Marking of Lovers thousands; who alive,
  Thanks only to her beauty rare, did pass.
To pry in glasses likes her: but afterward
She takes the nature of the stone most hard.
For whilst she cheerfully doth fix her eyes,
Gazing upon the brightness of the one;
Her heart, by th' other 's made, in strangy wise,
Hard as a rock and senseless as a stone:
  So that if Love this breaketh not in twain;
  It will a flint become, to others' pain.

XL.

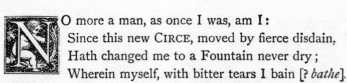

O more a man, as once I was, am I:
  Since this new CIRCE, moved by fierce disdain,
  Hath changed me to a Fountain never dry;
  Wherein myself, with bitter tears I bain [? *bathe*].
Then am I one who always eyes do bear;
And breast of water flowing only full.
Take heed, you Lovers all, of her! and fear
The sugared baits of this deceitful Trull!
  Lest by this CIRCE new, you be deceived,
  As I have been; and be of shape bereaved.

The Conclusion of the First Part.

THE Macedonian Monarch once did deign,
In cheerful sort, in kind and loving wise,
To feast in village with a homely Swain ;
Who entertained him, as in country guise,
With curds and creams, and such like knacks he
had.
Whereof the courteous Prince accepted glad.

So, Lady, boldly I presumèd have,
To invite you to a sorry banquet base ;
Nor to disdain the same, of you I crave !
Though cates too coarse for you ; too poor, the place.
I cannot, as I would, give curds and cream ;
But milk and whey : my fortune is so mean.

Yet (if you shall accept it graciously ;
And with your favour sweet, this board adorn)
The virtue which is in you, presently,
The whey, to curds ; the milk, to cream shall turn.
But if your look (you angry) turn away ;
The milk shall still be milk ; the whey, still whey.

Then as the sun in glorious wise doth shine
As well on valley low as mountain high ;
Vouchsafe one cheerful glimpse of favour thine
On poor me, from out that heavenly eye !
Unworthy I, such grace ! I do confess :
Yet worthy thou to do so, ne'ertheless.

R. T.

LAURA.

THE SECOND PART.

I.

F I somewhile look up into the Skies,
I see, fair Lady, that same cheerful light;
Which, like to you, doth shine in glorious
    wise:
And if on th' Earth, I chance to cast my
    sight;
The moveless centre firm to me doth show
The hardness which within your heart doth grow.
If Seas I view, the flowing waves most plain
Your fickle faith do represent to me.
So as I still behold you, to my pain;
When as the Skies, or th' Earth, or Seas I see:
    For in your seemly self doth plain appear
    Like faith; like hardness; and like brightness clear.

II.

ARVEL I do not, though thou dost not see
My griefs and martyrs; which I still sustain.
For thou, the Mole of Love dost seem to me;
But if a Mole, th' art only to my pain.
How comes it then that, seeing thou art blind,
Thou me consum'st, as if thou had'st thy sight?
Why, as thy nature by instinct doth bind,
Stayest not below? Pack hence, and leave this light!
    Either those eyes still shut, not me to grieve;
    Or under ground, in darkness, always live!

III.

IF whilom, in times past, that Spartan Lass
    (" The Flower of Greece," Dan PARIS's costly joy)
    Through her fair feature, the only causer was,
        So many Knights were slain at Siege of Troy:
Thou, LAURA, art unlike unto her far!
In this our Age, a much more blessed star.
For she brought Wars, Strife, Death, and Cruelty;
Where thou, alone, bring'st Peace and Pleasure still.
Ah, happy thrice, that ligs in love with thee!
And if, by chance, un'wares, thou sometimes kill:
    Thou, with thy smile, the wound canst heal again;
    And give him life, whom thou before hadst slain.

                                                    Pisa.

IV.

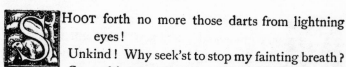

SHOOT forth no more those darts from lightning
        eyes!
    Unkind! Why seek'st to stop my fainting breath?
    Go, and invent some new kind exercise;
New weapons seek wherewith me to offend!
Play the right Tyrant! Choices use in death;
Whereby, I dying, content may rest thy will.
But tell me? Wouldst so fain my life should end?
And know'st not, *Sweet extremes do sudden kill*?
    Cruel, kiss me but once! and thou shalt see
    Ended my life with that same kiss to be.

V.

F what is heavy craves the Centre base;
    The earth below, as Nature wills the same:
    Heavy the woeful griefs are, in this case,
    Which inward in my heart I do sustain.
And if what 's light, by kind, aloft doth mount:
Then light 's my love with thee, of light account.
So that in doubtful dangerous extreme,
Wretch that I am! myself am sore afraid:
And doubt of thee, so far from Golden Mean;
Nor know I well out of this depth to wade.
    Lest that my life be shortened, or I die;
    Whether it heavy, falls; or light, ascends on high.

VI.

ADY, what time I seek in mournful note
    To show mine agonies and bloody moan,
    My Voice doth fail; and hoarse and harsh my
        throat:
And this doth come through you, through you alone
The whilst I think, by means of you in Song,
To mitigate some part of this my smart;
Instead thereof, you do me double wrong:
And with a glance you take away my Heart.
    So that I find great hurt by this your theft:
    Since where, before but Voice, now Heart, 's bereft.

VII.

S rocks become, exposed 'gainst waves and wind,
    More hard ; such is thy nature, stubborn Dame!
    Opposed 'gainst waters of my plaints most kind ;
    And winds of mine hot sighs, which inward flame,
That hardness such to increase 'bout heart is found,
  As to it, soft might seem the diamond.
Henceforward then, let no man think to move
By weeping or lamenting, to his will,
This self-willed Saint ; which too too well I prove
A senseless stone to be unto me still.
  Since, to my grief, from all good luck debarred ;
  With plaints and sighs, she doth become more hard.

VIII.

ARK, Lovers !   Hark, a strange miracle
    Of one, deprived of heart ; yet death doth 'scape !
    Mine L. a flower gave me, which sweet did smell ;
    And for the same, away my life did take.
So that I only breathe through scent of flower ;
And without heart, not without life, I live.
Then is not this, of might LOVE his power
A wonder strange ? which he for sport doth give :
  When that a flower sustaineth me alone
  With life ; who in my body, heart have none.

IX.

Hen I did part from thee the other night ;
　　Methought a foul black dog, with ugly shape,
　　Did follow me : and did me sore affright ;
　　And all the way did greedy on me gape.
　Nor I this cur, how he at me did howl,
　Can well as yet forget, with chaps most foul.
Then thinking of his colour, hateful black ;
Methought some ill, my thought did fear to come,
And said within me, " Turn again, turn back !
If forward thou dost go, thou art undone ! "
　Then pardon, Lady, if I back again
　Am come this night, with you for to remain.

X.

Y mourning Mistress's garments, black doth bear ;
　　And I in black, like her, attirèd am !
　　Yet diverse is the cause why black we wear ;
　　She for another's death doth shew the same.
I for another reason bear this suit ;
Only to show by this, my outward weed,
Mine inward grief (although my tongue be mute)
Of tender heart ; which deadly sighs doth bleed.
　Thrice happy I, if, as in habit [*dress*] we
　Are both in one, our minds both one might be.

XI.

F April fresh doth kindly give us flowers ;
 September yields with more increase the fruit.
 Sweetest, you have in bosom, Beauty's Bowers,
 Both these sweet tides : whence forth they
  always shoot
 Both flower and fruit. All only you, alone,
  Can give me, when you please ; or else can none.
O dainty bosom, bosom rich in price,
 Surmounting mountains huge of beaten gold ;
Whose whiteness braves the whitest snow that lies
On highest hills, whose height none can behold.
  In you, my soul doth hope, without annoy,
  Both Spring and Harvest, one day to enjoy.

            Roma.

XII.

RAWN, cunning Painter, hast thou with great art,
 The Shadow [*Image*] of my lovely LAURA fair ;
 Which object sweet not smally joys my heart :
 But little didst thou think, nor wast thou 'ware,
That where thou thought'st my fancy for to please,
Effect contrary sorts to my desire :
So that it breeds, in body mine, unease ;
And, senseless, burns my heart with feeling fire.
  O strange success ! What made was for content
  Doth most displease ; and, lifeless, doth torment.

XIII.

WHEN first the cruel Fair deigned graciously
　　To look on me with kind and courteous view;
　　And cast on me a lovely glancing eye:
　　She knew not that I was her servant true.
　.But She no sooner 'ware was of the same;
　　But that She turned her back with great disdain.
So as the wound I then close bare in breast;
I now, through grief, show outward in my face:
But if that She, by whom I woundèd rest,
Lives in compassion cold towards me, sans grace:
　　Hard hearted is She, cruel was She to her friend;
　　And wicked shall be, world withouten end.

XIV.

WHEN first the sun did shine upon her eyes,
　　Who fairest 'mongst her beauteous sex doth show;
　　The heavens her dainty corpse, in courteous wise,
　　Covered with chilly cold and whitest snow.
She, through the nature of that humour cold,
Both coldest Ice, at once, and purest White
Draws to herself. Then none, for strange should hold;
Though, to me, fair and cruel is her sight:
　　Since that the heavens, for favours, did impart
　　A snow-white corpse to her, and frozen heart.

XV.

THE dusky cloud in sky, with shadow dark,
　　Doth cover oft the sun's most clearest light:
　　So as his beams we cannot see, nor mark;
　　And he himself doth play at least in sight.
Ah were I such a cloud on earth to cover
My sweetest Sun! as doth that cloud, the other.
But if that cloud do vanish soon away,
And doth as momentary pass and vade;
Eternal would I be to hide her aye,
And of a harder mixture would be made.
　　O happy I!　O fortunate eclipse!
　　With kissing so to darken those fair lips.

XVI.

FROM milk of JUNO, as the Poets feign,
　　The Lily had its whiteness, passing white:
　　And from ADONIS' blood, that lovely Swain,
　　The Rose his colour red, which doth delight.
Thou, pretty Soul, hast both the colours rare
Of these sweet flowers; which others all exceed.
Thy breast 's a bed of beauteous Lilies fair;
Thy dainty cheeks, pure damask Rose breed.
　　O fruitful garden flow'ring; where appear
　　The Rose and Lily at all times of year!

XVII.

F constant love, I am the wasted fire ;
  The furious wind 's my Lady's angry eye :
  Who whilst She kindles both, through wrathful ire,
  The flame increaseth, mounting to the sky.
    In midst is LOVE, half dead of grievous pain ;
    And, doubtful, winds about like sparkling flame.
He fears the heat : and trembles, being turned
Unto this blast ; which still more sharp doth rise.
Nor is his fear in vain, when so he is burned :
For one of these must hap, in sudden wise,
    Either the fire must spoil him as his prey ;
    Or whirling wind else blow him quite away.

XVIII.

Y LAURA wonders that, in visage pale,
  I bear of Death itself, the lively show :
  But if She muse at this, her musing 's stale ;
  For this sad colour had I long ago.
The fire, close burning in my veins, doth make
That outward ashes in my face you view :
But if that She would on me pity take,
Who is the cause of this my palish hue,
    This kindled heat shall die, which now doth burn ;
    And my first colour shall again return.

XIX.

HILST foaming steed I spur unto the quick,
  To make him gallop to my Love amain :
  Love doth my thoughts, through Fancy, forward
      prick ;
The end of wishèd journey mine to gain.
  But light 's his hurt! 'Tis but a little smart!
  Where mine is mortal, sounding to the heart.
Run then, my gelding swift, like Pegasus !
Fly hence with wings ! for wings hath my desire :
Both of us, forced amain, are forward thus,
And kindled in us is a burning fire.
  Thou, through two spurs in flank, provoked art sore :
  But thousands inwardly, my heart do gore.

XX.

ICH is the diamond, a gem of price ;
  Yet such the nature strange is of the same,
  That who the powder thereof drinks, straight dies :
  And, as if poison 'twere, doth take his bane.
So thou another precious jewel art ;
In name and nature not unmuch alike :
Since death thou giv'st unto the loving heart ;
If but a kiss one sucks from thee most sweet.
  Whilst he doth swallow down his sugared bait ;
  The joy 's so great, it kills him through conceit.

XXI.

HE Grecians used to offer up their hair
  Unto their rivers : whom they did esteem
  As mighty gods ; and them great honour bare,
  As if no virtue small in them had been.
Do thou the like, sweet LAURA, unto me !
Who, for my love, deserves a greater fee.
Thy golden tresses on me do bestow !
Who hold whole rivers flowing in mine eyes :
Yet would not I, thou off shouldst cut them though.
Dost muse ? and ask, How this thou may'st devise ?
  I'll tell thee.   Give thyself to me for mine !
  So shalt thou give, uncut, thy tresses fine.

XXII.

NE lovely glance, which from the eyes did pass
  Of Lady mine, hath changed my gentle heart
  From hardest diamond to brittle glass :
  And now again (unto my bitter smart),
Through dreadful frown, she turns it suddenly
As 'twas before, from glass to diamond.
So if She will, She may (and presently,
As likes her) change me ; who to her am bound.
  If cruel She ; my heart is hard to break :
  If pitiful ; 'tis gentle, brittle, weak.

XXIII.

Wo winds, one calm, another fierce, to see;
    Th' one of the Spring, of Winter th' other right:
    I plainly, Lady, do discern in thee!
    The first, which makes me joy, breathes from
        thy sight
  Such dainty flowers, in diverse coloured show,
  As makes to blush Dame IRIS's rainy bow.
The second, which makes me to pine away,
Blows from thine inward breast, a deadly blast;
Where doth eternal hardness always stay,
Which I do see eternal aye to last.
  So as calm ZEPHYRUS, in face, thou art!
  But rough as boisterous BOREAS, in thine heart.

XXIV.

No sooner do I earnest fix mine eyes
    On my fair Sun: but that I her perceive
    To vanish like a cloud, in darkest wise;
    As if, eclipsed, her light it did bereave.
I know not, If She's troubled thus because
She doth disdain I should behold her so:
Or if for fear, this shadow to her draws;
Lest me her beams should hurt, which glistering show.
  Say then, sweet LOVE, for thou know'st best, if still
  I shall behold her; or no more, thou will.

XXV.

THAT I were sly PROTEUS! for to take
  On me that form which most I like or wish:
  Then would I change myself unto the shape
  Of that thy little whelp, thy joy and bliss.
Into that little worm thou so dost like;
And dallying, play'st with him both day and
    night.
Those savoury smacks, those busses, sweet which be,
Which thou to him dost give, should all be mine:
And I would make my heart to leap for glee;
Whilst I did lick that bosom fair of thine.
  But since I to despair of this am brought:
  My wish shall PROTEUS be; thy dog, my thought!

XXVI.

"SAy, gentle friend, tell me in courtesy,
  Before what was I? and what am I now?
  A senseless Shadow, or a Body, I?"
  "Neither of both. Mark, and I'll tell thee how.
No *Body* now: for that, by proud disdain
Of scornful She, dislived was. *Shadow* none;
For that did underground go with the same,
Unwilling it should wander all alone."
  "What am I then?" "Even one that doth not know
  What now he is: or what he was, can show."

XXVII.

THE Blazing Star foretells the hapless fall,
  And sudden death of others, soon to come.
  To me a Face, brighter than Comets all,
  Doth, with her looks, my fortune hard forerun ;
And with her shooting darts, from glancing eye,
Presageth that, ere long, I needs must die.
The Blazing Star death only prophesies ;
This doth foreshew to me a harder fate :
And dares me to mine end, in warlike wise ;
Nor how this Challenge know I to escape.
  Ah, cruel Star ! of death not only sign ;
  But murderer th' art of this poor life of mine.

XXVIII.

THE Crow makes war with the Chameleon ;
  And, being hurt, to th' laurel straight doth fly :
  And, through the fruit he findeth thereupon,
  Is healed of hurt, finds food, and lives thereby.
LOVE the Chameleon is ; the Crow am I :
And battle wage with him unto the death.
He wounds me deadly ; whereupon I hie
To thee, my LAURAL ! to restore my breath.
  Thou me reviv'st.   Such virtue 's in thee rife
  As thou, at once, dost give me food and life,

XXIX.

MONGST the Parthians is a kind of ground
 Of nature such as, though it far doth stand
 From fire : yet fire to take it straight is found ;
 And flying thither, burns it out of hand.
This prey so sure of Love am I, fair Dame !
And you to me, which burneth me, the flame.
So that if I, to you far off do show ;
You kindle straight in me a quenchless fire :
And yet, although within it burn me so,
Sweet is the heat whose fuel is desire.
 For rather I, in fire near you would be :
 Than freed from flame, you farther off to see.

XXX.

OVE, ope my heart ! Hot fire thou forth shall take.
 Open my LAURA's !   In it thou shalt find
 Cold frost.   Then of these two contraries make
 But one ; and that same one, frame thou more
  kind !
Of both our hearts, make but one loving heart !
And give it unto which thou please, of twain.
Give it to her !   To her do it impart ;
Or unto me !   It skills not much the same.
 I'll doubt no more, when but one heart we have
 Between us both : for this is all I crave.

XXXI.

NTO an Image may I right compare
My Mistress, since so crucl She 's to me :
Which standeth for a sign or shadow fair ;
To which the simple ignorant bow with knee :
And though with eyes, mouth, ears, and feet it show ;
Yet doth it neither see, talk, hear, or go.
So plays my Choice, when I appear in sight :
Nor see, nor speak, nor hear, nor stay She will.
So as an Idol, She resembleth right ;
Blind, mute, deaf, moveless, senseless standing still.
Then am not I worse than a lifeless block ;
To worship such a painted coloured stock.

Fiorenza.

XXXII.

OTH gems, and pearls, their proper value have ;
But yet unlike : for not alike 's their price.
Some sought for are, and each one doth them crave
Others, more base, do pass in worthless wise.
A jewel rich, and princelike gem, is She
Whom I esteem ; and such account of make :
Yet in herself no price hath for to see.
For it is holden at so high a rate
As all the gold, nor silver, which doth lie
In th' earth, or sea, the same, at worth, can buy.

XXXIII.

IF love, wherein I burn, were but a fire;
 I quenched it had, with water of my plaints:
 If water, these my Plaints; I this desire
 Had dried through inward heat, my heart that
  taints.
But LOVE, that in my griefs doth take delight,
Both fire and water turns, to work me spite.
Fly then, this LOVE! since such is his great power
As waves to fire, and fire to waves, he turns:
And with an absent Beauty, every hour,
My fainting heart with Fancy's fuel burns;
 And, 'gainst all sense, makes me, of CARe and IL
 More than of good and comfoRT, to have will.

XXXIV.

RIVERS unto the Sea do tribute pay.
 A most unconstant moving Sea art thou!
 And I, within mine eyes, bedewèd aye,
 A River hold of bitter tears as now.
Receive then, from these moistened cheeks of mine,
Into thy lap, the water forth I pour!
Of duty mine, and of thy debt, a sign:
And mix together with my sweet, thy sour!
 So shall the water to the water be
 More precious; and the Sea, more rich to th' Sea.

XXXV.

UCH is the virtue of the sunny heat,
    As seizing on the Cockle Shell (which lies
    On seaish shore), whereon his beams do beat,
    It makes it brightly shine, in orient wise :
So that, through secret power of radiant sun,
Of worthless shell, a pearl it doth become.
So, Lady, you, through force of Beauty's power,
If you shall deign to glance on me your eye,
And rain with grace on me a smiling shower,
A jewel rich you make me by and bye :
    And if no pearl ; at least a precious stone.
    This, only, can you do ; or else can none.

XXXVI.

HE blood of fair ADONIS, VENUS changed
    Into a flower: who, whilst he did pursue
    In forest thick, where as he hunting ranged,
    The savage boar to kill ; the boar him slew.
Do thou the like, sweet Love ! Do thou the same,
Whilst now my life doth languish, through thy power :
And whilst my wound makes me for to remain
Withouten blood, transform me to a flower !
    That where I, living, cannot ; dead, I may ;
    A loved flower in LAURA's bosom stay.

XXXVII.

AN ocean Sea of water calm am I ;
  Wherein kind LOVE the form of Fish doth take,
  Leaping alongst the shore most wantonly.
  Then, Lady, of a Fisher don the shape!
Ah, what sweet fishing shall you have to like ;
If LOVE you chance to catch, while he doth bite?
Come then, and naked into this water hie!
He cannot 'scape ; but, here, perforce must bide!
'Less to my heart, to save himself, he fly.
Then quickly strip thyself! Lay fear aside!
  For of this dainty prey, which thou shalt take ;
  Both Sea, Fish, and Thyself, thou glad shalt make.

XXXVIII.

RICH Damask Roses in fair cheeks do bide
  Of my sweet Girl, like April in his prime :
  But her hard heart, cold chilly snow doth hide ;
  Of bitter Januar, the perfect sign.
Her hair of gold shows yellow like the corn
In July, when the sun doth scorch the ground ;
And her fair breast, ripe fruit which doth adorn
September rich. So as in her is found
  Both Harvest, Summer, Winter, Spring to be :
  Which you in breast, hair, heart, and face may see.

XXXIX.

T H' immortal PARCÆ, fatal Sisters three,
　　Of mortal men, do sing the shunless fate :
　　What once Was, what Is now, and what Shall Be;
　　Their life, their death, their fortune, and theiɪ
　　　　state.
　Our Song let be like theirs ! for Three they were;
　And so our number is.　Three are we here.
Sing LAURA then ! Sing LOVE ! and sing will I !
Of dreary fortune mine, sing let us all !
Let 's sing in doleful tune most mournfully,
How 'Tis, how 'Twas, and hapless still Shall fall ;
　The Present, Past, and (which none can mend)
　What Shall Be, world to come, withouten end.

XL.

T H E heavens, their restless sphere do always move.
　　In thee doth move the faith, which thou didst
　　　　plight.
　　　And I, IXION-like, still in my love
Do roll ; and yet I roll my wheel aright.
So that, 'twixt us, continual motions wend.
But which is worse, unconstant Wench, I see !
The heavens will have their motions without end ;
Which, never ceasing, roll continually :
　And thou, like them, to roll dost mean thy fill ;
　And since 'tis so, I'll roll too, against my will !

The Conclusion of the Second Part.

Hus is the Second Course now servèd in.
A Course too coarse for such a dainty Dame :
Yet, Lady, though the cheer be bad and thin;
Because it comes of zeal, accept the same!
And though not worthy of your grace it be ;
Yet make it gracious through your courtesy!

Great sumptuous feasts the stomach doth dislike ;
Which oft, in body dangerous surfeits breed :
Where dishes few revive our sense and sprite ;
And Nature 's pleased on little for to feed.
This, as a sauce, your appetite to move,
Accept! where meat 's the heaRT, where
cook is LOVE:

Nor think the worse, though I have spun a thread
So fine (I mean your praise) I cannot mend :
Since 'tis a Work to ground the wisest head ;
And mar I should this loom, this cloth not mend.
So VENUS' matchless shape APELLES drew ;
But how to finish it, he never knew.

Far more 's my mind than is my feeble might.
My pencil, for thy picture is too weak.
The sun is only for the eagle's flight.
My strength's too small, this hardened ice to break.
Not painted, scarce I thee have shadowed here :
This task 's for such as have in skill no peer.

R. T.

LAURA.

THE THIRD PART.

I.

Ho joys in love? The Heart alone, to see.
Who languisheth in love? The Heart
alone.
Then is 't a thing impossible for me
To joy or languish: since I Heart have
none.
Withouten Heart! Then tell me, What am I?
Even bones and flesh united cunningly.
The Soul, where is 't? Love that hath ta'en away:
My Body only resteth in his place.
Deprived of Soul and Heart, how live? I say,
I live, maintained by love, in this strange case.
O wonder strange, the Body live to see;
The Heart and Soul in other place to be.
Napoli.

II.

HAT crimson gown, with drops of blood ywrought,
Which LAURA wears, a token is most true,
How that of blood desirous is her thought:
And that 'tis so, I best can tell to you.
My wrongèd heart too well doth find the same;
Who, thousand times, not once, hath wrongèd been
By her: and, now, to aggravate my pain,
(More cruel in desire for to be seen),
By outward habit [*dress*] covets She to show
What, inward, in her mind She hides below.

III.

HE flaming torch, a shadow of the light,
 Put out by hasty hand, doth colour change;
 And black becomes, which seemed before most
   bright :
Nor so to show is any marvel strange.
 So was I long a lively fire of Love;
 The heat whereof my body oft did prove :
But I, at last, by one who moaned my woe,
Extinguished was, by pitiful Disdain.
Then if my colour black in face do show,
You need not much to wonder at the same ;
 Since 'tis a sign, by part to know the whole,
 That Love made me a fire, Disdain a coal.

IV.

ARDONED of every wicked fact was he,
 To HEBE's Temple that, with prayers, came :
 And, of such grace in sign, his bonds, as free,
 He left hung up on high within the same.
I, Lady, errèd have; and humbly come
To thee, who art the Temple fair of Love :
Off'ring to thee my prayers, all and some,
To free me from my faults, thy heart let move!
 In token of which gift, with thee I'll leave
 My jealous thoughts; wherewith I did thee grieve.

V.

F thou art cold, as is the Winter's snow;
I, as the Summer, hot am most extreme:
Then let's unite thy heart, which cold is so,
To mine so warm; and make of both a mean!
So th' one a help to th' other still shall be;
And linked in concord, as two doves shall 'gree.
To form this frame, LOVE shall the workman play.
Then let's with July, January mix!
Let's make, between us, an eternal May!
An everlasting truce, twain betwix!
Thy Winter, with my Summer let us join!
My fire so warm, with frost so cold of thine!

VI.

HE cruel NERO used on golden hook,
The harmless fish to catch with sugared bait:
So courteous LOVE, fishing, me quickly took;
Whilst he with dainty prey for me did wait.
Yet far more fortunate am I in this:
For whereas NERO's hooks most sharp did kill;
The other hooks revive the taken fish,
Whilst they do hold him gently by the gill.
But hooks they are none! For hooks they are too fair!
Two golden tresses be they of fine hair!

VIL

WHEN She was born ; She came, with smiling eye,
    Laughing into the world, a sign of glee.
When I was born; to her quite contrary,
    Wailing I came into the world to see.
Then mark this wonder strange ! What nature gave ;
From first to th' last, this fashion kept we have.
She in my sad laments doth take great joy :
I, through her laughing, die ; and languish must,
Unless that LOVE, to save me from this 'noy,
Do unto me, unworthy, shew so just
    As for to change her laughter into pain ;
    And my complaints, into her joy again.

VIII.

IN LOVE his kingdom great, two Fools there be :
    My Lady 's one ; myself the other am.
The fond behaviour of both, which to see ;
    Whoso but nicely marks, will say the same.
Foolish our thoughts are.   Foolish, our desire.
Foolish our hearts in Fancy's flame to fry.
Foolish to burn in Love's hot scorching fire.
But what ?   Fools are we none.   My tongue doth lie.
    For who most foolish is, and fond, in love ;
    More wiser far than others, oft doth prove.

IX.

N O sooner LAURA mine appears to me ;
　　But that a dainty dye, or blushing red,
　　In both our faces showeth for to be.
　　　But who, alas, doth mine so overspread ?
O'er-fervent LOVE doth draw this shadow pure ;
Like cunning'st Painter, long for to endure.
Who painteth hers ?　Disdain, with pencil hard ;
Which turneth all my sweetness into sour.
So that all my designs are quickly marred ;
Except LOVE bind Love, by his awful power,
　　In Faith's firm bands.　Too high th' exchange will
　　　grow,
　　When love, for hate ; and not for like, shall go.

X.

P HŒBUS had once a bird, his chief delight,
　　Which, only 'cause he had an evil tongue,
　　He made him black ; who was before most white.
　　　So if all those who, Lovers true have stung
With spiteful speech, and have their loves betrayed ;
Or to their Ladies false be and untrue,
Setting at nought the promise they have made ;
LOVE would but change into this coal-black hue :
　　Thousands abroad, like sea-coal crows should show ;
　　Who, now unknown, for snowy swans do go.

XI.

IN silver stream, on shallow fountain's shelf,
The lively image saw he in the same;
Who was in love with shadow of himself:
Through pride forgetful how his likeness came.
Such one myself, by chance, I see to be;
When as in river I myself did see:
Yet I myself, instead of loving, hate.
And such strange hatred is this, and so strong;
That while he, loving, died by justest Fate,
Himself by seeing, whilst he himself did wrong:
I die will unto him contrary clean;
'Cause I, hating myself, myself too much have seen.

XII.

JOY of my soul! My blindfold eyes' clear light!
Cordial of heart! Right methridate of love!
Fair orient pearl! Bright shining margarite!
Pure quintessence of heaven's delight above!
When shall I taste, what favour grants me touch;
And ease the rage of mine so sharp desire?
When shall I free enjoy, what I so much
Do covet; but I doubt in vain, to aspire?
Ah, do not still my soul thus tantalise;
But once, through grace, the same imparadise!

XIII.

AINTER, in lively colours draw Disdain!
    Dost ask, How that may rightly shadowed be?
    I'll tell thee. If thou, fine, wilt do the same;
    My Lady paint! and thou Disdain shalt see.
Fond man! dost not believe? or think'st I jest?
If doubtful thou remain, then hear the rest!
Mark her but well; and thou shalt, in her face,
See right Disdain: which, coming from her eyes,
Makes her to look with most disdainful grace;
Then if thou seest it, in so plain a guise,
    Straight shadow [*paint*] her! For this one counterfeit
        [*picture*]
Of her, and of Disdain, shall show the shape.

XIV.

ITH gold and rubies glistereth her small hand;
    But if you match them with her lips or hair,
    They seem withouten brightness for to stand:
    The others have such lively colours fair.
O worthy Beauty! peerless A PER SE!
To whom all other Beauties are most vile.
O fairness such as fairer none can be!
Thou grace itself, of graciousness dost spoil!
    With rubies, thou right rubies dost disgrace!
    With gold, bright gold thou stainest in his place!

XV.

GENTLE tame deer am I, called a Hart :
The cruel huntress fierce my Mistress is.
With crossbow bent, she comes to me in Park ;
Paled in with pleasant thoughts of wanton wish.
She shoots, and hits me ; takes me for her prey :
And (having shot, hit, taken) flies her way.
Back she retires from me, with pleasant smile ;
Unloosing me, and heals my wound and pain :
When, as afresh incensed (alack the while !)
'Gainst me, desirous me to plague again,
She turns towards me, o'ertakes me, strikes me sore :
And, binding up my wounds, makes deadly more.

XVI.

HE golden tresses of a Lady fair ;
At first beginning were of this my love :
But now, at last, unto my double care,
To be the end of my sad life I prove.
Then did my doubtful spirit live in hope :
But now he fears, despairing as it were
Because he doth perceive in sudden broke
His hope, which dying heart did help and bear ;
Since that the hair, that Alpha me did bind
In love, of life the Omega I do find.

XVII.

" SWEET LAURA, in the water look no more,
    To see if feature thine be fair or no!
    Look in mine eyes! which tears rain streaming
      sore
Of bitter plaints; whose water clear doth show,
    As in a looking-glass, most bright to thee,
    Those favours which in that sweet visage be."
So said I to her: when She answered blive,
" And thou, my Love! say, Dost thou likewise wish
To see thyself in one that is alive?
Then in this breast, look where thine image is!
    Love shall alike in both our bodies rest:
    Bear thou me in thine eyes; I'll thee in breast!"

XVIII.

IF, cruel, thou desirous art of blood;
    Behold how I do bleed in streaming wise!
    Glut then thyself therewith, if thou think good;
    And do content, with blood, thy bloody eyes!
From breast it comes, where fainting heart doth lie;
And for a gift, I it present to thee!
Although I know, through this, I soon shall die;
And yet to die it little grieveth me:
    Since 'tis my wish, my blood with soul as one
    May rest; and that's with thee, or else with none,

XIX.

THAT ivory hand, a fan most white doth hold;
　And to the milky breast blows wind apace;
　And yet is full of chilly ice most cold;
　Disgrace to others, to herself a grace.
But I, who wistly mark these whiteness' three,
　Vouchsafe, sweet LOVE, this boon to grant to me!
Distil within the rolling of mine eyes,
By virtue of thy power, such hidden flame;
And let it tempered be, in such strange wise,
That, as I cast my look upon the same,
　It quite may take away her cruelty!
　Melt straight the ice! and fan burn suddenly!

XX.

THE snakes, amongst themselves, so carefully
　Love one another, wonder for to see!
　As if th' one want, the other straight doth die.
　Lady, unto these snakes unlike we be!
For if I die, thou diest not for my death;
But, through my pain revivest! Such is thy spite!
And pleasure tak'st to see me void of breath.
Ah, yet in love let 's unto them be like!
　Thou CUPID, work! that I, poor snake in love,
　This 'sdainful snake for to be kind may move.

XXI.

AURA is fair and cruel both in one;
And born was of a dainty diamond.
Then is it marvel, neither wonder, none;
Although her heart as hard as stone be found.
Nature that hardness, as a Keeper, gave
To her, her beauty thereby so to save.
But fond is he, and simple in conceit,
That thinks LOVE will not, one day, burst the same.
Then quickly, mighty Lord, quickly this break!
Break thou this stony heart, so hard, in twain!
Unto thy power, let Nature's force still yield!
And be thou Conqueror 'gainst her in Field!

XXII.

HE snow-white Swan betokens brightsome Day:
The coal-black Crow, of darky Night is sign.
Thou Day, or Night, bring unto me still may,
With those bright lamps, those glistering stars,
of thine.
But, cruel thou, thy heart is bent so hard,
As I that sun can never see with eyes
(That wished-for sun, from these my lights debarred):
Nor aught discern but mists, in foggy wise.
Then since I live in woe; and, blind, nought see:
A Crow, not Swan, thou still shalt be to me!

XXIII.

Ay, Cupid, since thou wings so swift dost bear;
Within my heart, alone, why dost thou lie?
Why dost not seek to lodge some other where;
And to some other place, why dost not hie?
Go unto her, who hath the lily breast!
Who though she hates me; yet I love her best.
If her, to entertain thee thou shalt find;
It is a sign she hateth me no more.
Straight then, return again; and show her mind
To my desire! who for this news longs sore.
 Then, prithee, go! No longer ling'ring stay!
 Lest, when thou wouldst, thou canst not go thy way.

XXIV.

N quicksedge wrought with lovely eglantine,
My Laura laid her handkercher to dry;
Which had before snow-white ywashed been.
 But after, when she called to memory,
That long 'twould be before, and very late,
Ere sun could do, as would her glistering eyes:
She cast from them such sparkling glances straight,
And with such force, in such a strangy guise,
 As suddenly, and in one selfsame time,
 She dried her cloth; but burnt this heart of mine.

XXV.

OLD upon gold, mine only Joy did plate,
   Whilst She did dress her head by crystal glass:
   But whilst She looked on it, it sudden brake;
   So as, amazed thereat, much grieved She was;
To whom I said, "To grieve thus, 'tis in vain:
Since what is broke, whole cannot be again.
Look steadfastly, with both thine eyes on me!
Who have my heart, through love, a glass new made."
She on my face looked; and herself did see:
Wherewith contented th'roughly, thus She said,
   "Most happy I! Since for to dress my head,
   For broken glass, of whole one I am sped."

XXVI.

HE heavens begin, with thunder, for to break
   The troubled air; and to the coloured fields,
   The lightning for to spoil their pride doth threat.
   Each thing unto the furious tempest yields.
And yet, methinks, within me I do hear
A gentle voice, hard at my heart, to say:
"Fear nothing, thou; but be of merry cheer!
Thou only safe, 'fore others all shalt stay.
   To save thee from all hurt, thy shield shalt be
   The shadow of the conquering Laural Tree."

Fano.

XXVII.

"OVE this fair Lass!" said LOVE once unto me.
 I loved her. "Love her now," saith he, "no
  more!"
 When thousand darts within my breast there be;
And if I love her, he me threateneth sore.
 He saith, "Himself is fallen in love with her;
 And that himself, 'fore others, he'll prefer!"
His sense is this. He, in her beauteous eyes,
Hath found such Amours as ne'er like were seen:
But thinks he, this shall serve, in cunning wise,
To make me leave? he cozening me so clean?
 In spite of him, I'll love! sith heart doth 'gree,
 With LOVE in love as rival for to be.

XXVIII.

Y Mistress writing, as her hand did shake,
 The pen did dash, which on her gown did spurt:
 One drop, more higher than the rest did take;
 And to presume to touch her breast it durst.
Upon her dainty bosom it did light:
Wherewith she blushed, in show like damask rose.
Presumptuous black! how dar'dst thou touch that white,
Wherein a World of gladsome pleasure grows?
 Yet, spite of envy, happed it for the best:
 To the white, more grace; more beauty, 'twas to th' breast.

XXIX.

ONE dares now look more on my LAURA's face,
So dangerous is her beauty to behold :
For he no sooner gives to her the gaze ;
But straight his heart, She takes from him so bold.
Such virtue 's locked within those ebon eyes ;
Where, dallying with Delight, Dan CUPID lies.
So sweetly rolleth She that radiant sphere,
As She, from whom She lists, robs suddenly :
So as to look on her, each one doth fear ;
And yet to look on her, spare will not I !
For though I lose my Heart, and him disease.
I like shall my Desire ; and her I'll please.

XXX.

UNBARE that ivory Hand !   Hide it no more !
For though it death brings to my tender heart
To see it naked, where is Beauty's store ;
And where moist pearl with azure doth impart :
Yet fear I not to die, in this sweet wise !
My fancy, so to see 't, is set on fire.
Then leave that glove ! (most hateful to mine eyes !)
And let me surfeit with this kind desire !
So that my looks may have of them their fill ;
Though heart decay, I'll take it for none ill.

Mantoa.

XXXI.

" **M**Y Mistress seems but brown," say you to me.
'Tis very true, and I confess the same :
Yet love I her although that brown She be ;
Because to please me, She is glad and fain.
I lovèd one most beautiful before ;
Whom now, as death, I deadly do abhor.
Because to scorn my service her I found ;
I gave her o'er, and chose to me this same.
Nor to be faithful, think I, I am bound
To one, in whom no kindness doth remain.
This is the cause, for brown and pitiful ;
I left a fair, but yet a faithless, Trull.

XXXII.

WHITE art thou, like the mountain-snow to see ;
I Black, like to the burnèd coal do show :
Then give some of thy purest white to me !
And I'll some of my black on thee bestow :
So will we these two contraries unite
Together ; which so joined, will show more fair.
Let 's both then make this change, for our delight ;
Unless to kill me, thou do little care !
But why of White or Black, talk I to thee ?
My blood not black 'tis ; which thou fain wouldst see.

XXXIII.

A S sacrifice unto a goddess bright,
My heart I offered with devotion great:
Thinking that She, Love's Temple had been
right.
But what, un'wares, I spied not then, in heat,
I, wary, now discern her for to be:
Of hell below, the rightest cruelty.
I was deceived, I do confess.   That smile,
That wanton smile, that bred in me delight,
Hid in those lips so fair, did me beguile.
O beauty false!   O cruelty most right!
Flee, flee my heart! flee then, if thou be wise,
Thy hurt! my burning heat, her treacheries!

XXXIV.

STRANGE is this thing!   My horse I cannot make
With spur, with speech, nor yet with rod in hand,
Force him to go; altbough great pains I take.
Do what I can; he still, as tired, doth stand.
No doubt he feels a heavy weight of me;
Which is the cause he standeth still as stone:
Nor is he 'ware that now he carrieth three;
He thinks, poor jade, I am on 's back alone.
But three we are, with mine own self I prove:
LAURA is in my heart; in soul is LOVE.

Pesaro.

XXXV.

HEN I, of my sweet LAURA leave did take:
Fair Fano's city, for a while to leave:
She gave to me, to wear it for her sake,
Of gold and pearl a dainty woven wreath.
Dear was the gift; because for love it came:
But dearer more; 'cause She gave me the same.
I look on 't still, and kiss it as my joy;
Kissing and bussing it, with it I play:
Which, at one instant, brings me mirth and 'noy;
And sighing oft thus to myself I say:
  " White pearls are these; yet hath her mouth more fair!
Fine gold is this; yet finer is her hair!"

Fano.

XXXVI.

ITH thousand bands of furious inward heat,
Love binds my soul; and burns my gentle heart:
And, two ways, LAURA, death to me doth threat
With Colour fresh; and wanton Eye, like dart.
This for reward for all my love I gain.
For my goodwill, two enemies I have:
LAURA and Love. Four plagues conspire my pain,
Because I like; and what 's but just, do crave:
  Fire, roseal Colour, Eyes, and cruel Band.
These, at the gaze of Beauty, make me stand.

XXXVII.

F scalding sighs, my faith may testify ;
   And brinish tears, of love may warrant be :
   Both th' one and th' other thou hast seen with eye !
   Then what wouldst have, hard hearted ! more of
      me ?
  But thou, perhaps, though much I have endured,
  Wouldst yet be better of my faith assured.
Then with thine eyes, into my breast do peer !
Which, for the nonce, I leave to open sight ;
And that which now thou doubt'st, see shalt thou clear.
Ah, mark it then ; and view what shows so bright !
  But too too cruel art thou, and precise ;
  That will not credit give to thine own eyes !

XXXVIII.

HE hapless ARGUS, happy in this same,
   The glory of the sun's surpassing light ;
   The brightness of the stars, the fire which stain :
   With hundred eyes, behold them always might.
  But I, alas, who have but only twain,
  Cannot behold the beauty of my Sun !
For which I live as blind, in endless pain ;
And count myself, for want thereof, undone.
  I can but wish that I an ARGUS were !
  With hundred eyes to view her everywhere.

XXXIX.

I N vasty sea, fain would my slender Muse
   Wade in thy praise! to praise thy beauty right :
   But, Lady, I for pardon crave excuse.
      To break such waves, too brittle is her might !
Meantime, with lowly verse, in humble show,
Along the shallow shore I'll wading go.
The time may come, perhaps ere it be long,
That this my Quill, more bold, may write thy praise :
And venture for to sail in th' ocean strong ;
Though now, on gravelled shore it fearful stays.
   And whereas now, to dip his foot he fears :
   He then shall dive himself o'er head and ears.

Fano.

XL.

W HEN I did part, my soul did part from me ;
    And took his Farewell of thy beauteous ey'n :
    But now that I, returned, do thee see ;
       He is returned, and lives through kindness thine :
And of thee looketh for a Welcome Home.
I then, not any more, to sorrow need ;
Now I am come : and if before, alone,
On Shadow then ; on Substance now I feed.
   So if my parting bitter was and sad :
   Sweet 's my return to thee, and passing glad.

The conclusion of the last Part.

TIMANTES, when he saw he could not paint
    With lively colours, to his lasting fame,
    Such works he took in hand; and found
        too faint
His cunning: seeking for to hide the same,
    He over them a subtil Shadow drew;
    So that his faults, or none, or few, could view.

So, Lady, I finding my wit too weak,
With current terms, your beauty forth to blaze;
And that to arrive, too blunt is my conceit,
Unto the height of your surmounting praise:
    With silence forcèd am, against my will,
    To shadow my defect, the want of skill.

Yet do I hope, the Shadow you'll not scorn:
Since Princes, in their stately arbours green,
Account of shade, as trees which fruit adorn;
Because from heat they welcome shelters been.
    The Shadow shields, 'gainst sun, your beauty fair;
    Which else his scorching heat would much impair.

Then though a Shadow without fruit I be;
And scarce yield leaves to cover this my bark:
Accept these leaves, thy Beauty's Shade, of me!
Where wealth doth ebb, goodwill doth flow from
    heart.
    Deign me, for all my love, but Shadow thine!
    Thy Substance 's too too high for fortune mine.

                    R. T.

A Friend's just Excuse about the Book and [the] Author; in his absence.

ITHOUT the Author's knowledge, as is before said by the Printer [at pp. 355, 356]; this Poem is made thus publicly known; which, with my best endeavour, the Gentleman himself, suspecting what is now proved too true, at my coming up, earnestly intreated me to prevent. But I came at the last sheet's printing; and find more than thirty Sonnets not his, intermixt with his. Helped it cannot be, but by the well judging Reader: who will, with less pain distinguish between them, than I, on this sudden, possibly can. To him then, I refer that labour.

And for the Printer's faults passed in some of the Books; I have gathered them in the next page.*

With the Author, bear, I pray ye! whom I must intreat to bear with me.

R. B.

* These four Corrections have been embodied in the text.

INDEX OF PROPER NAMES[1]

[1] The small Roman numbers refer to the text of the Introduction in Volume I.

INDEX OF FIRST LINES

Edinburgh : T. and A. CONSTABLE, Printers to His Majesty

223

MA